BIG BIBLE GUIDE

CREATION & BIBLE ANIMALS

Fun and Fascinating Bible Reference for Kids Ages 8 to 12

TRACY M. SUMNER
JANE LANDRETH

starts on page 3!

starts on page 161!

BARBOUR
PUBLISHING

Published by Barbour Books, an imprint of Barbour Publishing, Inc., P.O. Box 719, Uhrichsville, Ohio 44683, www.barbourbooks.com

Our mission is to publish and distribute inspirational products offering exceptional value and biblical encouragement to the masses.

Member of the
Evangelical Christian
Publishers Association

Printed in the United States of America.
Versa Press, Inc., East Peoria, IL 61611; April 2014; D10004468

KiDS'
Guide to
Creation

TRACY M. SUMNER

What's in This Book

Before You Get Started 7

Genesis 1: The Creation Story 11

1. Day 1, Part I: How It All Started—Heavens, Earth, and Water

(Genesis 1:1–2) 13

2. Day 1, Part II: Let There Be Light!

(Genesis 1:3–5) 27

3. Day 2: Our Earth's Atmosphere

(Genesis 1:6–8) 39

4. Day 3: The Oceans. . .the Land. . .and the Plants

(Genesis 1:9–13) 51

5. Day 4: Some Great Stuff God Made "Out There"

(Genesis 1:14–19) 71

6. Day 5: Things with Fins, Things with Feathers

(Genesis 1:20–23) 85

7. Day 6, Part I: All the Land Animals

(Genesis 1:24–25) 105

8. Day 6, Part II: Humans: Made in God's Image

(Genesis 1:26–28) 127

9. Day 6, Part III: Creation Complete. . .Now What?

(Genesis 1:29–31) 147

BEFORE YOU GET STARTED

Have you ever stopped to think about what the words "In the beginning God created" in Genesis 1:1 really mean? Just when was the beginning, and what did God create back then?

The simple but wonderful answer is that God created *everything*! And while only God knows exactly when the beginning took place, we can know without any doubt that He created a universe so big that people still don't know where it ends—or *if* it ends. He also created all the stars, including the one we call the sun. He created the planets that orbit the sun, including the planet we humans call home—Earth. And He created every living thing that lives here with us: every microbe, every plant, every fish, every bird, every mammal, every insect. . .the list goes on and on.

And, of course, He created us humans—the one thing He made in His own image and likeness—and designed us with the special ability to know and communicate with our Maker.

This book is about all the amazing things God created—starting with the heavens and the earth and ending with us humans. It's about the vastness of the universe God created, and it's about the amazing variety of things—things out there in outer space and things here on good old planet Earth—He made during those six days of work He spent creating everything you see. . .and some things you can't see.

Sometimes when we look at the wonder of God's creation, it's hard to fully comprehend that the God who lovingly and thoughtfully made everything—from the biggest galaxies, stars, and planets all the way down to the tiniest organisms (things you can't see with the naked eye) that live here on Earth—is the same God the Bible says loves each of us deeply and personally.

But the God who loves you is also the God who created everything around you. In fact, He created everything around you *for* you! It's true! Everything God made before He created us humans was with an eye toward preparing a place that would serve as a perfect home for each and every one of us. That's what the six days of creation were all about!

Some of God's creation is big and beautiful beyond description. Some of it is complicated and a little hard to understand. Some of it is funny to look at and think about. Some of it might even seem a little gross to you. But *all* of creation is amazing and wonderful—just like the God who used six days to accomplish all of it.

This book covers all six days of the creation story from the first chapter of Genesis. It gives you a fairly detailed "day-by-day" picture of what God made on each of those creation days. It covers the creation of the universe—or what some people call the *cosmos*—as well as the creation of the earth. . .and everything that lives on it, including an incredible number of plants, animals, and other living things.

Each of the nine chapters in this book includes not only a good overview of the things God made on each creation day, but also some fun, interesting, and sometimes weird special features having to do with the chapter's main subject.

Here is a list of the features you'll enjoy in this book:

- **"That's Weird!"**: Really strange things within different parts of creation—like black holes in space, Venus flytraps (plants that eat meat), and the duck-billed platypus (quite possibly the world's weirdest mammal).

- "Record Breaking": The biggest, the tallest, the farthest, and the most in all of creation!

- **"Exploring the. . ."**: Special experiments or studies you can do outside this book to learn more about the chapter's main topic.

- **"The Way It Used to Be"**: Really strange—and wrong—things people used to believe about different parts of God's creation.

- **"Did You Know. . . ?"**: Fun facts—some of them most people don't know—about the natural world God created.

- **"That's Amazing!"**: Some really astounding tidbits about the universe, the earth, and the natural world that makes its home on our planet.

This book won't teach you everything there is to know about the universe and the world God created for you to live on—or about the living things we share our planet with. For you to learn about every single thing God created, you would need a book many times longer than the one you're holding in your hands right now.

But by the time you're finished reading this book, you will have a pretty good idea how big and wonderful creation really is—and how big and wonderful the God who made it all is, too. You also might find yourself wanting to read and study to learn more! When you do that, you'll learn not only about the wonder of God's creation, but you'll also learn a thing or two about God Himself that you might not have known before.

GENESIS 1: THE CREATION STORY

[1] In the beginning God created the heavens and the earth. [2] The earth was formless and empty, and darkness covered the deep waters. And the Spirit of God was hovering over the surface of the waters.

[3] Then God said, "Let there be light," and there was light. [4] And God saw that the light was good. Then he separated the light from the darkness. [5] God called the light "day" and the darkness "night."

And evening passed and morning came, marking the first day.

[6] Then God said, "Let there be a space between the waters, to separate the waters of the heavens from the waters of the earth." [7] And that is what happened. God made this space to separate the waters of the earth from the waters of the heavens. [8] God called the space "sky." And evening passed and morning came, marking the second day.

[9] Then God said, "Let the waters beneath the sky flow together into one place, so dry ground may appear." And that is what happened. [10] God called the dry ground "land" and the waters "seas." And God saw that it was good. [11] Then God said, "Let the land sprout with vegetation—every sort of seed-bearing plant, and trees that grow seed-bearing fruit. These seeds will then produce the kinds of plants and trees from which they came." And that is what happened. [12] The land produced vegetation—all sorts of seed-bearing plants, and trees with seed-bearing fruit. Their seeds produced plants and trees of the same kind. And God saw that it was good.

[13] And evening passed and morning came, marking the third day.

[14] Then God said, "Let lights appear in the sky to separate the day from the night. Let them mark off the seasons, days, and years. [15] Let these lights in the sky shine down on the earth." And that is what happened. [16] God made two great lights—the larger one to govern the day, and the smaller one to govern the night. He also made the stars. [17] God set these lights in the sky to light the earth, [18] to govern the day and night, and to separate the light from the darkness. And God saw that it was good.

[19] And evening passed and morning came, marking the fourth day.

²⁰ Then God said, "Let the waters swarm with fish and other life. Let the skies be filled with birds of every kind." ²¹ So God created great sea creatures and every living thing that scurries and swarms in the water, and every sort of bird—each producing offspring of the same kind. And God saw that it was good. ²² Then God blessed them, saying, "Be fruitful and multiply. Let the fish fill the seas, and let the birds multiply on the earth."

²³ And evening passed and morning came, marking the fifth day.

²⁴ Then God said, "Let the earth produce every sort of animal, each producing offspring of the same kind—livestock, small animals that scurry along the ground, and wild animals." And that is what happened. ²⁵ God made all sorts of wild animals, livestock, and small animals, each able to produce offspring of the same kind. And God saw that it was good.

²⁶ Then God said, "Let us make human beings in our image, to be like us. They will reign over the fish in the sea, the birds in the sky, the livestock, all the wild animals on the earth, and the small animals that scurry along the ground."

²⁷ So God created human beings in his own image. In the image of God he created them; male and female he created them.

²⁸ Then God blessed them and said, "Be fruitful and multiply. Fill the earth and govern it. Reign over the fish in the sea, the birds in the sky, and all the animals that scurry along the ground."

²⁹ Then God said, "Look! I have given you every seed-bearing plant throughout the earth and all the fruit trees for your food.

³⁰ And I have given every green plant as food for all the wild animals, the birds in the sky, and the small animals that scurry along the ground—everything that has life." And that is what happened.

³¹ Then God looked over all he had made, and he saw that it was very good!

And evening passed and morning came, marking the sixth day.

CHAPTER 1
DAY 1, PART 1
HOW IT ALL STARTED—
HEAVENS, EARTH, AND WATER

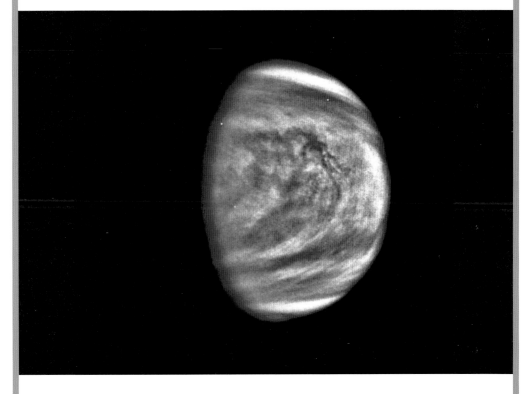

In the beginning God created the heavens and the earth. The earth was formless and empty, and darkness covered the deep waters. And the Spirit of God was hovering over the surface of the waters.

GENESIS 1:1–2

Have you ever really thought about the word *nothing*? When you look around you and see all the really cool things God created, it's hard to imagine that there was a time when there was literally nothing around—no Earth, no moon, no stars, no people, no animals, and no plants. There wasn't even a place for God to put all these things! What's more, there wasn't even any light!

The Bible tells us that God's work of creation began in the same place everything else begins: in the *beginning*! Before that day, the only thing that existed was God Himself. And on that first day of creation, He began laying the foundation for everything you see around you—and for a lot of things you can't see.

The Bible tells us "In the beginning, God created the heavens and the earth" (Genesis 1:1). That certainly seems like a good place to start, doesn't it? But the earth God started creating on the first day of creation wasn't at all like the earth you see around you now—at least not at first. The Bible tells us that at the beginning of creation, "the earth was formless and empty" (Genesis 1:2).

What does the phrase "formless and empty" sound like to you? It certainly doesn't sound like the earth would have been a very pleasant place to live back then, does it? In fact, it sounds like the earth was nothing but a huge ball of gases and solid materials that no human, animal, or plant could possibly live on. It sounds like it was more or less a big unformed blob of what God later molded and formed into the amazing planet Earth you live on now.

Some people believe that on the first day of creation, God made what scientists call *matter*. Matter is basically all the materials God would later need to really get the work of creation going.

One of the basic laws of science is that you can't make something out of nothing. But God can! And that's exactly what He did! On that first day of creation, God began an amazing process of putting together everything we see around us—starting with what the Bible calls "the heavens and the earth" (Genesis 1:1).

The Heavens. . .a Huge Area We Call Space

What the Bible calls "the heavens" in Genesis 1, we now call *space* or the *universe* or the *cosmos*. This is a huge area God created on that first day, then later filled with planets, stars, and other amazing things you'll read about later on in chapter 5.

But just how big is the universe? About 500 years ago, people believed the entire universe was only a little bigger than Earth. And it wasn't all that long ago when schoolchildren were taught that the universe is maybe only about 5,000 light-years across—much smaller than scientists have since discovered it really is. Today, when modern technology allows us to see deeper into the universe, we have learned that space is much bigger than anyone in the past could have possibly imagined.

It's hard for most of us to imagine just how big the universe really is. In fact, even the smartest scientists in the world today really don't know the exact size of outer space. Over the past few decades, scientists have come to believe the universe actually had a beginning (just like the Bible says it does) and that it is still growing and expanding. That means we may never know just how big it is—simply because the universe God created is still getting bigger all the time.

For now, scientists know that outer space extends away from Earth by at least 13 billion light-years. A *light-year* is how far light—which travels at about 186,000 miles per second—moves in one year. So you know that the distance between Earth and the farthest objects humans have seen out in space is probably far too huge for you to figure out with a pencil and paper—even if you're really good at arithmetic!

The visible universe covers an area that is about 28 billion light-years across. Scientists know that they are limited in what they can see in space, but they believe it's possible that what they have seen so far could actually make up a small fraction of the whole universe.

Even though the universe is bigger than most people can even imagine, you can know one thing about it for sure: Every inch of it was created by the same God who so carefully and thoughtfully created you and every other person who lives here on Earth, or who has ever lived here on Earth. And He's the same God who made sure during the process of creation that you would have everything you need to live your life here on Earth.

Most everyone has seen a magician make a rabbit appear from an empty hat. But you know it's just a trick. Only God can make something from nothing!

The Hubble Space Telescope floats more than 350 miles above the earth. From that far up, beyond Earth's atmosphere, the Hubble can take clear pictures of deep space objects.

What It's Really Like in Space

What do you think it's like in outer space—thousands or millions of miles away from Earth? Is it really cold out there, or is it really hot? What does outer space sound like? What could you see if you suddenly found yourself floating around in outer space?

When you think of outer space, you probably imagine a huge area filled with stars, planets, asteroids, comets, and other objects zipping around one another at light speed. . .and making lots of noise as they do it. But even though countless numbers of objects like these are out there, outer space isn't really all that crowded. Most of the objects we can see in space are many, many light-years apart, and even those objects that are relatively close to one another very seldom come all that close to one another.

And outer space is anything but noisy. In fact, it's the quietest place in all creation.

Have you ever seen one of those old science-fiction movies where a spaceship explodes and

THAT'S AMAZING!

As of now, the farthest we've seen into space is more than 13 billion light-years away. That tells us that the heavens God created are bigger than most of us can imagine! But as huge as outer space is, the farthest any human being has traveled in space is to our moon,

which is about 250,000 miles from Earth. On July 20, 1969, the spacecraft *Apollo 11*, which was commanded by Neil Armstrong, achieved the first manned landing on the moon's surface. Armstrong was the first to set foot on the moon, followed by Buzz Aldrin. After that mission, the United States' National Aeronautics and Space Administration (NASA) carried out five more manned moon landings, the last of which was in 1972.

One of the twelve humans to walk on the moon explores a deep hole called the Plum Crater. Notice the electric-powered "moon buggy" in the background. Look like fun!

gives off a loud *bang*? Outer-space explosions in movies can look and sound pretty cool. But did you know that if a blast like that happened in outer space, it wouldn't give off any sound at all?

In order for sound to travel, it has to have something to travel through. Sound travels by causing tiny particles of air—called *molecules*—to vibrate. Of course, sound can also travel through other kinds of molecules, like water, and even some solid objects like wood or metal. On Earth, where there is air, sound travels to your ears through vibrating air. But since there is no air or atmosphere of any kind in space, sound waves can't travel there.

Light, on the other hand, *can* travel through space. If you want quick proof, all you have to do is look up in the sky at night and see the stars. The light from those stars traveled many millions of miles before it reached Earth. Light can travel through space because it doesn't have to travel through anything like air or other matter. So if you were in outer space and a spaceship exploded, you could see the flash but you wouldn't hear the sound of the explosion.

Dust and hydrogen gas mix to form this giant
cloud in space. This photo, of the Eagle Nebula,
was taken from the Hubble Space Telescope.

Even though outer space isn't crowded with big objects bumping into one another, it is not really empty, either. Some of the huge gaps between planets and stars and other bodies in space are filled with huge amounts of gas and dust. A lot of that gas and dust is spread very thin in space. Some of it appears only as atoms or molecules. There are also many kinds of radiation in space. The sun gives off many kinds of radiation that make their way through space and arrive here on Earth. Some of the radiation in space is necessary for life on Earth.

The Size and Shape of Planet Earth

The planet you live on might seem pretty big to you, but com-pared with the rest of the universe God created, Earth is like a tiny speck of sand on a huge, sand dune-covered beach. The universe is that big!

But just how big is the earth? Actually, that depends on how you measure it. The earth's *diameter* (how wide it is) is about 7,900 miles, and its *circumference* (how big around it is) is about 24,900 miles. The earth's *radius* (the distance between the surface of the earth all the way down to its center) is about 4,000 miles. The earth's total surface area—including both land and water—is almost 197 million square miles.

Earth is huge to us but just a tiny part of the whole universe.

THAT'S AMAZING!

It might amaze you to know this, but people who lived before the time of Jesus had a pretty good idea of the earth's actual size. In about 200 BC, a Greek mathematician named Eratosthenes of Cyrene used the altitude of the sun in the sky on the first day of summer (the *summer solstice*) in a city called Syene (now Aswan, Egypt) and in Alexandria, Egypt, which was about 490 miles north of Syene, to calculate that the earth's circumference was about 25,000 miles. He was off by less than 100 miles!

Eratosthenes of Cyrene

While you probably didn't know how big around or how wide the earth is, you probably know that the earth is round. Or is it?

Actually, the earth isn't perfectly round. . .even though the globe in your school classroom— or maybe the one you have in your own bedroom—makes it look that way. Scientists call our planet an *oblate spheroid* because it bulges a little bit at the equator, which is the line that circles the earth and separates the Northern Hemisphere from the Southern Hemisphere. The earth is about 42 miles bigger around at the equator than it is when measured around from north to south.

That means that the earth isn't shaped like a fully inflated basketball but more like that same basketball if you let some of the air out of it, put it on the floor, and then lightly pressed down on it from the top.

THE WAY IT USED TO BE

One of the first things you probably learned in school about the earth is that it is round. But people didn't always believe that. Thousands of years ago, almost everyone believed that the earth was flat like a piece of paper and not round like a basketball. That began to change in the fourth century BC, when Greek scientists and philosophers—including Aristotle, one of the first to provide real evidence that the earth was not flat—began to teach that the earth was a sphere (like a basketball), or at least round in shape.

The Layers of the Earth

If you were to look at a cross-section of the earth—in other words, split it in half so you could see what is inside—you'd see that the earth is made of four different layers. . .sort of like the layers of an onion. The outermost layer of the earth is called the *crust*.

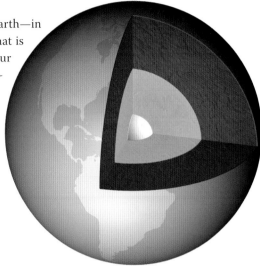

The earth's crust is about 25 miles thick underneath land but only about 6.5 miles thick underneath the oceans. The earth's crust is made up of relatively light and brittle materials that can crack during earthquakes. There are about 90 known elements in the earth's crust, and they combine in several natural ways to create materials known as *minerals*. There are about 3,700 known minerals in the earth's crust.

Underneath the earth's crust is what is called the *mantle*. The earth's mantle is the

Earth's four layers are seen in this cross-section diagram—the crust, or thin outer layer; the mantle, in brown; the outer core, in orange; and the inner core, in yellow.

thickest layer of the four. It extends from the bottom of the crust all the way down into the earth about 1,800 miles. The mantle is made up of thick, solid, rocky materials that make up about 85 percent of the earth's weight and mass. Scientists believe the first 50 miles or so of the mantle are made up of very hard rock. The 150 miles after that are made up of very hot (an estimated 4,000 to 6,700 degrees Fahrenheit) rock. The rest of the mantle is made up of very solid, strong rocky materials.

The next layer of the earth after the mantle is the *outer core*. The outer core is about 3,000 miles beneath the surface. Scientists believe the outer core is made up of very hot (about 6,700 degrees Fahrenheit) liquid metals—mostly iron and nickel. The earth's *inner core* is also very hot (around 6,700 to 8,500 degrees Fahrenheit) and is also made mostly of iron and nickel, but it is under such pressure that it is completely solid.

DID YOU KNOW. . . ?

The earth itself—not counting its atmosphere—is made up of several elements. *Elements* are substances that cannot be broken down by any natural chemical means. They are the basic building blocks of everything around us. The earth is made up of about 34.6 percent iron (most of which is in the inner layers of the earth), 29.5 percent oxygen, 15.2 percent silicon, 12.7 percent magnesium, 2.4 percent nickel, 1.9 percent sulfur, and .05 percent titanium.

The Earth's Surface—a Huge Jigsaw Puzzle

When you look at a map of the earth, you might get the idea that its surface is one solid shell that covers the entire planet. But the earth's crust is not one big solid outer layer. It is actually broken up into several huge, thick plates that sit on top of the earth's mantle. These plates are made of rock, and they are about 50 to 250 miles thick.

The seven largest of these plates are the African plate, the Eurasian plate (under Europe and Asia), the North American plate, the South American plate, the Australian plate, the Antarctic plate, and the Pacific plate. There are also several other smaller plates on the earth's surface, including the Arabian, Nazca, and Philippine plates. The places where the plates meet one another are called *plate boundaries.*

These plates don't just sit in one place. They move both sideways in different directions and up and down. The plates move very slowly—from under an inch to a few inches every year, depending on which plate it is. Sometimes the plates move away from each other, but sometimes they crash together or brush one another as they move. Most of the earth's volcanoes and earthquakes (what scientists call *seismic activity*) happen when the earth's plates move away from, toward, or into one another.

Scientist Andrea Donnellan uses special equipment to measure California's San Andreas Fault. Earthquakes often happen along the fault, where the North American and Pacific plates meet.

The Gift of Water

Earth is a one-of-a-kind creation because it is the only planet in our solar system—which includes our sun and the other planets that orbit it—known to have liquid water, which is absolutely necessary for the survival of all known life forms.

About 71 percent (almost three-quarters) of our earth's surface is covered with saltwater oceans. Continents and islands—as well as the freshwater rivers, lakes, and streams found on them—make up the rest of the earth's surface.

Scientists estimate that there are more than 326 million *trillion* gallons of water on our planet. That's an awful lot of water! But where do you think all that water is at any given time? If you guessed that most of it is in the oceans, you'd be right! Around 97 percent of the earth's water at any given time is in the oceans, seas, and bays. Less than 3 percent of the earth's water is freshwater, and most of that water is found in ice caps, glaciers, and other frozen forms.

Though you can see the evidence of water in our atmosphere in the form of clouds, the amount of water in the atmosphere (.001 percent) is a very small part of the total water on Earth. It might surprise you to know that the world's freshwater lakes and rivers also account for a very small amount of the total water on Earth.

A scuba diver skims through the clear blue water of the Caribbean Sea.

Even though there is an amazing amount of water on the earth's surface, a small percentage of it is drinkable. Most of the earth's water is found in seas and oceans—about 97 percent—and is too salty to drink. Another 2 percent is frozen in ice caps and glaciers. That leaves less than 1 percent of all the water on Earth that is fresh and clean enough for humans and animals to drink.

What's So Important about Water?

When God created the earth, He made sure that the people, animals, and plants He created it for would have everything they needed to live, grow, and reproduce. That included the most common—and most important—substance in the world: water!

Without water, life as we know it on Earth simply can't exist. Many kinds of plants and animals live in the water, but they aren't the only ones who need water to live. People, as well as all land animals, plants, and other living things, must have water in order to survive. In fact, we humans can live for weeks without eating food, but we would survive less than seven days without water.

Water is important to all living things because it has the ability to dissolve other substances. That helps water to carry needed nutrients to cells and to carry waste away from them. The bodies of almost all living things are more than half water. Some organisms' bodies are up to 95 percent water. Water makes up about 60 to 70 percent of the weight of your body, and about 83 percent of your blood is water. Even your bones are 25 percent water! The human brain weighs about 3 pounds, but if you squeezed all the water out of your brain, it would weigh only 10 ounces.

Jellyfish are approximately 95 percent water. This one is called a "moon jellyfish."

The Wonder of Water

You've probably heard water called H_2O. Have you ever wondered what that means? When you look at a glass of water, what you're seeing is millions of tiny particles of water called *water molecules*. Each water molecule is made up of two atoms of hydrogen (the H_2 part) and one atom of oxygen (the O part).

You'd need a very good microscope to see what this model imitates—two hydrogen atoms attached to an oxygen atom, making up a molecule of water.

When these three atoms come together to form a water molecule, the bond is very hard to break. That is partly why nearly all the water on Earth now has been here since the beginning of creation. That means that the water we are using today is the same water that people all through history used and the same water the animals God first created used. Just think! Someone famous in history may have bathed in the very same water that you brushed your teeth with this morning! (Don't worry. . .all the *impurities*—the gross stuff you wouldn't want to put in your mouth—are long gone, so when you use water from your tap to brush your teeth, you're using just the water.)

Today, we find water on Earth in three forms. Water appears as a *liquid* (just plain water), as a *solid* (ice), and as a *gas* (steam or water vapor). The fact that water can take on these three forms helps the earth to distribute its water through ocean currents, through the movement of ice, and through precipitation (rain and snow).

In its natural form, water freezes and takes on solid form at 32 degrees Fahrenheit. Water boils and begins to turn to gas at 212 degrees Fahrenheit. But water doesn't have to reach 212 degrees Fahrenheit to be turned to gas or vapor. Water also turns to vapor in the form of clouds and fog when water from the ocean evaporates and forms

Water appears in its three forms—liquid, solid, and gas—off Greenland.

tiny water droplets. The tiny droplets of water are invisible until they condense enough in the atmosphere to form clouds and fog.

THAT'S WEIRD!

Water really is an amazing substance. You may have learned in school that water is the only material on Earth that exists as a solid, liquid, and a gas in natural conditions on our planet. But in the right conditions, water can actually take on other forms. When water is cooled down very quickly to colder than around negative 184 degrees Fahrenheit, a weird thing happens: The water turns to the thickness of molasses. At negative 211, the water turns solid but has no crystal structure, like normal ice has. Scientists call this phenomenon glassy water—because the frozen water is completely clear, just like glass.

"Altocumulus" clouds are generally dark in the center and puffy white on the edges...
unless there's a dramatic red sunset behind them!

CHAPTER 2
DAY 1, PART II
LET THERE BE LIGHT!

Then God said, "Let there be light," and there was light. And God saw that the light was good. Then he separated the light from the darkness. God called the light "day" and the darkness "night." And evening passed and morning came, marking the first day.

GENESIS 1:3–5

Can you imagine being in a place where there is absolutely no light? We're not talking about the kind of darkness you can experience on a really dark night away from the city lights when the moon isn't shining overhead. That's dark, but it's not *absolute* darkness because there is always some light. (If you're ever out on a night like that, you'll find that your eyes will adjust and you will be able to see at least a little bit.) We're talking about absolute blackness—the kind where you literally can't see your hand in front of your face.

The Bible says that in the beginning, "darkness covered the deep waters" (Genesis 1:2). This was before God created light of any kind, so it's easy to imagine that creation up to that point was covered in absolute darkness. Not only wasn't there much to be seen (remember, the earth was just a formless mass at that time), there wasn't even any light to see it!

But it wasn't long before God put a stop to that incredible darkness by simply speaking the words, "Let there be light." In an instant, God had taken that first step in preparing the earth as a suitable place for people, plants, and animals to live on. Not only would the light God created allow us humans and the animals to see, but it would also be the basis for all life on planet Earth.

LET THERE BE LIGHT!

The sun helps plants to grow...and the plants help you to grow!

Why Light Is Important

How would you answer if someone were to ask you why light is important? Probably the first thing that would come to your mind is that you need light to see! But let's imagine for a moment that every living thing on Earth—including us humans—had every sense we have now. . .except sight. Would light still be important to us? If so, *how* would it be important?

Light, which comes from the sun to the earth, is an absolute necessity for everything that lives here. Without light, nothing could live on Earth. That includes the plants and animals that live above ground, as well as the ones that live underground. And it includes people!

One reason light is important is because plants need it to grow and produce energy—or food. This happens during a process called *photosynthesis*, which you'll read more about in chapter 4. Plants are the foundation of all food here on Earth. All animals on Earth eat either plants or other animals that eat plants. Without light, plants would stop growing and die, and if that happened, all other life here on Earth, including humans, would soon die of starvation.

Light from the sun is also important because it heats the earth. Without the sun's light, there wouldn't be enough energy on Earth to keep us warm enough to live here. God placed our planet just the right distance from the sun to allow its light to heat our atmosphere to just the right temperature.

When God created light, He created the foundation for all the life He would later carefully design to live here on Earth. God thought far enough ahead in His plan of creation to know that before any living things could be placed here on Earth, there had to be light to support them and feed them.

THAT'S WEIRD!

As crazy as it may sound, scientists have proved that light itself can be bent or moved by intense gravity from objects such as stars. Gravity can also change the energy of light. The astrophysicist Sir Arthur Eddington proved the effect of gravity on light during a solar eclipse in 1919. With the sun completely blocked and the sky dark enough to see stars, Eddington photographed the stars that appeared close to the sun in the sky and observed that their light had actually been bent as it passed by the sun.

In a total solar eclipse, the moon almost exactly blocks the sun, leaving only the sun's "crown" (or corona) in view.

What Is Light Really?

Maybe all you really understand about light is that you need it in order to not trip over things when you walk into a room. When you walk into your bedroom at night, the first thing you probably do is reach for a light switch so you can see where you're going.

But there's a lot more to light than just how it allows us to see things. Light is a fascinating creation of God that has some amazing scientific properties—some of which you probably never even thought of before.

Light is sometimes called *radiant energy* or *electromagnetic energy* because it is both electric and magnetic. There are many kinds of light. There is the light you can see, and there is light you can't see—like gamma rays, X-rays, ultraviolet light, and radio waves. While you may not have thought of some of these things as light, by all scientific definitions, they really are forms of light.

Sir Isaac Newton (1642–1727)

For centuries, people argued over whether light travels as a *wave* (like waves in water, only without what scientists call a *medium*) or as *particles* (like tiny pellets from a shotgun blast). In the seventeenth century (about 400 years ago), the great English scientist Sir Isaac Newton studied light and came to the conclusion that it was more or less a stream of particles (he called them *corpuscles*). Around that same time, another great scientist named Christiaan Huygens, who lived and worked in Holland, taught that light traveled in waves.

As it turns out, they were both right!

During the twentieth century, scientists started to believe and teach that light travels as both particles and waves. This idea is called *wave-particle duality*. Scientists began believing this because light behaves like a wave in some ways and like a particle in others. They call the particles of light *quanta*—which is plural for *quantum*—or *photons*.

Christiaan Huygens (1629–1695)

How Light Travels. . .and What It Does When It Gets Here

When you're outside on a sunny day, you probably don't think much about how the sunlight you're enjoying made it through space to Earth. But sunlight doesn't just leave the sun and arrive here on Earth in an instant. In fact, the light and warmth you feel from the sun actually left the sun's surface about 8 minutes, 18 seconds before it reached you.

Light travels through space at about 186,000 miles per second. When light leaves the sun, it travels in a straight line—in all directions. But when it hits something either here on Earth or somewhere else—even air—it starts to act very differently. And you can be thankful that it does!

When it comes to your ability to see things, the most important thing light does when it runs into things is reflect. If it weren't for reflection, you couldn't see anything around you. That's because when light hits something here on Earth—a person, a car, a tree. . .anything you can imagine—it bounces, or reflects, off that object and into your eyes, allowing you to see it. If light were somehow stopped from reflecting off of things, they would still be there, but you wouldn't be able to see them.

The speed and direction of light also changes when it runs into materials like water, glass, or plastic. When light waves hit these materials, they slow down and bend. This is called *refraction*. You can see the effects of refraction when you look at someone standing waist-deep in the water in a swimming pool. From where you stand, it looks like the water has changed the angle of the person's legs. But the water hasn't done anything at all to that person; it's just that light bends and changes direction when it hits water, and that makes it look like the person's legs have been bent at the wrong angle.

Humans have made great use of the refraction of light. For example, the lenses of eyeglasses, which are usually made of glass or plastic, are curved enough to refract (or bend) the light that enters a person's eyes and allow him or her to see things more clearly than he or she could without glasses. Refraction is also used in cameras, binoculars, camcorders, and other things designed with lenses.

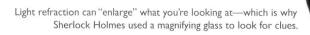

Light refraction can "enlarge" what you're looking at—which is why Sherlock Holmes used a magnifying glass to look for clues.

Why Is There Color? Because of Light!

One of the coolest things about light is that it allows us to see different colors. But did you know that light itself is actually a big collection of colors? It's true! If there were no colors in light, especially sunlight, you wouldn't be able to see any colors at all.

Here's a quick explanation of how color comes from light.

Light waves come in many different frequencies. The *frequency of light* is the number of light waves that pass through a certain point during a certain time period—usually one second.

Imagine that light waves are like waves in the ocean. Waves in water have a *crest* (a high point) and a *trough* (a low point). Depending on how the wave started, these crests and troughs can be of different sizes and can be farther apart or closer together. The same thing is true of light. In light, the distance between the crests and troughs is called the *amplitude*, and it determines the light's brightness. The distance between the crests of each wave is called the *wavelength*, and it determines the light's color.

If you could see the actual waves of light, you would see that *low frequency* light waves are a lot like slow, rolling waves in water—with more distance between each wave's peaks. *High frequency* light waves are like higher waves in water with less distance between them.

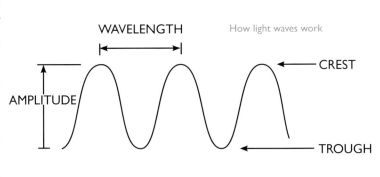

Low frequency light has lower energy, and high frequency light has higher energy. The light with the highest frequency are *gamma rays*, and the light with the lowest frequency are *radio waves*—both of which are invisible to the human eye. The visible light with the highest frequency is *violet light*, and the visible light with the lowest frequency is *red light*.

Your eyes can only see light that is more or less in the middle of the frequency spectrum. This range is called the *visible spectrum* or *visible light*. You can't see infrared light because it is just below the frequency of the visible spectrum, and you can't see ultraviolet light because it is just above the visible spectrum.

Your eye can tell apart around 10,000 different colors or shades of visible light. For example, you can see many different shades of each color. Most of the time, though, the visible spectrum of light is made up of a list of the seven major colors you can see in a rainbow. In order from the longest wavelength to the shortest, these colors are red, orange, yellow, green, blue, indigo, and violet. This list is often referred to as ROY G. BIV (go back and write down the first letter in each color of the rainbow in order, and you'll see why).

THAT'S WEIRD!

All electromagnetic radiation is considered light, but we humans can only see the light that is within a certain frequency or wavelength. But that doesn't mean that light we humans can't see is invisible to every living thing on planet Earth. Scientists have somehow figured out that certain kinds of reptiles can see infrared light and that many fish, reptiles, birds, and insects can see ultraviolet light. Both of these frequencies of light come from the sun, and both are completely invisible to us humans.

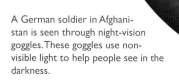

A German soldier in Afghanistan is seen through night-vision goggles. These goggles use non-visible light to help people see in the darkness.

God created the rainbow as a promise to never again flood the entire earth. See the whole story in Genesis 9:12–15.

How We See Colors

When you see sunlight on your hand or on some other object, it looks like it's pretty much one color—kind of yellowish white. That is why sunlight is sometimes called *white light*. But in reality, sunlight is made up of all the different colors all mixed together. When you look at a rainbow, what you're seeing is droplets of water splitting sunlight into its different colors by bending (or refracting) different colors of light.

So how do we see different colors here on Earth? Why is an apple red? Why are the leaves on plants green? It has a lot to do with how different things react to sunlight, and it also has to do with how our eyes receive light and color.

When sunlight hits a red apple, the red part of the sunlight is reflected off the apple's peel, while other colors are absorbed into the apple's skin so that you can't see them. On the other hand, if you were to look at the same red apple with sunlight shining on it that had been filtered through a piece of green plastic, the apple wouldn't appear red but would look black or gray. That's because the apple absorbed the green light instead of reflecting it back to you.

Everything on Earth is designed in such a way that it absorbs certain colors of light but reflects others. That's as true of your skin and hair and eyes as it is of green plants, red apples, and anything else on Earth that we see as having a particular color.

THAT'S AMAZING!

The first person to prove that sunlight is a mixture of all colors was Sir Isaac Newton, the great seventeenth-century English scientist. Newton passed sunlight through a glass prism to separate the colors into a rainbow spectrum. He then took a second prism and a lens and combined the two rainbows. You might think that the result was one big rainbow of colors, but you'd be wrong. What Newton produced when he combined the two spectrums was white light. This proved that white light isn't just white but is a mixture of light of many different colors or frequencies.

The First Day and the First Night

When God created light on that first day of creation, He also separated the times when it was dark outside and when it was light. Another way to say that is to say that God created night and day. Even though God wouldn't make the sun until the fourth day of creation, He started things out on the first day by designing the earth and light so that there would be night and day once about every twenty-four hours.

People use the terms sunrise and

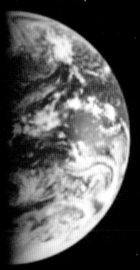

The Galileo spacecraft took this picture of earth-half bathed in the light of the sun—from almost four million miles away!

sunset to describe the daily appearance and disappearance of the sun. But in reality, the sun doesn't rise or set at all. The sun mostly stays in the same place—at least in relation to the earth—all the time. So when you see the sun appear in the east every morning and disappear in the west every evening, it's because the earth is spinning on an axis as it orbits (or circles) the sun. In other words, it's the earth that is moving in relation to the sun, not the other way around.

When it's dark outside where you live, it's because the sun is shining on the other side of the earth. That means that it's always daylight somewhere on Earth and that while you are sleeping, people on the other side of the world are busy doing some of the same kinds of things you do when it's daytime where you live.

One tradition says that in leap years, a woman can propose marriage to a man. This postcard, from more than 100 years ago, has some fun with that idea.

If someone were to ask you how long it takes the earth to *rotate* (make one complete spin) on its axis (in other words, how long a day on Earth lasts), you'd probably answer, "Everyone knows it's 24 hours!" But the earth doesn't rotate quite that long. It actually takes the earth only 23 hours, 56 minutes to completely rotate in relation to the sun. But here's another interesting fact: The time it takes the earth to *orbit* (or circle) the sun is actually a little more than a 365-day calendar year. The earth actually orbits the sun once every 365 days plus one-quarter of a day. That's why we have a February 29 once every four years in what is called a *leap year*.

When God Created Time

Even though all Christians agree that God created the earth and everything in and around it, some of them disagree over how long it took God to do it. Some believe the earth is very young—between 6,000 and 10,000 years old—while others believe the earth is very old. . .maybe billions of years old.

People will probably never completely agree on the answer to the question of how old the earth really is—at least not in this lifetime. But one thing we can probably all agree on is that God actually created time as we know it on the first day of creation when He separated day from night.

Has anyone ever asked you to define the word *time*? It's probably not as easy as you think! People mostly think of time in terms of seconds, minutes, hours, days, and years. But those are just *measurements* of time. It's hard to define time, so we'll just say that *time* is the means people use to measure the periods between certain events.

Probably the most basic measurement of time is the day. Since each day has a certain amount of daytime and a certain amount of nighttime, people use 24-hour days to measure time. But time is also measured by years. On Earth, a year is measured by the time it takes for the earth to completely orbit the sun. But even that measurement of time isn't perfect. You see, a year on Earth doesn't last exactly 365 days but about 365 days and 6 hours.

We humans are limited by time. We all begin our time on Earth when we are born, and one day our time on Earth will end. Not so with the God who began the process of making everything around us on that first day of creation. God exists outside the bounds of time. God is eternal. That means that He has always existed and will always exist. And when He created time on the first day, it was just the beginning of the process of showing His own greatness and love through making everything you see around you.

CHAPTER 3
DAY 2
OUR EARTH'S ATMOSPHERE

Then God said, "Let there be a space between the waters, to separate the waters of the heavens from the waters of the earth." And that is what happened. God made this space to separate the waters of the earth from the waters of the heavens. God called the space "sky." And evening passed and morning came, marking the second day.

GENESIS 1:6–8

You probably don't give a lot of thought to air when you take a deep breath, but the air you breathe is part of what makes it possible for you—and every other person and every other living thing—to live here on Earth.

Another word for the air you breathe is *atmosphere*. Earth's atmosphere is made up of three main gases: *nitrogen*, *oxygen*, and *argon*. About 78 percent (more than three-quarters) of our atmosphere is made up of nitrogen, with oxygen accounting for about 21 percent. Argon accounts for a little less than 1 percent of our planet's atmosphere, with the remainder made up of carbon dioxide and small traces of other gases. In addition to the gases in our atmosphere, there are also small particles of dust, water, and pollen floating around.

When you breathe in air, you breathe in everything that's in it. Nitrogen and argon are what are called *inert gases*, which means they don't react chemically with other substances. So when the nitrogen and argon enter your lungs when you inhale, they do an about-face and leave your lungs when you exhale. . .without affecting your body in any real way. The same is not true of oxygen—and it's a good thing, too!

Oxygen is the life-sustaining part of Earth's atmosphere. Nearly every living thing on Earth needs oxygen to survive. Every cell in your body requires oxygen to work properly. Your body gets the oxygen it needs when you breathe air—or atmosphere—into your lungs.

Oxygen is one of Earth's ninety-four *naturally occurring chemical elements*—meaning a substance that can't be broken down by any natural means on Earth. While nitrogen and argon are inert gases, oxygen reacts easily with many other elements and chemicals. For example, in your body, oxygen reacts with carbon to create carbon dioxide, which leaves your body when you exhale. Oxygen is not only important because most living things breathe it in, but because things on Earth need it to *combust*—or burn.

DID YOU KNOW. . . ?

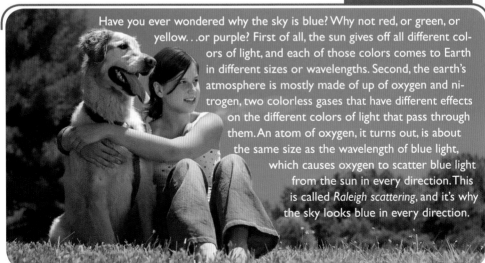

Have you ever wondered why the sky is blue? Why not red, or green, or yellow. . .or purple? First of all, the sun gives off all different colors of light, and each of those colors comes to Earth in different sizes or wavelengths. Second, the earth's atmosphere is mostly made of up of oxygen and nitrogen, two colorless gases that have different effects on the different colors of light that pass through them. An atom of oxygen, it turns out, is about the same size as the wavelength of blue light, which causes oxygen to scatter blue light from the sun in every direction. This is called *Raleigh scattering*, and it's why the sky looks blue in every direction.

How Our Atmosphere Is Put Together

You can think of the earth's atmosphere as a thin layer of air surrounding the entire globe. The atmosphere is held in place by the earth's gravity. The higher you go above the earth's surface, the thinner the atmosphere becomes. That's because gravity pulls the atmosphere down so that it compresses on itself at lower elevations.

The main part of the earth's atmosphere is about 300 miles thick, with smaller parts of the atmosphere extending out about 6,000 miles. Most of the gases and other materials in the atmosphere are found in the first ten miles above the earth's surface.

The air pressure of our atmosphere at sea level is about 14.7 pounds per square inch, which is just about right for people and most other living things to breathe comfortably. This is called *atmospheric pressure*. But the atmosphere's air pressure decreases the higher up you go. At about 18,000 feet, the atmosphere's air pressure can be as low as half what it is at sea level.

If you've ever visited a place that is high above sea level—like on a high mountaintop or in a city like Denver, Colorado—you might have noticed that it was a little harder to breathe. That's because there is less oxygen in the air at higher altitudes, which means your lungs have to work harder to collect enough to keep you going.

The atmosphere not only keeps oxygen where humans and other life forms need it to be, but it also acts like a blanket that insulates the earth and keeps it from becoming extremely hot or extremely cold.

BE AWARE OF THESE HIGH
ALTITUDE HAZARDS:
ALTITUDE SICKNESS
REGARDLESS OF FITNESS
LEVEL, 'LIGHTHEADEDNESS"
AND DISORIENTATION OFTEN
OCCUR AT THIS ELEVATION.
YOU MAY FAINT OR UNDER-
ESTIMATE OTHER DANGERS.
IF YOU EXPERIENCE ANY OF
THESE SYMPTOMS AVOID
PHYSICAL EXERTION AND
BREATHING TOO SLOW AND
TOO SHALLOW. EXERCISING
CAUTION, RETURN TO A
LOWER ELEVATION. IF
SYMPTOMS DO NOT SUBSIDE,
SEEK MEDICAL ASSISTANCE.
LIGHTNING
IF A STORM APPROACHES,
TAKE SHELTER IMMEDIATELY
OR CROUCH LOW WITH ONLY
YOUR FEET IN
CONTACT WITH THE GROUND.
ONE OF THE SAFEST PLACES
IS INSIDE A VEHICLE.
HYPOTHERMIA
STAY DRY, WEAR A
COAT AND HAT.

This warning sign, on Colorado's Mount Evans, warns visitors of the dangers of "thin air."

41

The Layers of Our Atmosphere

In chapter 1, you read about how the earth is made up of several different layers, each of which was constructed very differently from one another. The same thing is true of the atmosphere that surrounds Earth.

The layer of the earth's atmosphere closest to the ground—the part we live in—is called the *troposphere.* Our troposphere goes up from the earth's surface about 11 miles. The troposphere is where all Earth's weather occurs, and it's also where most of the gases in our atmosphere are concentrated.

The next level of Earth's atmosphere is a thin transitional layer between the troposphere and the stratosphere called the *tropopause.* The *stratosphere* begins about 11 miles from the earth's surface and ends around 31 miles up. This is where the earth's ozone layer is found. *Ozone* is a form of oxygen that is crucial to the survival of life on Earth because it absorbs much of the sun's ultraviolet light, which is very dangerous to people and other living things if they are exposed to it in high doses.

The earth's stratosphere is followed by a layer called the *mesosphere*, which begins about 31 miles above the earth's surface and ends about 50 miles up. Next is the *ionosphere*, which starts between 43 and 45 miles up and continues out about 400 miles. The ionosphere is followed by the *exosphere*, which goes from about 400 miles out to about 800 miles above Earth's surface. The exosphere and part of the ionosphere together make up what is called the *thermosphere.*

Weather. . .an Important Function of the Atmosphere

Take a look outside right now and ask yourself what the weather is like. Is it sunny and warm? Is it cloudy and rainy? Or is it windy and cold? We use the word *weather* to describe what our atmosphere is doing around us on a given day—whether it's warm and dry, cool and rainy, clear and warm. Weather includes factors like cloudiness, *precipitation* (rain, snow, hail, and other kinds of moisture that fall from the sky), windiness, temperature, and *humidity* (how much water vapor is in the air).

Wet, cool weather can sometimes be a disappointment when you want to be outside enjoying yourself. Who wouldn't rather be outdoors on a nice sunny day than stuck inside on a rainy and cold one? But different kinds of weather serve different purposes—and all of them are important for life on Earth. For example, when it rains, water falls on the soil plants grow in and gives them the moisture they need to continue growing. And when the rain stops and the sky clears, those same plants receive an extra shot of sunlight, which is also necessary for them to grow.

Rain is produced when water evaporates and rises up to the sky, forming clouds. When the clouds start moving, the water vapor condenses, forming larger drops of water. When the drops become big and heavy enough, gravity from the earth pulls them downward. When that happens, we have rain!

Snow happens basically the same way, but with a few differences. Snow forms when the temperature in the clouds is cold enough for water vapor to condense and turn into ice. The tiny drops of moisture then start to stick together and become ice crystals. When enough of the ice crystals have gathered together, they begin to fall from the sky (again, getting some help from gravity). If the temperature between the clouds and the ground is cold enough, the ice crystals reach the ground as snowflakes. If not, they reach the ground as rain or a mixture of rain and snow called *sleet*.

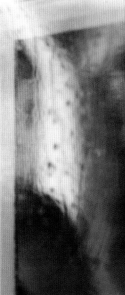

Hail also starts as droplets of water. When a strong upward wind from the surface of the earth pushes the drops above the freezing level, the droplets freeze. When they become heavy enough, they start to fall toward Earth. At that point, these balls of ice usually either melt and fall as rain or stay solid and fall as hail. Sometimes, if the upward wind is strong enough, the wind pushes the hailstones back up above the freezing level, where they become bigger hailstones.

These baseball-sized hailstones fell on Wisconsin in 2007.

THAT'S WEIRD!

Late in December of 2006, a couple living in Folsom, California, reported what had to be the strangest weather event they had ever seen. It was *raining fish*! Even if the story seems a little hard to swallow, in truth there are several instances of fish falling from the sky worldwide every year. It can happen when *waterspouts*—tornadoes over water with winds as high as 200 miles per hour—suck fish out of the water and drop them over land. People as far as 100 miles inland have witnessed raining fish.

Like a tornado, a waterspout is made up of whirling winds—which suck up water from lakes or seas.

How Do Clouds Work?

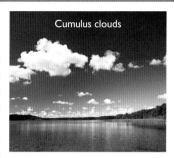
Cumulus clouds

Clouds are actually collections of tiny droplets of water or ice that are small enough for wind to carry them upward from the earth's surface. Most clouds form when water evaporates in the ocean or other big bodies of water, but some clouds can form over land—that is, when there is enough moisture in them.

There are four main types of clouds: cumulus, cirrus, stratus, and nimbus. When you see white, fluffy clouds in the sky—you know, the ones that can sometimes look like animals or people... if you use your imagination—you're seeing *cumulus clouds*. But sometimes cumulus clouds can be thick and gray. When you see a big, gray cumulus cloud, then it will probably rain soon. Cumulus clouds are formed when warm air carries water vapor from the ground. When that warm, wet air meets cold air in the sky, the vapor condenses into droplets of water and forms a cumulus cloud.

Cirrus clouds

Cirrus clouds are the thin, wispy clouds you sometimes see high in the sky—even on a very nice day. Cirrus clouds look the way they do because they are made of ice crystals instead of water droplets. Cirrus clouds form high enough in the sky where it is cold enough for water droplets to freeze.

Stratus clouds look like big, gray blankets hanging low in the sky. If you see stratus clouds, then you can be pretty sure that it's going to rain—or snow if it's cold enough outside. Stratus clouds can hang so low from the sky that they touch the ground. That is what we call *fog*.

Stratus clouds

When you see a *nimbus cloud* headed your way, it's probably a good idea to get inside. That's because nimbus clouds are often the source of thunderstorms—and sometimes tornadoes. Many times when you see a nimbus cloud on the horizon, you can already see that it has rain—or snow, or sometimes hail—falling out of it. You might even be able to see the flashes of lightning, too!

Nimbus clouds

There are a few other kinds of clouds, and most of them are combinations of the basic four listed above. There is the *cumulonimbus* cloud, which is a cumulus cloud with rain coming out of it. This cloud can be the source of some really bad weather—even tornadoes. There is also the *stratonimbus* cloud, which is a stratus cloud that looks like a gray blanket with rain falling out of it.

What's with the Wind?

Do you like really windy days? Some people like windy days, but some don't like them at all. Some people are even afraid of really strong wind. But wind is an important part of how our earth keeps itself from overheating. That's because wind helps move heat around and equalize it, and also because it moves heat away from the earth's surface and up into the higher parts of the atmosphere.

This barometer measures changes in atmospheric pressure to predict the weather.

Wind happens when air moves from a place where the air pressure—also known as *barometric pressure*—is high to a place where the air pressure is low. How strong the wind blows depends on how big the difference in air pressure is between two places. When there are big differences in air pressure between two places, the wind will be stronger. Sometimes the differences are so great that violent storms like hurricanes and cyclones start. But when the difference isn't too great, the wind will be weaker—maybe even a nice, gentle breeze.

Several different factors can cause the differences in air pressure that result in wind. These factors include heat from the sun. Different parts of the earth receive different amounts of heat and light from the sun. This causes the temperatures to be hot near the equator and cold at the North Pole and South Pole. Extreme heat causes low pressure and extreme cold causes high pressure. That's because hot air tends to rise while cold air tends to stay close to the ground. These extreme differences in temperatures cause differences in barometric pressure, which causes wind.

EXPLORING THE WORLD OF WIND

If you're looking for a good illustration of how wind works, try this. Take two balloons that are about the same size. Blow one of them up until it is filled with air—don't tie it off. Blow the other balloon up halfway so that it is still soft and squishy. Now, hold each balloon at the bottom, then let them go at the same time. You'll probably notice that the balloon you filled completely flies around the room faster and longer than the one you filled halfway. That's because the balloon you filled completely has higher air pressure inside it so the air comes out of it faster as the air inside the balloon tries to equalize itself with the air outside the balloon.

Climate and Weather: What's the Difference?

There are many factors that determine what kind of weather you see around you. One of those factors is the *climate* you live in. Climate isn't exactly the same thing as weather, but it has every-thing to do with the kind of weather you usually see where you live.

Weather is what happens in a small area of the world during a short period of time. Weather can and does change often. For example, it might be rainy and cool where you are today, but to-morrow it just might be sunny and warm. Or if it's cold and snowy this week, next week it might be warmer and rainy.

On the other hand, the *climate* of a certain part of the world is usually determined by the kind of weather that area experi-ences over a long period of time—usually about 30 years. The climates of different parts of the world can be dry or wet, warm or cool—and everything in between. But that doesn't mean that the area won't sometimes experience weather that doesn't exactly fit in with the climate it is known for.

Some parts of the world are known for extreme climates. For ex-ample, the Sahara Desert in north-ern Africa is known for very dry, very hot weather. Antarctica, which is located in the extreme southern part of planet Earth, is known for extremely cold weather—way too cold for people to live there.

Bedouins—people who live in the desert—cross the Sahara with their camels.

Tourists bundle up to watch Antarctic penguins—who watch the people in return.

RECORD BREAKING

Here's the classic image of Death Valley—a bleached cow skull baking on dry, cracked soil.

Most of us are lucky enough not to be living in places where the temperatures get extremely hot or extremely cold. But there are places in the world where records are set. The hottest daily temperature on record took place in a place called El Azizia, Libya (Libya is a country in North Africa). Way back on September 13, 1922, the temperature there reached 136 degrees Fahrenheit. The hottest temperature ever recorded in the United States was 134 degrees Fahrenheit, recorded on July 10, 1913, in Death Valley, California. The coldest temperature ever was recorded was on July 21, 1983, in Vostok Station in Antarctica (it is winter in Antarctica in July), where it reached negative 128.6 degrees Fahrenheit.

The plants in Washington's Olympic National Park like all that rain—it's one of the wettest places in the United States.

If you don't like rain, then the Atacama Desert in Chile might be the place for you. This area receives an average of about one inch of rainfall a year, but in some spots there has never been measurable rainfall recorded since people started keeping track of weather. Nothing lives in the driest parts of the Atacama Desert, not even cactus plants! On the other hand, if you like rain—*really* like rain—then you would probably like Mawsynram, a village in northeastern India, which receives around 467 inches—almost 39 feet!—of rain each year.

Things that Affect Climate

There are several factors that affect climate in different parts of the world. These factors include an area's distance from the equator, its distance from the ocean, its altitude, and its distance from mountains.

The equator receives more direct sunlight than the rest of the world, so it is warmer. If you were to travel north or south from the equator, you would probably notice that the weather gets cooler and cooler the farther you get from the equator. By the time you reached the North Pole or South Pole, you'd look around you and see that everything is covered in ice and snow.

Coastal areas are usually cooler and wetter than inland areas. That is because clouds form over water when warm air collides with cool air from the sea. Areas close to large bodies of water also tend to be more humid because water from the ocean, sea, or lake evaporates. Generally, the closer you are to the ocean or sea—or other large body of water—the wetter and cooler the air will be where you live. On the other hand, the farther you live from big bodies of water, the drier it will be where you live. That's because moisture from these bodies of water evaporates before it can reach you.

Altitude, meaning how far above sea level a certain place is located, affects climate because places that are farther away from sea level receive less heat and energy from the sun. You can easily see evidence of that fact when you look at a mountain—or a picture of one, if you don't live near a mountain range. Even when the ground is dry, the mountaintop (if it is in a climate where it is possible for snow to fall) is covered in ice and snow. That's simply because it's colder up there!

That seems a little backwards, doesn't it? You would think that since higher places are closer to the sun, then they would be warmer. But it doesn't work that way. Actually, the atmosphere isn't warmed directly by the sun's rays. The earth's surface absorbs most of the heat from the sun, and as it warms up, it heats the atmosphere. The lower levels of the atmosphere—the ones close to the earth's surface—absorb and trap most of the heat, leaving very little of it to reach high altitudes.

Mountains can have a huge effect on the climate of the lands around them. In some coastal areas, mountains block rain from reaching inland areas. In situations like that, land on one side of the mountain may be very rainy, but the other side will be drier. In the Pacific Northwest, for example, the Coast Range and the Cascade Mountains each keep inland areas from receiving as much rain as they would have. That's why it's very rainy on the Oregon and Washington coast, less rainy in the inland parts of the states, and drier east of the Cascade Mountains.

Skiers are glad that air gets colder as you go up a mountain!

CHAPTER 4

DAY 3

THE OCEANS...THE LAND... AND THE PLANTS

Then God said, "Let the waters beneath the sky flow together into one place, so dry ground may appear." And that is what happened. God called the dry ground "land" and the waters "seas." And God saw that it was good. Then God said, "Let the land sprout with vegetation—every sort of seed-bearing plant, and trees that grow seed-bearing fruit. These seeds will then produce the kinds of plants and trees from which they came." And that is what happened. The land produced vegetation—all sorts of seed-bearing plants, and trees with seed-bearing fruit. Their seeds produced plants and trees of the same kind. And God saw that it was good. And evening passed and morning came, marking the third day.

GENESIS 1:9–13

During the first two days of creation, God laid the groundwork for a world that would look very much like it looks today. From the beginning, God intended that our earth would include oceans and land area that would serve as homes to the amazing number of plants, animals, and other living things He would create just a few days later.

On the third day of creation, God took what had been a fairly shapeless earth and turned it into one with oceans and other bodies of water separating huge pieces of land that would later be home to us humans. Not only that, He stocked the entire earth with plants—the living things that would later support all life on Earth.

Water, Water Everywhere!

Planet Earth is a one-of-a-kind creation because it is the only planet circling our sun that has oceans. In fact, no other planet known to humans has liquid water, which is necessary for supporting all known forms of life.

The oceans cover about 71 percent of the earth's surface and hold about 97 percent of all water on Earth. The Pacific Ocean is by far the biggest ocean in the world. It covers more than 64 million square miles of the earth's surface and has an average depth of about 14,000 feet. The Pacific is almost twice as big as the second largest ocean, the Atlantic. The Indian Ocean is the third biggest ocean in the world, followed by the Southern Ocean and the Arctic Ocean.

Up until the year 2000, there were four oceans recognized—the Pacific, the Atlantic, the Indian, and the Arctic. That doesn't mean that the earth suddenly developed a new ocean. It means that another area of saltwater was recognized as an ocean. In the spring of 2000, the International Hydrographic Organization recognized the Southern Ocean, which surrounds Antarctica deep in the Southern Hemisphere.

While there are only five oceans in the world, there are more than eighty-five seas. Seas are filled with saltwater, just like oceans, but they are usually smaller than oceans. In fact, many seas are smaller parts of oceans. For example, the Caribbean Sea, which is located southeast of the Gulf of Mexico, is a part of the Atlantic Ocean. The Pacific Ocean has more than thirty seas. Some seas aren't part of oceans but are completely surrounded by land. These are called *landlocked seas*, and they include the Dead Sea and the Caspian Sea.

Salt collects on the shore of the Dead Sea in Israel.

Even though humans have named five different oceans, all the world's oceans are actually connected with one another through currents that flow around the world. The five named oceans are divided up according to continents and other features in the ocean, such as ridges on the ocean floor. This huge body of saltwater is sometimes called the *World Ocean* or *global ocean*. The World Ocean covers about 139 million square miles of the earth's surface and has an average depth of about 12,230 feet.

THAT'S AMAZING!

The deepest water on Earth is called the Challenger Deep, a spot located in the Mariana Islands group at the southern end of the Mariana Trench in the Pacific Ocean—south of Japan, north of New Guinea, and east of the Philippines. No one knows for sure how deep the water there really is, but estimates tell us that it is more than 36,000 feet (almost seven miles) deep! Also amazing is the fact that scientists have found life on the floor of the Mariana Trench, including sea cucumbers, scale worms, shrimps, and other small organisms.

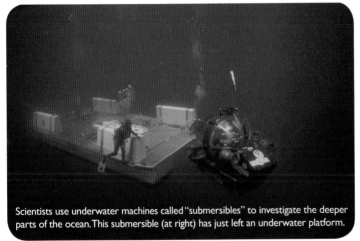

Scientists use underwater machines called "submersibles" to investigate the deeper parts of the ocean. This submersible (at right) has just left an underwater platform.

Why the Oceans Are Important to Us

Even if you don't live near an ocean, the world's oceans play a bigger part in your life than you realize. First of all, oceans are important to all life on Earth because they have a huge effect on weather and temperatures all over the world—even places that are far from any ocean.

Oceans help keep most of the surface of the earth from getting too hot or too cold because they absorb a lot of heat and light from the sun. They influence the entire world's weather by moving the warmth they absorb from the sun around the world through ocean currents and winds.

Oceans are also the source of most rain that falls on land all over the world. When water from the ocean evaporates, it leaves the salt and other materials behind and forms clouds. The clouds that form from the evaporated water then move over land, where the water in them condenses and then falls as life-giving rain.

Oceans are also important to people because they are huge sources of food such as fish, shrimps, crabs, and lobsters. Millions of people worldwide eat food that comes from the sea. That includes about 29 million tons of fish every year.

Another reason oceans are important to people is that many of the world's important goods are moved by ships that travel the ocean between the world's seaports. Those shipped goods include food, petroleum, and other important products you and your family use every day.

A fisherman pulls a net from the Atlantic Ocean, off the west African nation of Sierra Leone.

DID YOU KNOW. . .?

Have you ever wondered why oceans and other big bodies of water have high tides and low tides every day? Believe it or not, it has to do with gravity. . .from the moon! The moon's gravity pulls at the water in the oceans so that they begin to bulge out in the direction of the moon. If you think that's amazing, then wait till you hear this! The water in the oceans on the side of the earth facing *away* from the moon also bulges out and forms tides. That's because Earth is being pulled toward the moon and away from the water on the opposite side of the earth. High tides and low tides happen twice each day because the earth is rotating, which means that one-half of the earth is always facing away from the moon.

The moon reflects off the Mediterranean Sea over the French Riviera.

THE WAY IT USED TO BE

Up until the late 1400s, many European explorers traveled to other places in Europe and to Africa, but they wouldn't sail into the Atlantic Ocean. And why not? First of all, no one had ever done it, and the explorers didn't want to risk sailing into unknown waters. But they were also afraid of the myths they heard about the Atlantic—that the water far from shore was boiling and filled with horrible sea monsters. That all changed when in 1492, Christopher Columbus and his crew sailed across the Atlantic— without seeing any boiling water or sea monsters.

In the 1600s, when this map was created, some people still imagined monsters lurking in the world's seas.

The Ocean: A Perfect Home for Lots of Living Things

One of the reasons God created the oceans and seas was to provide a home for millions of different forms of life He would be making a few days later. To this day, the oceans are home to an amazing variety of creatures and plants that simply couldn't live anywhere else.

A big part of what makes oceans different from freshwater lakes and rivers is the saltiness of the water. Ocean water is salty because more than 30 different elements, ions, and compounds are dissolved in it. Six of those—chloride, sulfate, sodium (a scientific word for salt), magnesium, calcium, and potassium—make up about 99 percent of the total. The average saltiness of the ocean is about 35 parts per thousand. That means that for every thousand ounces of seawater, 35 of those ounces are made up of "sea salt."

The chemical makeup of saltwater makes it possible for the oceans and most of the seas to support countless kinds of life. Many kinds of animals and plants are designed to live in and near saltwater. That includes tiny creatures called *plankton*, which are food for many other ocean creatures, all the way up to the world's biggest animal, the blue whale. Whales, seals, fish, crustaceans, jellyfish, and many other animals live in the ocean. There are more than 15,000 known species of fish that live in the ocean, with many new kinds of saltwater fish being discovered and named every year. Also, there are more than 200,000 other animals and plants living in the world's oceans.

THAT'S AMAZING!

The Great Barrier Reef is a place where the waters "swarm with fish and other life" (Genesis 1:20 NLT).

The Great Barrier Reef, which is located off the coast of Queensland in northern Australia and stretches to a length of 1,616 miles, is such an amazing wonder of nature—and the creativity of God—that it has been called the largest living organism in the world. An amazing 4,000 species of mollusks, 1,500 species of fish (including 125 species of sharks), 400 species of corals, 215 species of birds, 500 species of seaweed, 17 species of sea snakes, and 6 species of sea turtles make their home there. Take the time to look up the Great Barrier Reef and see what kinds of animals and fish live there.

Lots of dry land—in the African nation of Namibia.

Land: The Other Part of the Earth's Surface

About 29 percent (less than one-third) of the earth's surface is dry land. This part of the world is called the *continental area*. Most of the dry land on Earth is joined together in big masses we now call *continents*. Most people recognize seven continents: North America, South America, Africa, Asia, Europe, Australia, and Antarctica. More than two-thirds of the continental area is north of the equator.

KIDS' GUIDE TO CREATION

Not everyone agrees that there are seven continents on Earth. That's because some continents are joined to one another by land. Some people also believe that Europe and Asia are parts of a huge continent called *Eurasia*. Some even believe that Eurasia and Africa is one continent, which they call *Eurafrasia*. Some believe that North America and South America combined is actually one continent called the *Americas*. And some people believe that Australia is only one part of a larger continent that includes New Zealand and the Pacific Islands. They call that continent *Oceania*.

Asia is by far the largest of the seven most commonly recognized continents. Asia covers more than 17 million square miles, which is almost 30 percent of the world's total land area. Asia is the only continent that borders two other continents—Africa and Europe—which are to the west of Asia. It is bordered to the east by the Pacific Ocean.

RECORD BREAKING

Asia is not only the world's largest continent, it is also home to some other kinds of world records—namely the highest point on Earth and the lowest point on land. The peak of Mount Everest, which is located on the border of Nepal and Tibet, is the highest place in the world at more than 29,000 feet above sea level. The lowest point on land is the Dead Sea, which is located between Israel and Jordan and sits around 1,370 feet *below* sea level.

Mount Everest, lit by the late afternoon sun

The Great Wall of China is one of Asia's best-known landmarks. Here, it crosses mountain tops near Beijing.

The Asian continent is so big that it is divided into five subregions: Northern Asia, Middle East, Southern Asia, Eastern Asia, and Southeastern Asia. Asia is also the continent with the most people living on it. Right now, six out of ten people alive on Earth live in Asia.

Africa is known for its fascinating wildlife. "Safaris"—special trips for tourists—allow people to see animals up close, like these elephants in Tanzania.

Africa is the world's second biggest continent at more than 11 million square miles, or about 20 percent of the world's total land area. Africa sits on the equator and stretches about 4,970 miles from its most northern point to its most southern tip. At its widest point, Africa is about 4,700 miles wide.

Niagara Falls connects the two largest nations of North America—the United States and Canada. Notice the boat in the river below the falls!

The third largest continent is North America, which includes the United States, Canada, Mexico, and the Caribbean and Central American nations. North America is also home to Greenland, the world's largest island. North America covers more than 9.4 million square miles of the earth's surface and accounts for about 16.5 percent of the world's land.

A giant statue of Jesus—"Christ the Redeemer"—overlooks one of South America's most important cities, Rio de Janeiro, Brazil.

South America is the world's fourth largest continent, covering more than 6.8 million square miles and making up about 12 percent of the earth's land. South America is home to some amazing natural wonders, including the Amazon River, at more than 3,900 miles long—the second longest river on the planet, as well as the largest tropical rain forest in the world. The Andes Mountains stretch the entire length of the continent.

Antarctica, which is the fifth largest continent by area, accounts for around 9.2 percent of the earth's land mass. Antarctica is almost completely covered year-round by a thick layer of ice. It is the coldest place on Earth, with temperatures in some parts of the continent sometimes dipping all the way down to below negative 100 degrees Fahrenheit! That's why Antarctica is last in total population. No one lives in Antarctica permanently, but a few thousand scientists work there during the summer, with only around 1,000 of them staying through the winter.

Ice, snow, and penguins are among the main features of Antarctica. What you won't find are many people!

Europe is the world's second smallest continent by area, covering just over 3.9 million square miles, or about 6.8 percent of the world's land mass.

The Eiffel Tower in Paris, France, is one of Europe's best-known landmarks. It was built in the late 1880s for a world's fair.

Australia is the smallest continent by area, accounting for about 5.9 percent of the world's land.

Ayers Rock, also called Uluru, is one of Australia's most famous natural landmarks. It's nearly six miles around— that's a big rock!

Where Do Continents End and the Oceans Begin?

Nearly all continents are surrounded from their beaches out toward the ocean by an extension of underwater land in the shallow part of the oceans called the *continental shelf*. The water over the continental shelf is usually not more than 500 to 650 feet deep. How wide a continental shelf is depends on the continent and its geological features. Some areas have almost no continental shelf, while some have continental shelves wider than 250 miles. For areas that do have continental shelves, the average shelf is about 50 miles in width. The largest continental shelf is called the Serbian Shelf. It is located in the Arctic Ocean and stretches 930 miles from shore.

The continental shelf is actually made up of several parts. The first part of the continental shelf starts just outside the shoreline of the continent. As you move from the shoreline out into the deeper parts of the ocean, the shelf slopes smoothly until it reaches what is called the *continental shelf break*. The continental shelf break usually starts in ocean waters about 430 feet deep. After the continental break, the floor of the ocean turns quickly downward. This feature of geology is called the *continental slope*. Farther out from the continental slope is the *continental rise*, which is a deposit of sediments that form as a result of runoff from the continent's streams and rivers. After the continental rise is what geologists call the *abyssal plains*, which is a scientific way of saying the deepest parts of the ocean.

The continental shelf isn't always flat. Some parts of the continental shelf include deep valleys as well as tall mountains and hills. Some of these mountains reach up past the surface of the sea, creating islands. Islands that stand on a continent's continental shelf are considered part of that continent.

The continental shelf is home to most of the kinds of plants and animals that live in the ocean—including fish and other living things that humans harvest and eat. This part of the ocean supports the most kinds of life because it receives more sunlight and because the sediment that washes into the ocean from the continent's rivers and streams provides nourishment for microscopic plants and animals that larger animals—such as fish—feed on. The continental shelf also supports the largest amounts of plants and animals that live on the ocean floor.

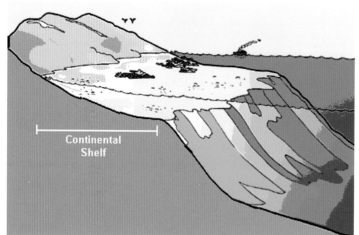

Continental Shelf

The continental shelf is a shallow, underwater plain that makes up a continent's true outer edge. It can be a few miles to more than 200 miles wide, before dropping off quickly to the deep ocean floor.

Islands Big and Small

It might surprise you to hear this, but today one out of every ten people living in the world live on islands. But when you realize that 200 million people live in Indonesia—which is made up entirely of islands—and that more than 60 million live on the island of Great Britain, it's not hard to imagine how so many people live on islands today.

Islands are bodies of land that are surrounded on all sides by water. Continents are also surrounded by water, but they are much larger and are therefore classified as continents. For example, Australia is surrounded by water, but it covers almost three million square miles. That's why Australia is considered a continent. Greenland, which is the world's largest island, is about one-fourth the size of Australia and is therefore considered an island.

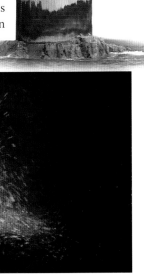

Bishop Rock island is just big enough to hold this lighthouse!

It's hard to say how many islands there are in the world. Today, people live on more than 100,000 of the world's islands, and there are many times more islands that people don't live on. The Asian island nation of Indonesia leads the world with a total of 13,667 islands, 6,000 of which are inhabited by people.

There are many kinds of islands in the world. Islands that sit on the continental shelf of a certain continent are called *continental islands*. The nations of Great Britain, Ireland, New Guinea, Barbados, and several others are all considered continental islands. Islands that sit in the ocean away from continental shelf are called *oceanic islands*. Scientists believe that almost all oceanic islands were made as the result of volcanoes. The Hawaiian Islands are examples of volcanic islands.

The smallest island in the world is Bishop Rock, which is located at the southwestern part of the United Kingdom. Actually, Bishop Rock is little more than that: a rock, sticking up out of the water. Greenland, on the other hand, covers about 840,000 square miles.

Red-hot lava bursts out of a volcano called Piton de la Fournaise, on the Indian Ocean island of Réunion.

Here's some good trivia to remember: The second tallest mountain in the world is called K2, or Mount Godwin-Austen. It's near the border of Pakistan and China.

RECORD BREAKING

You probably already know that Mount Everest, which is located in the Himalayas at the border of Tibet and Nepal, is the highest mountain peak in the world. The peak of Everest is an amazing 29,028 feet above sea level. But it might surprise you to know that Everest is not really the world's tallest mountain. That honor goes to Mauna Kea, a dormant volcano in Hawaii. Mauna Kea's peak is 13,796 feet above sea level, less than half the elevation of Everest. But if you measured from the base of Mauna Kea, which is deep on the ocean floor, you'd find it was more than 32,800 feet tall, far taller than Everest.

Observatories—buildings that house large telescopes—sit atop Hawaii's Mauna Kea. It's one of the best places in the world to see the stars.

All Land on Earth Is Not Equal

When God created the earth, then separated the water from the land, He designed many types of land masses. That includes mountain ranges, forests, deserts, valleys, canyons, plains, and other kinds of land we see on Earth today.

Some of the most amazing formations of land in the world are mountains. There are many mountains and mountain ranges on the earth. Geologists say that about 25 percent of the earth's surface is mountainous. Asia is the capital continent for mountains. More than half of Asia is covered in mountains, and all of the world's 50 tallest mountains are located there. Mountains are important to people, animals, and plants because they serve as barriers to weather and because they collect snow in the winter, which runs off the mountain when the weather warms and provides people with fresh water.

There are several kinds of mountains on Earth today. Some mountains were formed when huge plates on the earth's surface pushed against one another and caused the mountains to arise. The Rocky Mountains in North America are examples of those kinds of mountains. Other mountains were formed as the result of molten rock, or *magma*, pushing up from under the earth's crust. Sometimes the magma erupts and piles up on the surface, making what

Giant farm machines called combines harvest wheat on the plains.

is called a *volcanic mountain*. Mount St. Helens in Washington state is a volcanic mountain.

Some areas of land on Earth have no hills or mountains and receive enough precipitation to make them suitable for farming. These areas are called *plains*. The Great Plains of North America, which are located west of the Mississippi River and east of the Rocky Mountains, produce about 25 percent of the world's wheat, oats, barley, rye, sorghum, and corn.

Some areas of the world receive enough rain and snow each year to support large numbers of plants and other life. But other areas are so dry that only certain kinds of plants and animals can live there. *Deserts* are usually defined as areas of land that receive less than ten inches of rain or snow every year.

Camels can go a long time between drinks of water—which allows them to live in desert areas. This one is in China's Gobi Desert.

When God Made the World Come Alive

Imagine if someone set up a terrarium at school one day. He'd add the rocks, the sand, the water—maybe even some natural-looking decorations. Now. . .what do you think is missing? That's right! Plants and animals! No terrarium is complete without living things, even if they're just plants.

Creation wasn't complete until God began adding the living things He prepared Earth for in the first place. He had already finished making planet Earth a suitable home for all animals and other living things, so now it was time to begin the process of giving the earth life by filling it with every kind of living thing you can imagine—and some you can't.

The first living things God created were ones that don't move. . .at least not on their own: plants.

Plants live and grow just about anywhere there is sunlight and water. Plants can be found on land, in oceans, and in freshwater. Not all plants need the same amount of sunlight and water to live and grow. But God designed each and every one of them to be able to live and grow and reproduce in the different kinds of surroundings He placed them in.

There are many different types of plants living on Earth today. There are many kinds each of trees, grasses, flowers, bushes, herbs, ferns, mosses, vines, and some kinds of algae. Scientists estimate that there are about 350,000 species of plants living on Earth today, but so far almost 288,000 kinds of plants have been identified and named.

The arrival of land animals on Earth wouldn't begin for another few days. But in the meantime, God created living things that were like animals in some ways but very different in others. Plants are different from animals in three important ways.

First, plants have chlorophyll in them. *Chlorophyll* is what makes plants green and also allows them to produce their own food by absorbing sunlight. Second, the cell walls of all plants are made of a very sturdy material called *cellulose*. The cells of animals, on the other hand, don't have rigid walls the way plants do. Third, plants don't move on their own. Sure, they may seem to move as they respond to sunlight—like when a sunflower points toward the sun so that it can absorb more sunlight—but no plant can just get up and move on its own.

Why the Earth Needs Plants

Have you ever stopped and thought about how important plants are to all life on Earth? They're probably more important than you realize. First of all, plants are necessary for food for all animals—even the ones that eat mostly meat. Nearly every living creature that lives on Earth depends on plants to survive. All animals either eat plants or they eat other animals that eat plants.

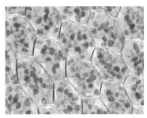

Chloroplasts, the parts of a plant cell that carry on photosynthesis, show up as green circles in this highly magnified picture.

The ability of plants to produce food is an amazing part of God's design for life on Earth. When He made plants, He gave them the ability to collect energy directly from the sun. In a process called *photosynthesis*, almost all plants use the chlorophyll stored in their leaves to convert the energy they collect from the sun into food. The plants store this energy in the form of natural sugar or *carbohydrates*—which are the basis of all food that animals and people eat. That means there are no naturally produced foods that aren't somehow based on plants.

Plants supply the earth with much more than food. During the process of photosynthesis, plants also absorb carbon dioxide and then release oxygen into the atmosphere.

Scientists estimate that plants—from microscopic ones that live in the ocean to the biggest trees growing on land—produce as much as 98 percent of the breathable oxygen in the earth's atmosphere.

All this means that without plants, there would be no life on Earth—at least as we know it today. It also means that God, who created all the earth and everything that lives in it, thought ahead enough to provide all living things with all they needed to live and grow and reproduce here on Earth.

Would you eat a fungus? If you like mushrooms, you would!

If you've ever been in the produce department at your local supermarket, you've probably noticed that mushrooms are placed in the produce department—along with fruits and vegetables, all of which come from different kinds of plants. But mushrooms aren't plants and don't come from plants. They belong in what is called the fungus kingdom. . .along with spores and molds. That's right! Mushrooms aren't vegetables, even though your grocer puts them in the same department as fruits and vegetables. They are a part of the same kingdom of living things as molds and fungi (the plural of *fungus*).

The First Kingdom on Earth: The Plant Kingdom

By the time God was finished creating all the living things on Earth, there were millions and millions of species of plants, animals, and other life forms. Since then, *biologists*—scientists who study living things—have sorted and classified all living things by how they are different and how they are alike.

The largest classes of living things are called *kingdoms.* All living things are classified into one of five different kingdoms, and all plants are placed in the plant kingdom (or, as some people call it, *Kingdom Plantae*).

Biologists have broken down the plant kingdom into smaller and smaller divisions based on different things that are true about different kinds of plants. The two largest divisions are between plants that can circulate water and other liquids through their roots, stems, and leaves, and plants that need to absorb all their water from their surroundings.

Spores of a mossy plant

Most plants can circulate water through their roots, stems, and leaves. Biologists call these *vascular* plants. These types of plants are then broken down by how they reproduce. Most plants reproduce through seeds, but some reproduce through spores. Plants that reproduce through seeds are called *spermatophytes.* Plants that reproduce through spores are called *pteridophytes*, and they include some mosses and ferns.

Pine cone

Some plants reproduce through seeds that aren't encased in anything. These plants are called *gymnosperms*. Many of these types of plants are very important to humans because they are a source of wood. That includes different species of cedars, firs, pines, spruces, redwoods, and others. These plants reproduce through seeds, but the seeds are stored in female cones until they are fertilized by the pollen of male cones. After the seeds mature, they are dropped out onto the ground, where they sprout and eventually mature into a fully grown plant.

Apple, showing seed inside

Most plants reproduce through seeds that are encased in things people and animals eat. You know how apples, cucumbers, pears, and other types of fruits and vegetables have seeds inside them? That's so they can reproduce and make more of their own kind. These kinds of plants are called *flowering plants*, or, more scientifically, *angiosperms*.

More Reasons to Like Plants with Flowers

Can you remember the last time you saw a beautiful flower? How about the last time you enjoyed a fresh piece of fruit or a juicy, sweet piece of corn on the cob? How about the last time you wore something made of cotton? If you can remember the last time you did one of those things, then you can remember the last time you benefited from a group of plants scientists call the *angiosperms*.

All these types of plants have one thing in common: flowers.

Not all flowers are as colorful or showy as a rose or a daffodil. . .or even a daisy. Many flowers are very small and not all that colorful. Sometimes you wouldn't even think of them as flowers. For example, oak trees, grass, and wheat plants all have flowers, but they aren't much to look at, so you don't really notice them. But all flowers, even the ones that aren't as pretty as others, serve the same purpose: reproduction of the plant.

When you hear the word *flowering*, you probably think of pretty flowers like roses, pansies, daisies, and other kinds of popular flowers. But did you know that most of our food comes from flowering plants? All grains, beans, nuts, fruits, vegetables, and spices come to our dinner tables as a result of the reproduction process of flowering plants. So do drinks like coffee, tea, and cola. Flowering plants also help us in the production of a lot of our clothes. Cotton and linen are produced from the fibers of flowering plants. A lot of the medicines we use are also made from flowering plants.

The plant world includes some of the strangest of all God's created things. Did you know that there are plants that eat meat? It's true! Instead of taking all their nourishment through their

Look out, fly—you're about to become lunch!

roots and from sunlight, like most plants do, these plants trap and eat insects and sometimes (are you ready for this?) small amphibians, reptiles, birds, and mammals. Probably the best known of the carnivorous plants is the Venus flytrap. But there are several other plants that eat meat. They include bladderworts, butterworts, pitcher plants, sundews, and cobra lilies.

Flowering plants reproduce through a process called *pollination.* Pollination happens when male plant spores (the pollen) combine with the female reproductive cells. Once pollination takes place, the plant begins to produce seeds and fruit. Pollen from a flowering plant is dusty-looking stuff that is most often yellow but can also be black, white, green, orange, or just about any other color you can think of.

Different kinds of flowering plants pollinate in different ways. Some plants need the help of birds and bats, as well as bees and other insects to pollinate. Other kinds of plants are pollinated when the wind picks up their pollen and spreads it out onto other plants of the same species. A few plants, such as peanut plants, just pollinate themselves.

Pollination is a necessary part of a flowering plant's life cycle. Without pollination, flowering plants can't reproduce. That means they couldn't bear fruit or seeds. If pollination were to suddenly stop, then almost all the earth's plant life would soon begin to die off.

CHAPTER 5
DAY 4
SOME GREAT STUFF GOD MADE "OUT THERE"

Then God said, "Let lights appear in the sky to separate the day from the night. Let them mark off the seasons, days, and years. Let these lights in the sky shine down on the earth." And that is what happened. God made two great lights—the larger one to govern the day, and the smaller one to govern the night. He also made the stars. God set these lights in the sky to light the earth, to govern the day and night, and to separate the light from the darkness. And God saw that it was good.

And evening passed and morning came, marking the fourth day.

GENESIS 1:14–19

On the fourth day of creation, God made things that have amazed and confused humans since the beginning of time. On that day, He made the things that aren't really part of the planet Earth but that are still important parts of His creation. That includes the objects we can easily see in the sky, like the sun, the moon, and some of the stars and planets. But it also includes things in outer space it took thousands of years for people to figure out how to see from here on Earth. All of these things that God made and placed out in space on the fourth day of creation make up what we now call the *universe*.

When you start to understand some things about what God really did on the fourth day of creation, you'll be amazed. But you'll also begin to understand that even though our planet is very, very big, it is really just a tiny speck in an unbelievably huge universe.

One of the great things about knowing a little something about the stars, planets, galaxies, and other things God made on that fourth day of creation is that it helps you to understand just how big and awesome the God who made all those things really is!

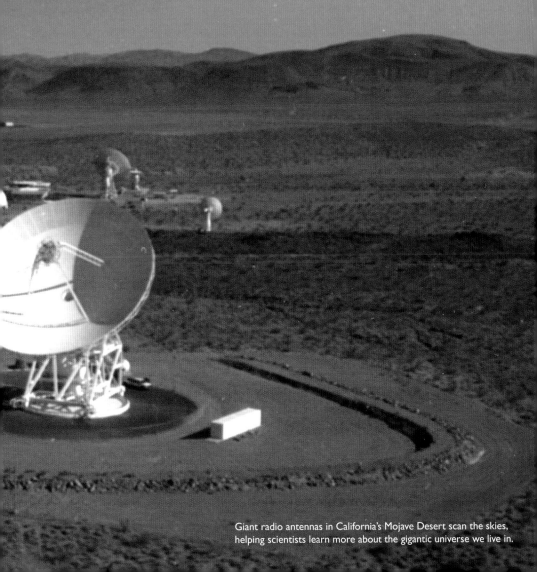

Giant radio antennas in California's Mojave Desert scan the skies, helping scientists learn more about the gigantic universe we live in.

Just How Big Is the Universe Anyway?

Almost since we first noticed the sun, the moon, the stars, and other mysterious objects in the sky, we humans have tried our best to discover what's out there in that enormous universe God created.

Thousands of years go, people started to get the fact that the universe God created was really big and really amazing and that it included some amazing creations. But it wasn't until the past several hundred years that we started to understand just *how* big it really is.

No one really knows for sure how big the universe is. So far, *astronomers*—scientists who study things in outer space—have located objects as far away from Earth as 10 to 13 billion light-years (for a quick reminder of how far a light-year is, look back at page 15 in chapter 1). Some of these objects are called *quasars*. Scientists believe quasars are formed when two *galaxies* (huge collections of stars, which you'll read about later in this chapter) collide with one another. They believe quasars are probably huge points of light that are fueled by enormous black holes in outer space.

How many miles are in a light year? Let's see...

Light travels 186,000 miles a second...
There are (x) 60 seconds in a minute...
There are (x) 60 minutes in an hour...
There are (x) 24 hours in a day...
There are (x) 365 days in a year...

So light travels about

5,865,696,000,000 miles in a year!

What Stars Are and How They Work

If you've ever been on a camping trip or just been outside during a really dark, clear night, you have probably seen thousands of stars in the sky. But during the day you can see the most important star to us humans: the sun! The stars you see at night look very tiny from Earth, but they are all actually huge balls of burning gas—just like our sun.

Our sun—photographed by the Solar and Heliospheric Observatory spacecraft—shoots out flares on two sides. Doesn't that look hot?

Even though stars give off huge amounts of heat and light, they don't burn the same way things burn here on Earth. For a fire to start here on Earth, you need three things: fuel, oxygen, and something to ignite the fire. Stars have plenty of fuel in the form of hydrogen, but since there is no oxygen inside stars, they have to burn another way. That way is called *nuclear fusion*, and it happens in stars when gravity from inside the star—which is many, many times as strong as the earth's gravity—pulls hydrogen inward and causes four atoms of hydrogen to fuse together to form one atom of helium. When that happens, part of the mass from the hydrogen atom is left over, and that extra mass is converted into heat and light.

Even though all stars look pretty much the same when you look at them from Earth, there are actually several kinds of stars. Some stars are very small, at least compared to other stars, and some stars are many times bigger than our sun. The smallest stars in the universe are called *neutron stars*. These are actually dead stars that are no wider than a city. The biggest stars in the universe—in fact, the biggest objects of any kind in the universe—are called *supergiant* stars. Some supergiants are more than 1,000 times bigger than our sun.

Most stars fit into a class astronomers call *main sequence stars*. Our sun is a main sequence star. Main sequence stars come in many different sizes, and many of them burn a lot brighter than others. But like our sun, all main sequence stars convert hydrogen into helium in their cores and release amazing amounts of heat and light.

RECORD BREAKING

Sirius is often called the Dog Star, because it's part of the "big dog" (Canis Majoris) constellation.

The biggest star known to humans is called VY Canis Majoris. It is located in the constellation Canis Majoris, which also includes Sirius, the brightest star in the sky. Scientists estimate that VY Canis Majoris is up to 2,100 times the diameter of our sun and that if it were to replace our sun, it would stretch all the way out to Saturn, the sixth planet in our solar system. VY Canis Majoris is so big that if you could hollow it out, it could hold 7 billion stars the size of our sun inside it.

Constellations: Random Puzzles in the Sky

From Earth, some of the stars in the sky are grouped in a way that makes them look like connect-the-dots puzzles of animals, people, and other things. These are called *constellations*.

There is a total of 88 named constellations. You've probably seen the Big Dipper, the Little Dipper, and other easy-to-find constellations. What constellations you see at night depends on where you live and what time of the year you look. The ones you can see in the Northern Hemisphere are different from the ones you can see in the south. For example, people in the north can see the Big Dipper and people in the south can see the Southern Cross.

Even today, some people believe that where the constellations appear in the sky affects life here on Earth. But in truth, constellations are nothing more than imaginary formations of stars in the sky. Even though the constellations may *look* like pictures of animals, people, or other things, most of them are made up of stars that are many light-years apart in space. One exception to that rule is the Big Dipper. The Big Dipper is made up of stars that really *are* close together—at least when you compare the distance between them with the distances between other stars.

People in North America call this constellation "the Big Dipper"—but in England, they're more likely to say "the Plough."

Here is an artist's idea of how a "black hole" can swallow a star: The star (left) comes within the black hole's extreme gravity, and begins to break apart (center), finally swirling into the dark void (right).

Have you ever heard of a black hole? It's an object in space with such strong gravity coming from it that nothing, including light, can escape from it. Scientists believe that black holes are created when massive stars run out of fuel and die. When that happens, the star's gravity pulls its material inward and compresses its core, which creates a supernova explosion. What is left over after the explosion is the star's core. The core's gravitational pull is so strong that not even light can escape it. The object is now a black hole. Although scientists can't really see black holes, they can find them by watching how objects around them are affected.

What Happens When a Really Big Star Dies? A Supernova!

All stars have a certain amount of fuel they can burn to produce light and heat. When the fuel in a really big star runs out, that star begins to die. When that happens, the star explodes and forms what astronomers call a *supernova*. A supernova is a gigantic explosion that makes the star brighter than all the other stars.

When the supernova is finished, what is left is a huge cloud called a *nebula* and a compressed star called a *neutron star*. If the star that exploded is one of the biggest stars in the universe, then it leaves behind a nebula *or* what is called a *black hole*.

Supernovas are very rare events. But every year astronomers see about 300 supernovas in other galaxies. Almost a thousand years ago, astronomers in China, Japan, Korea, and Arabia recorded a supernova that was so bright that it could be seen during the day. That supernova formed what is now known as the Crab Nebula.

See the bright star to the lower left of the "spiral galaxy"? That's a supernova—brighter than other stars, because it's in the process of exploding!

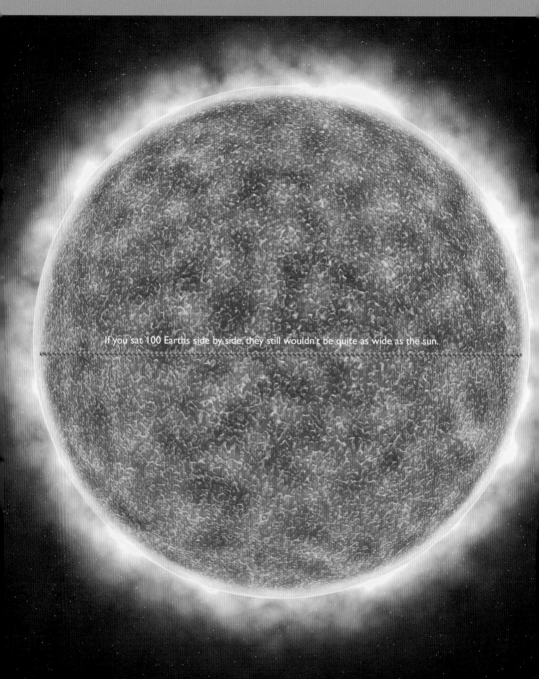

If you sat 100 Earths side by side, they still wouldn't be quite as wide as the sun.

Earth's Own Star: The Sun

When you see the sun, you're actually seeing a medium-sized star. The sun is made up of about three-quarters hydrogen and one-quarter helium. The sun's gravity holds planets and other objects in our solar system and keeps them orbiting around it.

The earth gets all its heat and light from the sun. Without that heat and light, plants and animals and people couldn't live on Earth. Our planet can support the different forms of life that live here because it is the perfect distance—about 93 millions miles—from the sun. If it were too much closer, the earth would be too hot to live on. If it were any farther away, it would be too cold to live here.

Maybe you haven't given much thought to the sun. . .other than how much you like it when it shines when you're outside. But here are some facts about the sun that just might amaze you. The temperature on the sun's surface is about 10,000 degrees Fahrenheit. Think that's hot? Try this: The temperature deep *inside* the sun is about 27 *million* degrees. The sun is about 870,000 miles wide—about 109 times wider than the earth.

Why We Have Seasons

Have you ever wondered why it's cold in the winter and hot in the summer? Or why the days get longer in the spring, then start getting shorter in the fall? The sun always gives off about the same amount of heat and light, so it can't be that someone just turns down the heat every winter.

Here's how it *really* works.

The earth travels all the way around the sun about once every 365 days. But it doesn't orbit the sun with the same spots on the planet pointing directly at the sun all the time. Earth leans to one side as it orbits the sun, so different parts of the earth point more directly at the sun than others during different times of the year. This means that different amounts of sunlight reach different points on the earth during different times of the year. The different amounts of sunlight cause different kinds of weather during those different times. In other words, it's colder when where you live on Earth is farthest from the sun and hotter when it's the closest.

During the summer in the Northern Hemisphere, that part of the earth is pointed more directly at the sun, so it receives more heat and light from the sun than it does in the winter. At that same time, the Southern Hemisphere is *farthest* away from the sun, so it receives less of the sun's heat and light. That means that when it's summer in the Northern Hemisphere, it's winter in the Southern Hemisphere.

Astronomers Call It a Satellite. . . . We Call It the Moon

The earth is one of eight planets that orbit the sun. Most of those planets have what scientists call *satellites* orbiting them. Our earth has a satellite of its own—one you can see in the sky most nights. You know this satellite better as the *moon*.

Even though the moon looks small from the earth, it is actually very large. The moon is about 2,160 miles across, which is about one-fourth the size of Earth. It only looks small because it is about 238,900 miles from Earth. Just as the sun's gravity holds the earth and other planets orbiting in place, Earth's gravity keeps the moon in place and orbiting the earth.

A few people have walked on the moon, but the moon can't support the kinds of plants and animals—or people—that live on Earth. That's because the moon has no air on it. The moon has no air on it because the gravity there is about one-sixth what it is on Earth. That's not even enough gravity for the moon to hold an atmosphere! Also, because the moon has no atmosphere to block out the sun's light or to help it trap heat, temperatures on the moon's surface range from up to 253 degrees Fahrenheit during the day, all the way down to minus 387 degrees Fahrenheit at night.

Even though the moon is the brightest object in the nighttime sky, it doesn't give off its own light. When you see the moon shining brightly, it's because the moon is reflecting light from the sun back to Earth. The moon orbits the earth, and it spins on its axis in about the same time it takes to orbit the earth. That's why we always see the same half of the moon's surface from Earth. The other half of the moon is called the "far side" of the moon. Some people have called that side of the moon the "dark side," but that isn't correct because the sun does shine on the side that is facing away from Earth.

Sometimes the moon looks like a big, shiny circle in the sky. But sometimes it is shaped like a crescent. At other times it looks like a sliver of light in the sky. That is because the moon shines on Earth in what are called *lunar phases*. It takes the moon about 29.5 days to complete the cycle of lunar phases and 27.3 days to orbit the earth. The moon looks different during its lunar phases because light from the sun is shining on it at different angles—at least as we see it from Earth. When the moon is full, it's because the sun is shining on the entire surface that we on Earth can see.

Only 12 humans have ever visited the moon, all of them from the United States: Neil Armstrong (the first to step onto the moon's surface), Buzz Aldrin, Charles "Pete" Conrad Jr., Alan Bean, Alan Shepard Jr., Edgar Mitchell, David Scott, James Irwin, John Young, Charles Duke Jr., Eugene Cernan, and Harrison Schmitt.

Our solar system. From right to left: the sun, Mercury, Venus, Earth, Mars, Jupiter, Saturn, Uranus, Neptune, and Pluto. This picture only shows the order of the planets—it's not to scale. The planets are much farther away from each other, and the sun is much, much larger than shown here.

Our Solar System: The Place Our Sun Calls Home

Our earth is part of a *solar system*. A solar system is made up of a star that has planets and other things orbiting around it. Our solar system includes the sun, a total of eight planets, some *dwarf planets* (more about them later), and other objects such as *comets* and *asteroids.*

Many astronomers believe that our solar system may be only one of many billions placed in the Milky Way Galaxy, the galaxy our solar system is located in, alone. There are more stars in the universe than we can actually count, and astronomers believe that if even a small fraction of those stars are centers of solar systems, then there could be countless hundreds of billions of solar systems in the entire universe.

Our sun is the center of our solar system. But it's a lot more than that. The sun is far bigger and heavier than the rest of the bodies in our solar system combined. The sun actually accounts for 99.9 percent of all the mass in our solar system. That means that if you put a value of $1,000 on all the material in our solar system, the sun would be worth $999, with all the rest of the material worth one buck!

THE WAY IT USED TO BE

Galileo Galilei
(1564–1642)

Hundreds of years ago, people really believed that the earth was the center of the universe. That means they believed that the sun, the moon, the stars, and the other planets revolved around the planet we live on. That began to change when astronomers like Galileo and Nicolaus Copernicus (1473–1543) began watching the rotations of the movement of the planets. It took awhile, but in time people came to accept the fact that the earth revolved around the sun, not the other way around.

Nicolaus Copernicus
(1473–1543)

Our Neighbors in the Solar System

The eight planets in our solar system are the biggest objects orbiting our sun. Those eight planets—from the closest to the sun to the farthest away—are Mercury, Venus, Earth, Mars, Jupiter, Saturn, Uranus, and Neptune.

Up until 2006, scientists believed there were nine planets in our solar system, because they had classified Pluto as a planet. Pluto is still out there just like it always has been, but scientists have now placed it in a new class of objects in the solar system called *dwarf planets*. Dwarf planets are a lot like planets. They are sphere-shaped (like a basketball), and they orbit the sun. Some astronomers hold that dwarf planets are different from planets in that they orbit in areas of the solar system where there are many other objects also orbiting.

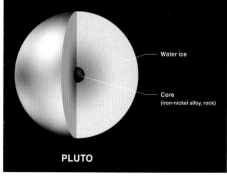

PLUTO

Scientists believe Pluto is mainly frozen methane, with a small center of metal and rock. Far from the sun, Pluto is very, very cold—hundreds of degrees below zero.

Mercury is the smallest planet in our solar system. It is only a little bigger than our moon. Venus is sometimes called Earth's Twin Sister because it is almost the same size as Earth. Mars is a little over half the size of Earth. Uranus is about four times bigger than Earth. Saturn is the second biggest planet in the solar system. At about 75,000 miles in diameter, it is about ten times wider than Earth. Jupiter is the largest planet in our solar system. Jupiter's diameter is about eleven times the diameter of Earth. Scientists estimate that Jupiter is so big that about 1,000 planets the size of Earth could fit inside a hollowed-out Jupiter.

Listed from the smallest to the largest, our solar system's planets are Mercury, Mars, Venus, Earth, Neptune, Uranus, Saturn, and Jupiter.

Earth is the only planet that can support life as we know it. First of all, other planets are either too hot (like Mercury and Venus) or too cold (like Mars) for humans or other forms of life on Earth to live on. Secondly, there's no air—at least the kind we have here on Earth—or liquid water on the other planets. And never mind the fact that Jupiter and Saturn are made mostly of gases we can't breathe!

THAT'S WEIRD!

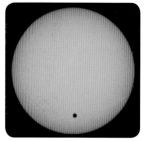

Venus, the second closest planet to the sun in our solar system, spins in the opposite direction compared to the earth and most other planets. Because of that, the sun rises in the west and sets in the east on Venus. But even if you could live on Venus, you wouldn't see the sunrise or sunset very often. That's because one day on Venus is equal to about 243 Earth days.

What's that black spot on the sun? It's the planet Venus, passing between the sun and the earth. This rare event, called a "Venus transit," was photographed in 2004.

More Cool Stuff in Our Solar System

Planets and dwarf planets are not the only objects that orbit our sun. There are also some really amazing objects out there that fit into their own classifications. That includes asteroids and comets.

Asteroids are a lot like planets, only smaller. Asteroids orbit the sun like planets do, and they can't make their own light. Most asteroids are made out of rock, but some are made out of metal.

There are tens of thousands of known asteroids in our solar system, with thousands of new ones being discovered every month. Most of the known asteroids orbit the sun between the orbits of Mars and Jupiter in what is called the *main asteroid belt.*

Astronomers believe there are between one million and two million asteroids bigger than half a mile across in the main asteroid belt and millions of smaller ones. A few asteroids are more than 300 miles wide! At 605 miles wide, Ceres (which was also classified as a dwarf planet in 2006) is the biggest object in the asteroid belt.

Halley's Comet streaks through space at 103,000 miles an hour in this photograph from 1986. The "tail" you can see behind the comet is about 450,000 miles long.

While asteroids are made of rock and metal, comets are dirty, dusty balls of ice. That is why they are often called *dirty snowballs.* Many comets orbit the sun differently than the planets and asteroids. Some comets orbit from outside the solar system, then into the solar system, and then back out into outer space.

The word *comet* comes from a Greek word meaning "long-haired." Comets got that name because when they have long tails they are visible from Earth. Comets grow tails when they move close to the sun, where solar heat causes the frozen gases and dust to partially melt and form a long trail of vaporized gas, dust, and rocks.

The most famous comet is Halley's Comet, which can be seen from Earth once every 76 years as it passes close to the sun. But a comet called Shoemaker-Levy 9 became famous in July of 1994 when 20 fragments of the comet crashed into the planet Jupiter.

THE WAY IT USED TO BE

People throughout history have seen bright comets in the night sky, and they believed that when they saw them it meant bad things were going to happen. They believed comets actually entered the earth's atmosphere, and they blamed wars, famines, and death on them. Some people wouldn't even leave their homes when there was a comet overhead! We now know that comets aren't signs of anything good or bad—just another part of God's creation.

In an ancient tapestry, astrologers (left) predict trouble for England's King Harold II (far right), because of the appearance of a comet (top center) during his reign. Harold was king of England from 1022 to 1066.

The Milky Way Galaxy: A Good Home for a Solar System

This galaxy—called NGC 7331—probably looks very much like our own Milky Way galaxy. The photo was taken by the Spitzer Space Telescope

The sun at the center of our solar system is just one of literally billions of stars God placed in what is called the *Milky Way Galaxy*. The Milky Way Galaxy is more than 100,000 light-years across and is home to between 100 and 400 billion stars.

A *galaxy* is a huge gathering of stars and other objects organized into a certain shape. Up until the 1920s, the Milky Way was the only known galaxy in the universe. But in 1924 an American astronomer named Edwin Hubble proved that there were several other distant galaxies in space. Since then, we have learned that there are hundreds of billions of galaxies in the universe. Most galaxies are tens of thousands of light-years across and contain billions of stars.

Galaxies come in many different shapes and sizes. The Milky Way Galaxy is what is called a *spiral galaxy*. Spiral galaxies are shaped like giant, spinning wheels with a *hub* (a center that all the stars spin around), and curved *arms* sticking out from the center. The arms of the spiral galaxy are actually tight groups of stars. There are several types of spiral galaxies, and they are classified by the tightness of their arms.

Elliptical galaxies are egg-shaped collections of stars. These are the biggest galaxies—as large as 18 million light-years across. The third kind of galaxy, an *irregular galaxy*, has an unusual shape, so it can't be put in other groups.

Galaxies spin on their hubs at amazing speeds. That includes the Milky Way. In fact, the sun and all the planets and other objects in our solar system are zipping around the center of the Milky Way at around 150 miles per second. And if that seems fast, think about this: Our entire galaxy is traveling through space at about one million miles per hour!

EXPLORING THE HEAVENS

Even if you don't own a telescope or live near a planetarium, you can still learn about some of the wonders of God's creation as they appear in space. It's as easy as stepping outside, looking up, and writing down what you see! Try this: Check out a book on astronomy at the library and look up the names of the constellations (there are eighty-eight of them), and see what they look like and which stars are in them. After you've done that, step out your front door, look up, and see how many of them you can find in the night sky.

CHAPTER 6
DAY 5
THINGS WITH FINS, THINGS WITH FEATHERS

Then God said, "Let the waters swarm with fish and other life. Let the skies be filled with birds of every kind." So God created great sea creatures and every living thing that scurries and swarms in the water, and every sort of bird—each producing offspring of the same kind. And God saw that it was good. Then God blessed them, saying, "Be fruitful and multiply. Let the fish fill the seas, and let the birds multiply on the earth."

And evening passed and morning came, marking the fifth day.

GENESIS 1:20–23

By the end of the fourth creation day, God had already made everything He knew would be needed for all the different kinds of animals to live on Earth. He made the earth itself and had separated dry land from the water, and He had stocked the earth with plenty of water for the animals to live in and to drink. He had provided the sunlight that is so vital to the growth of plants that would feed the animals and that would supply them with oxygen to breathe.

God had prepared everything perfectly for the animals He was about to create on the fifth and sixth days of creation. It was now time for Him to create what we now call the *animal kingdom*. He started His work of populating the world with animals by creating fish and birds.

Natural Kingdoms

The Bible doesn't list every type of living thing God created. It doesn't even list what humans would later call *kingdoms*. Maybe that's because He just wanted us to know the basics of creation. Whatever the reason, we can know that He created everything that lives on Earth today.

Not everything that lives on Earth is considered an animal. Over the years, scientists have broken down the world of all living things into what they call *kingdoms*. All living things are divided into five kingdoms: the *Monera kingdom* (includes single-celled creatures called *bacteria*), the *Protista kingdom* (some kinds of algae and single-celled creatures called *protozoa*), the *Fungi kingdom* (molds, spores, and mushrooms), the *plant kingdom*, and the *animal kingdom*.

On the fifth day of creation, God began making the animal kingdom. The animal kingdom includes worms, insects, arachnids (animals with eight legs, like spiders and scorpions), mollusks (such as clams, oysters, and octopuses), crustaceans, fish, reptiles, amphibians, birds, and mammals. It also includes creatures you might not have known are animals—creatures such as sponges and corals.

All these living creatures have some special traits in common that make them animals. All of them are made up of many individual cells, and all of them rely in some way or another on other living things for their nourishment. Also, most animals eat their food and digest it inside themselves.

Moving Down the Family Tree

Scientists not only break down all living things into the five kingdoms, but they also break down the animal kingdom into smaller groups called *phyla* (the plural of *phylum*). Most scientists believe there are 38 animal phyla and that most animal species belong to the nine biggest of them.

Each phylum includes smaller groups of animals called *classes*. Classes of animals are then divided into smaller groups called *orders*. Orders are divided into *families* (and sometimes subfamilies), and each family includes a number of different *genera* (the plural of *genus*). Finally, each genus is broken down into one or more *species* of animal.

A red-billed tropicbird photographed over the Caribbean Sea

Fish and birds—the animals God made on the fifth day of creation—are part of the phylum Chordata, which includes all animals that are considered vertebrates. *Vertebrates* are animals that have backbones. *Invertebrates*, on the other hand, are animals that don't have backbones—like crabs, spiders, and insects. Those three animals are called *arthropods*, and they belong to the phylum *Arthropoda*.

Birds all belong to one class of animals called *Aves*. But there are several classes of fish living in the world today.

A blue-spotted stingray photographed off Thailand

Fish's Big Place in the Animal Kingdom

Altogether, there are about 28,000 different species of fish populating the world's waters—with new species still being discovered every year. Some *ichthyologists* (scientists who study fish) say there may be many thousands more fish species yet to be discovered and named.

If you were to look at a chart of different kinds of fish, you would see at the top of their family tree the *superclasses* and *classes*, then what are called *subclasses*. The subclasses are followed by *infraclasses*. If you kept moving down the chart, you'd see the *superorders* of fish, followed by the *orders*, then the *superfamilies* and then the *families*.

There are three superclasses of fish living today, and each of them includes several classes. The biggest superclass of fish is *Osteichthyes* (fish with skeletons made of bone). This class of fish includes the subclass *Achtinopterygii*, which scientists call "ray-finned" fish. If you can't pronounce the word Achtinopterygii, don't worry. You can just think of them as typical fish, because for the most part they look like you'd expect a fish to look. This class of fish includes around 27,000 species, making it not only the largest class of fish but the largest class of vertebrates.

The *Agnatha* superclass of fish is known for having skeletons made of cartilage and not out of bone, like most fish. They also don't have jaws. This class includes lampreys and hagfish. And here's something really strange about this class of fish: They have digestive systems, just like any other fish, but they don't have stomachs!

The *Chondrichthyes* superclass of fish, which also has skeletons made of cartilage, includes sharks and rays. This class of fish includes some species you have no doubt heard about, including the whale shark, the largest fish alive on Earth today, and the great white shark.

There are literally hundreds of families of fish, but one-third of all species belong to the nine largest families. The family with the most species (at about 2,400) is called the *Cyprinidae* family, which includes carps and minnows. Since goldfish are carps, they belong to this family of fish.

To help you better understand the basics of how scientists classify fish, take a look at the chart below, which shows you where a common goldfish fits in the animal kingdom:

- Kingdom: *Animalia* (all animals)
- Phylum: *Chordata* (animals with backbones)
- Class: *Actinopterygii* (all ray-finned fish)
- Order: *Cypriniformes* (carps, minnows, roaches, and their relatives)
- Family: *Cyprinidae* (carps, minnows, and barbs)
- Genus: *Carassius* (Crucian carps)
- Species: *Carassius auratus* (the goldfish)

RECORD BREAKING

At up to 40 feet long and weighing up to 15 tons, the whale shark is the world's biggest fish. If you ever saw a whale shark, you wouldn't need to worry about being attacked, even if you were in the water with it. A whale shark eats only *plankton*—tiny plants and animals that live in the sea—and other small organisms, which it catches by taking water into its huge mouth and then straining out the food through its gills. In fact, it has been reported that whale sharks are gentle creatures that sometimes seem to enjoy playing with divers.

A diver swims with a whale shark in the Indian Ocean.

What Makes a Fish a Fish?

Fish are some of the most amazing members of the animal kingdom. All fish are vertebrates, which means they have backbones. All birds and mammals, including human beings, are also vertebrates, but more than half of all known species of vertebrates living in the world today are fish.

On the fifth day of creation, God made fish and many other forms of life that live in the water. That included many types of life that are not fish, even though they may have some of the same characteristics as fish. Different species of jellyfish, starfish, shellfish, sea anemones, coral, crustaceans (crabs, shrimps, lobsters, and others), and thousands of other animals also live in the earth's water, but they aren't fish.

So what makes a fish a fish? Fish come in every size, color, and shape you can imagine—and some you probably can't—but they all have certain things in common. . .other than having a backbone, that is. All fish are *cold-blooded*, meaning that their body temperature adjusts to the temperature of the water they live in. All fish have gills that absorb oxygen from the water into their bloodstreams. All fish have fins, though some species have more than others. And most fish have scales that protect their bodies.

THAT'S AMAZING!

Even though there's a lot of mystery around what kinds of fish and other sea creatures live in the deepest part of the world's oceans, scientists know that the record for fish living in the deepest waters goes to a type of fish in the brotulid family. These fish live in the ocean at depths of 23,000 feet or more. One species of fish—with the tongue-twisting scientific name of *Abyssobrotula galatheae*—was captured in the Puerto Rican Trench from an amazing depth of almost 27,500 feet—or more than five miles down. Most fish living at these depths have lost the use of their eyes—if they have eyes at all—simply because sunlight can't penetrate that deep into the ocean.

Where Fish Live

Fish live in just about any area of the world where you can find bodies of water. Some live in the saltwater of the world's oceans and seas. But many also live in freshwater lakes, rivers, streams, and other bodies of water. Some freshwater fish live in slow-moving or still water (in lakes and ponds), but others tend to live in fast-moving streams and rivers. Still other species of fish live in what is called *brackish* water, which is a mixture of saltwater and freshwater found in some coastal areas. One place you'll never find a fish living is in very salty bodies of water, like the Great Salt Lake in Utah.

Some types of fish live in places where the conditions would kill most other forms of life. There are fish that live in streams and pools in caves where no sunlight reaches them. Some fish live in the deepest parts of the ocean, several miles down. Some fish live in desert ponds and streams that dry up every year. These fish have the amazing ability to bury themselves in the mud, hibernate for up to two years, then swim free when the water returns. Some fish even live under the polar ice caps!

THAT'S WEIRD!

Can you imagine walking down the street and seeing a fish crawling along in front of you? That's exactly what happens sometimes in some neighborhoods in Florida, where a really strange fish called the walking catfish is sometimes seen crawling on dry land from one body of water to another. This weird species of fish has the ability to "walk" (actually, they crawl using their pectoral fins as legs) on dry land for a short time and breathe air as it moves from one body of water to another. The walking catfish first came to the United States in the 1960s, when they were imported from Asia for home aquariums.

How Fish Breathe

A fish's gills are amazingly designed organs. The gills are made up of tiny threadlike strands filled with tiny blood vessels. The fish breathes by taking water in through its open mouth and then forcing the water over the filaments when it closes its mouth. The filaments absorb the oxygen and move it into the fish's bloodstream.

Even though all fish have gills to collect oxygen from the water, some fish also take oxygen out of the air, using specially designed organs that do the same work your lungs do. Some species of lungfish can bury themselves in the mud when the body of water they live in dries up. These fish can survive on oxygen from the air for up to two years, or until the water returns.

Some kinds of fish have labyrinth organs that they use to breathe air from the atmosphere so that they can survive in oxygen-poor water. They still have gills just like any other fish, and they get most of their oxygen from the water. These fish are called *labyrinth fish*, and they include the betta (or Siamese fighting fish), a fish you can find in just about any pet store or aquarium shop.

How Fish Reproduce "After Their Own Kind"

When God created the different species of fish, He designed them to reproduce in a variety of ways. Most fish reproduce by laying or scattering their eggs in the water. This process is called *spawning*, and it happens when the female fish releases her eggs into the water and the male fertilizes them with his sperm. Some fish give birth to live babies. That means that the male fish must deposit his sperm inside the female fish, where her eggs are fertilized and later grow into baby fish that are born alive. Most fish leave their eggs or young to fend for themselves, but some are very good parents that protect their nests and babies until their offspring are able to take care of themselves.

Most fish reproduce in the same water they live in their whole lives. But some fish begin their lives in freshwater, migrate to saltwater, where they spend most of their lives, then return to freshwater to spawn. These are called *anadromous* fish, and they include salmon, smelt, shad, striped bass, sturgeon, and others. On the other hand, there are fish that are born in saltwater but live most of their lives in freshwater, only to return to saltwater to spawn. These are called *catadomous* fish, and they include most kinds of eels.

DID YOU KNOW. . . ?

While most fish lay their eggs or give live birth to their young and then pay no attention to them (other than to eat them, in some cases!), some species of fish are very good parents. For example, many species from the cichlid (pronounced "sick-lid") family—some of which are kept in freshwater aquariums as pets—are some of the most devoted, protective parents in all creation. Some species of cichlids fiercely guard their eggs and young from any and all predators—even those that are far bigger than they are! Probably the best examples are the mouthbreeders, which care for their eggs and young by carrying them in their mouths.

EXPLORING THE WORLD OF FISH

If you're interested in exploring the world of fish, you don't need to go any further than your local pet store or aquarium shop. When you go, take a pencil and notepad, and as you look

at the different kinds of fish, write down what you see, including the name of the species. Then go to your library—or log on to the Internet—and see what you can learn about the fish you've just seen: what they eat, how they reproduce, where they live in the wild. As you do these things, you'll learn to understand and appreciate God's creativity in making these fish you've just seen.

Birds, Birds Everywhere!

Birds live all over the world. They are found on every continent and in almost every kind of climate. Leading the world with the most species of birds—3,200—is South America. That includes the nations of Colombia, Bolivia, and Peru, each of which is home to around 1,700 species. About 2,900 species of birds live in Asia, and Africa is home to about 2,300. North America—which includes the United States and Canada—accounts for about 2,000 species, with another 1,000 living in Europe. There are even 65 kinds of birds living in Antarctica!

Of course, there are far more kinds of birds living in more ordinary climates where there are no extremely hot or extremely cold temperatures. But God also has designed and equipped certain birds to live in places where it's hard to imagine any living thing surviving for very long.

Birds are found in the hottest, driest deserts. Others are found in the coldest parts of the Arctic and Antarctic. Different kinds of birds live in open grasslands, in forests and jungles, on cliff faces and mountaintops, and on river banks and seashores. Some birds like to make their homes in manmade structures like barns, mineshafts, and the roofs of houses.

Some birds live only near or in water. These kinds of birds, which are called *aquatic birds*, also get most or all of their food from the water. Some species of aquatic birds, such as loons, tend to live near freshwater lakes, and some tend to live near saltwater. Some aquatic birds live near both saltwater and freshwater. Birds like ducks, geese, and swans—birds called *waterfowl*—live near freshwater lakes, ponds, and marshes.

Birds that live in different kinds of environments look and behave very differently from one another. The easiest differences for you to see are the bird's size, body shape, color, beak or bill shape, and the length of the legs and neck. None of these differences happened by accident. They happened because the same God who created the environment where the bird lives also designed each bird to live in the environment He placed it in.

Doesn't he look cold? This "chinstrap penguin" of Antarctica is named for the black line that runs under his beak.

Tiny hummingbirds have long, thin beaks they use to suck nectar from delicate flowers.

Large macaws have short, tough beaks they use to crack nuts.

Sparrows are common birds, and a good example of passerines, birds that perch.

The common loon is a duck-like bird of North America.

Some turkeys are raised on farms. This is a "wild turkey," showing off his plumage (tail feathers).

The budgie, a type of parakeet, is a common pet bird.

The Bird Family Tree

Earlier, you read about the long and complicated "family tree" of the world's fish. Birds have their own family tree, too, but it isn't nearly as large or complicated as that of fish.

Like all fish, all birds are part of the phylum *Chordata*, which means they are all animals with backbones. But unlike fish, all birds belong to just one class of animals. That class is called *Aves*. *Ornithologists*—scientists who study birds—have placed birds into about two dozen groups called *orders*. Those orders are divided into about 160 families, which are then grouped into birds of the same genus. Finally, the genus is divided into the different species of birds.

There are about 10,000 known species of birds living all over the world today, and more than half of them are from the order *Passeriformes*. They are more often called *passerines*, and they are from the order scientists have listed as *perching birds*. These birds' toes and legs are designed so that they can balance themselves on tree limbs, twigs, and telephone wires. Common birds like sparrows, finches, warblers, crows, blackbirds, thrushes, and swallows are all considered perching birds.

There are other orders of birds that include kinds of birds you have probably either seen or heard of. That includes the order *Anseriformes*, which includes ducks, geese, swans, and other kinds of waterfowl. The bald eagle, as well as other kinds of birds of prey like hawks and falcons, belongs to the order *Falconiformes*. Turkeys and chickens, both important birds for food, are from the order *Galliformes*. And the parrots, macaws, parakeets, and several other kinds of birds you see at your local pet store? They are from the order *Psittaciformes*.

When you get down the family tree for birds to the branch scientists call the *genus*, then you'll start to see how much certain kinds of birds are very much like other kinds in that genus. For example, the white stork and the black stork are from the same genus (called *Ciconia*) and look very much alike (except for the color), but they are two different kinds of birds.

To help you better understand how scientists have put

together the family tree for birds, take a look at the following chart. It will show you where the American robin, a bird you have probably seen many times, fits in:

- Kingdom: *Animalia* (all animals)
- Phylum: *Chordata* (animals with back bones)
- Class: *Aves* (all birds)
- Order: *Passeriformes* (perching birds)
- Family: *Turdidae* (all thrushes)
- Genus: *Turdus* (similar thrushes)
- Species: *Turdus migratorius* (the American robin)

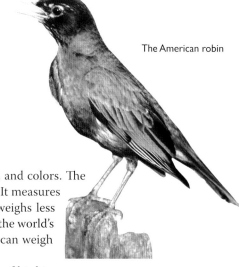

The American robin

What Makes a Bird a Bird?

God created birds in many different sizes, shapes, and colors. The tiny bee hummingbird is the smallest bird known. It measures less than 2.5 inches long when fully grown and weighs less than .10 ounces. Ostriches, on the other hand, are the world's largest bird. Ostriches can grow to 8 feet tall and can weigh more than 300 pounds.

But no matter how big or small a certain kind of bird is, no matter what color its feathers are, and no matter where it lives or how it eats or nests, it has certain things in common with all other birds.

Like fish, birds are vertebrates, and that means they have backbones. But instead of fins and scales, birds have wings, feathers, and a beak (or bill) with no teeth. Birds are also *warm-blooded*, which means that their body temperature stays pretty much the same all the time. All birds reproduce by laying eggs.

The bee hummingbird—the smallest known bird—lives in Cuba. This is a female, which is slightly larger than the male.

Most species of birds can fly, and they use that ability to hunt for food, to escape predators (including other birds sometimes), and to migrate from one place to another so they can get away from weather that is too cold or too hot. Birds that can fly are designed to be some of the world's greatest athletes. They have strong, hollow bones, powerful muscles, and strong hearts and lungs. They also have amazingly designed wings and powerful flight muscles that give them the ability to take off, to stay in the air, and to reach sometimes amazing speeds in midair.

But do you know what one characteristic sets birds apart from all other animals? It's not the fact that they all reproduce by laying eggs. Most species of fish, reptiles, and amphibians—as well as a few mammals—lay eggs. So do insects and many other living creatures. It's not the fact that they all have wings and that most of them can fly. Bats are mammals, but they have wings and can fly. So can most insects. It's not even the fact that they all have beaks or bills.

RECORD BREAKING

A peregrine falcon snatches a smaller bird in flight.

The peregrine falcon, which lives almost everywhere on Earth, is not only the world's fastest-flying bird but also the fastest creature of any kind on Earth today. Peregrines can fly at speeds of well over 200 miles per hour. They use their speed to hunt for food. They swoop from great heights to catch prey on the ground and other birds in midair. Peregrines eat mostly medium-sized birds, but they also sometimes eat small mammals and reptiles and insects.

If you want to know for certain if an animal is a bird, remember this: *If it has feathers, it's a bird!* In all the animal kingdom, only birds have feathers. Not only that, *all* birds have feathers!

God didn't put feathers on birds just to make them look pretty. Different types of feathers on a bird's body serve different purposes. The long, wide feathers on the bird's wings and tail allow the bird to fly (the tail feathers help the bird to steer itself while in flight), and the softer feathers that grow close to the skin help insulate the bird from heat or cold. Some male birds have big, colorful feathers they use to attract their mates, while the females usually have duller-colored feathers that help them to blend into their surroundings while they nest. That way they can escape the notice of predators that like to eat eggs. . .or the mother bird herself.

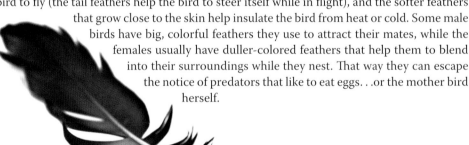

You probably know that ostriches can't fly. Their bodies are too heavy and their wings are too small for them to even attempt flying. But did you know there are actually 40 species of birds living on Earth today that can't fly? The list also includes several different species of kiwis, which live in New Zealand, as well as the emu, which is a native of Australia. Penguins, which live in the earth's Southern Hemisphere, are also flightless birds, but they use their wings for swimming. In case you're wondering, chickens don't fit on the list of flightless birds because they can actually fly.

Drivers in New Zealand see this sign, to warn them of kiwis ahead!

How Birds Reproduce

All birds reproduce by laying eggs with hard shells. The number of eggs the female bird lays at one time depends on the species. Some birds lay one egg per nesting, while others lay more than a dozen at a time. All birds' eggs are fertilized during mating while they are still inside the female bird's body.

Most birds build nests to protect their eggs from weather and predators. What the nest looks like and where the bird builds it depends on the species of bird. Many birds nest in trees, but others nest on the ground or underground. Some birds like to nest in man-made structures like housetops, gutters, barns and sheds, and other places. Some birds weave beautiful nests of grass, twigs, feathers, and other materials, but some nest in hollowed-out trees. Other kinds of birds, like eagles, nest in high treetops, while others just dig out a hole in the sand or dirt to nest. Some birds even nest in underground burrows.

Almost all birds sit on their eggs to keep them warm until they hatch. Most bird "couples" stay together during the nesting time and take turns sitting on the eggs so both the male and the female have a chance to feed. That is not true for all birds, though. Male emus do all the sitting and also care for the babies once they hatch. The male emperor penguin cares for his mate's egg during its incubation period. Once the egg has hatched and the female penguin returns from the

The Southern Masked-Weaver is an African bird that "weaves" its nest from grass, reeds, and other natural materials.

sea where she has been feeding, she begins helping care for the newly hatched chick.

When most baby birds first hatch, they are completely dependent on their parents for food. Both parents feed the young, whose mouths are always open waiting for Mom and Dad to feed them. Some birds feed their young by eating and partly digesting the food, then vomiting it into their chicks' mouths. That's called *regurgitation*, and although it might sound kinda gross, for the baby birds it's as tasty and nutritious as a big pancake breakfast is to you!

Some baby birds are able to eat on their own almost as soon as they hatch. Baby ducks, geese, chickens, quails, and other types of birds get up and walk soon after they hatch, but they stay close to their mothers, who protect them and take them to places where they can find food.

THAT'S WEIRD!

The killdeer is an amazing—and really noisy—bird that uses a really strange method for protecting its nest. When a predator, looking for a quick egg breakfast, gets too close to the killdeer's nest, the mother will use a broken-wing act to distract the predator. The bird will walk away from the nest, then start flopping around on the ground and squawking as if it is injured and can't fly. Once the mother has distracted the predator into thinking it has found an easy meal, she suddenly seems to get better. She then flies away and circles the area before she returns to her nest.

THAT'S AMAZING!

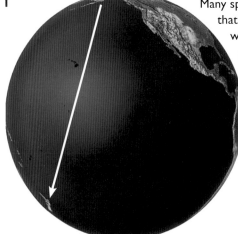

Many species of birds are *migratory*, which means that they travel during certain seasons to find warmer weather or to mate. In 2007 a bar-tailed godwit—a wading bird that mates in the Arctic coasts and tundra—made an amazing journey ...in an amazingly short period of time. Scientists tracked the bird as if flew south from Alaska to New Zealand—a distance of 7,145 miles—in just nine days. This amazing bird never stopped to eat, drink, or rest, and it lost more than half its body weight by the time it touched down in New Zealand.

Eating Like a Bird

Ever hear the phrase "eats like a bird"? That is usually what people say about someone who doesn't eat very much. But the truth about birds is that most of them consume a lot of food for their size. They have to eat a lot because they use up so much energy flying.

What a bird eats depends on the kind of bird it is. Many birds eat almost nothing but fruit and seeds, while others eat green plants. Birds such as hummingbirds eat nectar they find in flowers. Many species of birds eat insects and other bugs. Some birds of prey eat fish, small reptiles, and rodents, while others eat mammals and other birds they catch. Some birds, like vultures, are scavengers that eat only the bodies of dead animals.

The size and shape of a bird can tell you a lot about how it finds food and how it eats it. Every bird is equipped with everything it needs to gather or catch the kind of food it eats. For example, if a bird has long legs and a long neck—like a crane or flamingo—it probably spends most of its time walking on land or wading in water. Birds with long legs need long necks so they can reach food on the ground or in the water.

Eww, gross! The deader the better for scavenging birds like vultures.

Hummingbirds have long, thin beaks and slender tongues they use to dip into flowers to gather nectar. Swallows, swifts, and other birds that eat insects have short beaks and wide mouths that are perfect for catching flying insects. Parrots and other seed-eating birds have powerful, curved beaks that help them in cracking open nuts to eat.

These ducks aren't shy—they're looking for food underwater!

Birds of prey, such as eagles, hawks, ospreys, and owls, use their sharp eyesight and hearing to find food. They also use their strong claws (or *talons*) and hooked beaks to kill and eat their prey once they catch it. Some species of owls swallow their prey whole once they catch it, then vomit up the bones, fur, and other parts of the animal they can't digest.

Pelicans, geese, and swans all swim well and also have short legs and long necks that allow them to submerge their heads in the water to find food. Other water birds—such as cormorants—are considered diving birds. Their bodies are shaped a lot like torpedoes, and that allows them to dive deep and fast into the water to catch fish.

EXPLORING THE WORLD OF BIRDS

Whether you live in a big city or out in the country, you live in a place where you can see many types of birds. One good way to get a good look at the species of birds in your area is to set out a bird feeder. . .then just watch who comes to have a free meal! When birds come to eat at your feeder, take a good look at them—and take pictures of them if you can—then see if you can identify which species of birds live near you.

Why Fish and Birds Are Important to You

The Bible tells us that the very first animals God created were fish (and other creatures that live

Many of the eggs we eat come from large farms. These eggs are being processed on a conveyor belt.

in the water) and birds. When you look at the variety of fish living in the earth's bodies of water and at the different kinds of birds that live on Earth, you can see that God really likes variety.

But there's something else we can learn about God as we look at the living things He placed on Earth. As you will read later on in this book, God didn't just create all the animals that live on Earth so that He could have a huge zoo and aquarium to enjoy for Himself. God created all these things for the benefit of the most valuable and important part of His creation—us!

The fish and birds God created are important gifts to us humans for a lot of reasons. First of all, fish and birds are an important source of food for people in nearly all cultures. Fish are plentiful in many parts of the world and serve as a source of protein as well as useful fatty acids that help keep people's hearts healthy and operating properly.

Some kinds of birds are important sources of food. Can you remember the last time you had a chicken dinner with your family? Or when you had scrambled eggs or an omelet for breakfast? And you know that every Thanksgiving holiday many Americans cook a big turkey dinner to celebrate with their friends and families. People also often eat geese, pheasants, ducks, grouse, quail, and other game birds. In some parts of the world, people even eat the meat of emus and ostriches.

People also enjoy fish and birds for recreation and as pets. Both saltwater and freshwater sport fishing are popular in many parts of the world. So is hunting for birds. Many people in different parts of the world enjoy keeping aquariums in their homes so that they can enjoy caring for and breeding different types of fish.

Colorful birds like parrots, cockatiels, parakeets, and other species are kept as pets because they are pretty to look at. Some birds are also popular because they can be taught to copy human speech.

Some people also enjoy just going out and watching birds in the wild. These people call their activity *birding*—even though you probably know it better as *bird-watching*. Some bird-watchers just go out with a pair of binoculars to enjoy seeing birds in their natural habitat, but some enjoy taking cameras along so they can "collect" pictures of wild birds.

Birds are intelligent pets that enjoy bright, noisy toys.

So the next time you enjoy a nice fish or chicken or turkey dinner, or the next time you have eggs with your breakfast, don't forget to thank God for both His creativity and for providing you with the foods you eat. And the next time you go out fishing with your family, or watch fish in an aquarium (at home or anywhere else), or watch birds enjoying life in the wild, remember that it was God who made these creatures for you to enjoy.

THINGS WITH FINS, THINGS WITH FEATHERS

A bird book, binoculars, and a camera are nice for birdwatching—but not necessary. You can observe birds anywhere at any time!

CHAPTER 7

DAY 6, PART I
ALL THE LAND ANIMALS

Then God said, "Let the earth produce every sort of animal, each producing offspring of the same kind—livestock, small animals that scurry along the ground, and wild animals." And that is what happened. God made all sorts of wild animals, livestock, and small animals, each able to produce offspring of the same kind. And God saw that it was good.

GENESIS 1:24–25

When the sixth day of creation started, the earth had already been completely formed and filled with all kinds of plants, fish, and birds. God's next step in preparing our planet for us humans to live on was to create the different kinds of animals that live on land.

When you think of the animals that live on land, your mind probably goes to the animals that people are closest to—like dogs, cats, and horses. Some animals just seem to be designed for people to enjoy in special ways. Many people keep dogs and cats in their homes and treat them like members of the family. Other people like horses because they can train them and ride them and enjoy spending time with them.

But many of the land animals God created are important to humans for other reasons. Many land animals are sources of food. Other animals help people do their work. Amazingly enough, God had a purpose for *all* the land animals He created—from the biggest mammals (like elephants) to the tiniest insects (like ants).

Land Mammals. . .Including You!

Did you know that you are a mammal? It's true! People are mammals because they share some of the same features as animals like horses, cats, dogs, cattle, and all the rest of the 4,000 to 5,000 kinds of mammals living in the world today.

Land mammals come in a large variety of sizes, shapes, and colors. The smallest mammals are so tiny that it's likely you wouldn't see them if you were standing right next to them. The largest land mammals—the elephants—would be hard for anyone to miss! (The blue whale is actually the world's largest mammal, but it lives in the ocean and was probably created on the fifth day of creation.)

This picture is about the same size as a real mouse.

Some of the land mammals God created are known for their physical beauty. Who can't look at a Bengal tiger or a leopard and appreciate how beautiful and majestic God made those big cats? But some animals will never win any beauty contest. In fact, some land mammals are among the funniest-looking creatures in the entire animal kingdom. One example is the star-nosed mole, a species commonly found living near swamps and ponds in the eastern part of the United States. The star-nosed mole has a snout made up of 22 fleshy tentacles that make its nose look like a starfish with too many arms.

The aye-aye is related to monkeys but looks kind of like a cat—until you see those long, skinny fingers.

One of the weirdest-looking—and most misunderstood—land mammals is a small primate (the same family of animals as apes and monkeys) called the aye-aye. The aye-aye, which uses its long, slender middle finger to find and scoop insects to eat out of trees, is far from the most handsome animal in the world (go ahead and look it up!). It has large, yellowish-colored eyes and long, slender fingers. The residents of Madagascar, where it lives, often kill it because they think it is an evil spirit or a sign of bad luck. That is one reason the aye-aye is an endangered species.

Not only does the star-nosed mole have a strange face, look at the size of those paws! They're extra big to help him dig through the soil.

RECORD BREAKING

You probably already know that the elephant is the biggest land animal on Earth today. But there are actually several species of elephants, including the biggest one of all: the African bush elephant. This species of elephant can weigh 225 pounds when it is born, and most of them grow to around 20 to 24 feet long and 10 to 12 feet tall at the shoulder, and weigh between 13,000 and 20,000 pounds. The biggest African bush elephant on record weighed 27,060 pounds and stood almost 14 feet tall.

DID YOU KNOW. . .?

You have probably heard that no two people have exactly the same fingerprints. (Yes, that means your fingerprints are yours and yours alone.) But did you know that each giraffe and each zebra also has its own one-of-a-kind identifiers? It's true! No two giraffes have the exact same pattern of spots, and no two zebras have the same pattern of stripes. That means that each giraffe and each zebra is a one-of-a-kind creation with its own identity—just like you!

Where Land Mammals Live

Land mammals live in almost all kinds of environments. Polar bears and some kinds of seals live in the coldest parts of the world, while camels and other animals live in some of the hottest. Moles and other burrowing animals live underground, and bats live in caves and other places where they can keep out of the sunlight during the day. Other animals live in forests and jungles, in deserts and open fields, and in mountains and valleys.

Like the other kinds of life God created, the way different mammals look and behave can tell you a lot about the kind of surroundings they live in. God equipped the cold-weather specialists like polar bears with thick fur and layers of fat to help keep them warm. He also equipped animals that live in hotter areas with thick fur and skin that help insulate them from the heat. And He gave the animals that live in warmer areas of the world the ability to pant or sweat in order to release extra heat from their bodies.

God also designed different animals to eat different kinds of food. He gave animals that eat only plants the kind of teeth and digestive systems that work best for eating grass, grains, fruits, and vegetables. These mammals are called *herbivores*. He also gave animals that eat meat—they are called *carnivores*—strong jaws and sharp teeth that work best for eating the meat from other animals. God also equipped some carnivores with the speed and strength they need to hunt their prey.

A female cheetah chases a young gazelle in Kenya.

Without a doubt, the cheetah is the top track star out of all the land mammals. Cheetahs, which are found in Saharan Africa, can go from 0 to 45 miles an hour in less than two seconds and can reach top speeds of up to 70 miles per hour. Cheetahs are built for speed. They have long, slender legs and a tail they use for balance when they make quick cuts. They use their amazing speed and agility to catch their prey, which includes impalas, gazelles, rabbits, birds, and other small animals. Even though cheetahs are fast, they can only reach their top speeds in short bursts.

The Land Mammal Family Tree

Scientists have classified and named mammals the same way they have classified and named the fish and birds that live on Earth. The different kinds of mammals are broken down into one class—called *Mammalia*—that includes about twenty different orders of animals—give or take an order or two, depending on who you talk to. Each order of mammals is broken down into families and sometimes subfamilies, and each of the families is broken down into one or more genera (remember, that's the plural of *genus*). Each genus includes a certain number of kinds of animals that are all very much alike in many ways.

The "Indiana bat" is a tiny mammal!

This will probably surprise you, but nearly one-fourth of all species of mammals have the ability to fly. Strange but true! There are about 985 species of bats, which accounts for just over 23 percent of all known kinds of mammals. Though there are a few mammals that can glide through the air—such as flying squirrels and flying possums—bats are the only mammals that can really fly. Most bats are *insectivores*, meaning they eat bugs, but some eat nectar and pollen, while others eat fish, frogs, lizards, small rodents, birds, or other bats. A few species of bats drink fresh blood.

A chimp gets a piggyback ride from her human handler, who is preparing the animal to return to the wild.

Scientists have placed us humans in the same order of mammals as apes and monkeys. This order of mammals is called *Primates*. That means that out of the entire animal kingdom, the mammals that are most like us are the apes—including gorillas, chimpanzees, and orangutans—and monkeys, as well as other members of that order. While these kinds of animals lack some of the special traits God gave only humans (you'll read more about that in chapter 8), they are like us in many ways. For one thing, they are among the most intelligent animals in all creation.

It might surprise you to know that the order of mammals with the most species is *Rodentia* or rodents. There are as many as 2,277 different kinds of rodents living in the world today. Mice

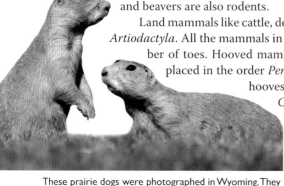

and rats are rodents, and so are squirrels, chipmunks, gophers, hamsters, gerbils, guinea pigs, prairie dogs, and groundhogs. It may surprise you to know that porcupines and beavers are also rodents.

Land mammals like cattle, deer, pigs, and camels are placed in the order *Artiodactyla*. All the mammals in this order have hooves with an even number of toes. Hooved mammals like horses, donkeys, and zebras are placed in the order *Perissodactyla*. All animals in this order have hooves with an odd number of toes. The order *Carnivora* includes meat-eating mammals like cats (the ones that live in the wild, like lions, tigers, and cougars, as well as cats people keep as pets), dogs (including wolves, foxes, and coyotes), bears, raccoons, and many others.

Some kinds of animals are placed in

These prairie dogs were photographed in Wyoming. They generally live west of the Mississippi River.

Did you know that male donkeys are called "Jacks," and female donkeys "Jennies"?

smaller orders because they have some very unusual traits. For example, the order *Marsupialia* includes only animals that carry their babies in a pouch—like the kangaroo. And the order *Proboscidea* is made up of only one family of mammals: elephants! It might make you laugh to read this, but the name *Proboscidea* means "eats with the nose." That name comes from the fact that elephants use their noses—which are really called *trunks*—to gather food and put it in their mouths.

The opossum is a marsupial, because—like the kangaroo—it carries its babies in a pouch. But these babies are big enough to ride on mom's back!

What Makes a Mammal a Mammal?

Like fish and birds, mammals are all part of the phylum *Chordata*. Remember, most animals from that phylum are considered vertebrates, which means they have backbones. All mammals are also warm-blooded. Remember, *warm-blooded* means that an animal's body is designed to stay at a certain temperature, no matter how warm or cold it is where it lives.

But there are a lot of animals living today that have spinal columns and are warm-blooded. Fish and birds—the first animals God created—all have backbones. So do all reptiles and amphibians. And birds are warm-blooded, just like mammals. So in order to know what makes a mammal a mammal, we're going to have to narrow things down a bit.

So, what else do you think all mammals have in common?

First of all, every mammal has hair or fur. It's pretty easy to see hair on most mammals. Most dogs and cats have thick hair and fur all over their bodies. So do bears, cattle, horses, and many

113

other mammals. Even mammals whose hair is hard to see have hair. That includes mammals that live in water, like dolphins and whales. Even though you can't easily see hair on these animals, it's there—it's just really small.

Not only do all mammals have hair or fur, but they are the only animals on Earth that do. "Wait a minute!" you might be saying. "I've seen pictures of tarantulas, and they are covered in hair!"

RECORD BREAKING

The smallest mammal in the world is the Kitti's hog-nosed bat, which lives in Thailand and feeds on small insects. This tiny bat grows to only 1.14 to 1.3 inches long and weighs just .07 ounces when it is fully grown. At that size, it is a lot smaller than a lot of insects. The Kitti's hog-nosed bat barely beats out Savi's pygmy shrew—also known as the white-toothed pygmy shrew—as the world's smallest mammal. These tiny creatures, which are found in southern Europe, grow to less than 1.75 inches long and weigh less than .10 ounces as adults.

Hair on a dolphin? You'll have to look very closely…

Breakfast time for a kid—of the goat variety

It's true that tarantulas and other creatures that aren't mammals *look* like they are covered in hair. But what seems like hair on a tarantula isn't really hair at all. Real hair is made up of dead strands of a substance called *keratin*. It's the same stuff your hair and fingernails and the hooves and horns of animals are made of. The difference is that what looks like hair on a tarantula actually contains living parts of the spider.

Another way that all mammals are alike is that they feed their babies with milk that comes from the mother's body. From the biggest elephant in the world to the tiniest mouse or bat, every mammal mother gives her baby the nourishment it needs to grow in the form of milk. Because mammal babies rely on their mother's milk to live and grow, mammal mothers all care for their young.

So there you have it! If an animal is a warm-blooded creature with a backbone and has hair on its body and feeds its young with milk, then it's a mammal! If an animal lacks any of those things, then it's something else.

THAT'S WEIRD!

Ever seen a duck-billed platypus? Other than having a strange name and also looking really funny, the platypus, which lives in eastern Australia, is one of only a few mammals that lays eggs instead of giving birth to its young. When scientists from Europe first saw the platypus—which has a mouth like a duck, a tail like a beaver, and feet like an otter—they thought someone was playing a joke on them. But it was real! And it's one of the weirdest-looking mammals God created!

The platypus is not only strange looking, it can be dangerous. Male platypuses can sting other creatures with a venom that comes through a sharp "spur" on their ankles.

Mammal Moms

Nearly all mammal mothers carry their babies inside them before giving birth. The amount of time the baby spends in its mother's body before it is born is called the *gestation period*. The amount of time it takes for the mammal baby to develop before it is born depends on the kind of mammal. Baby opossums are inside their mother's body just 12 days before they are born. And baby hamsters take 16 days to develop. Human babies are born about 266 days after the mother's egg is fertilized. The longest gestation period in the mammal world? The Indian elephant, at an amazing 624 days!

As a group, mammal mothers are just about the best in all creation. They care for their young, protect them from predators and other dangers, and, of course, they feed them every day. Because all baby mammals rely on their mother's milk to live and grow, the mother must care for the young at least until they are able to feed themselves and survive on their own. That means that mammal moms spend all of their time caring for their babies. The length of time a mammal mother cares for its young depends on the kind of animal. Some mammals—like certain kinds of rodents—care for their young for just a few weeks.

Nearly all mammal babies, including humans, have baby teeth or *milk teeth*. That makes it easier for the mother to feed its young the milk they need to live and grow. The exception to this rule in the mammal world is anteaters and a few other species of mammals that never grow teeth.

Reptiles: Land Animals with Scales

Out of all the animals that live on Earth, reptiles probably have the hardest time being accepted by humans. Some people are afraid of reptiles. Maybe it has something to do with the fact that all reptiles are covered with scales. Or maybe people just don't like animals that crawl or slither on the ground. Even though there are some kinds of reptiles that are poisonous—like some snakes and lizards such as Gila monsters—they are still important members of the animal kingdom. Reptiles are helpful to humans in several ways. Many reptiles eat rodents and other "pests," which helps farmers and other people who grow food for humans. In some cultures people eat certain reptiles, and some people enjoy keeping them as pets.

There are about 8,200 to 9,000 different species of reptiles living on Earth today. That includes many species each of turtles, snakes, crocodiles, lizards, and others. Reptiles live on every continent on Earth except Antarctica. Reptiles come as small as the dwarf gecko, which grows to less than an inch long, and as big as the saltwater crocodile, which can grow to more than 17 feet in length and weigh more than 3,000 pounds.

Is It Just the Scales?

Like other members of the animal kingdom, all reptiles have certain special traits that make them a part of their own family of animals. In reptiles, the two most important traits are that they are all cold-blooded and that they are all covered in scales.

Since a reptile is cold-blooded, its body temperature adjusts to its surroundings. That means that when a reptile gets too hot, it must move to water or shade to cool itself off. And if it gets too cold, it has to move to a sunny place to warm itself up.

This close-up of a python shows the many small scales that cover a snake's body. This snake is from the Pacific island nation of New Guinea.

One of the myths about reptiles, especially snakes, is that they are slimy to the touch. Actually, since all reptiles have scales, they are anything but slimy. The skins of some reptiles are very smooth because they are covered with very small scales. Some reptile skins are used to make people's clothing and shoes.

Most reptiles reproduce by laying eggs, but a few kinds give birth to live young. All turtles, tortoises, crocodiles, and alligators lay eggs. So do most lizards. All boas, vipers, and garter snakes give birth to live babies. So do a few species of lizards called *skinks*.

Most reptiles lay their eggs or give birth to their young, then leave them on their own. A few kinds of reptiles protect their eggs until they hatch. Alligators and crocodiles are known for guarding their nests and for helping their babies emerge from their eggs. Female pythons are known for coiling their bodies around their eggs to give them protection from predators and to keep them at the right temperature.

The skink (not skunk) eats mainly bugs— like crickets, grasshoppers, and beetles.

117

The eastern milk snake is a colorful species found in North America and South America. It got its name because in the past people believed they often went into barns and sucked milk from dairy cows. Of course, this story wasn't true. Actually, snakes don't drink milk at all! Milk snakes are actually beneficial to farmers because they help keep the population of rodents, which they eat, in check. Although milk snakes look a lot like the poisonous coral snake, they aren't venomous.

The Reptile Family Tree

All reptiles have backbones, and that means that they are all vertebrates from the phylum *Chordata*. There is only one class of reptiles, which scientists refer to as *Reptilia*.

Why are they called "snapping turtles"? Because they can snap at you with those sharp beaks!

Scientists have placed reptiles that live on Earth today in four orders and a few suborders. The largest order of reptiles (about 7,900 species) is *Squamata*. This order includes lizards, snakes, and creatures in the family *Amphisbaenids* (better known as worm-lizards). The second biggest order of reptiles (300 species) is *Testudines*. It includes the shelled reptiles—turtles, tortoises, and terrapins. The order *Crocodilia* includes 23 species of crocodiles, alligators, gavials, and caimans. The order *Sphenodontia* includes just two lizardlike species that live in New Zealand.

The orders of reptiles are broken into families and subfamilies. The order Squamata, for example, includes about 20 different families of lizards and about 18 different families of snakes. Each of these families is broken down into different genera, and each genera includes a certain number of species.

There are almost 5,000 species of lizards living in the world today, making them the most common of reptile species. Second among the reptiles as far as the number of species is concerned is snakes. There are about 2,700 different kinds of snakes; only 375 of them are poisonous.

This tiny worm lizard is found in the Virgin Islands.

The Mystery of the Dinosaurs

The biggest reptiles ever to live on Earth were the dinosaurs. All dinosaurs are extinct now. That means that they no longer live on Earth. No one knows for sure why all the dinosaurs became extinct. What scientists *do* know is that there were many kinds of dinosaurs in many shapes and sizes. They know that because they have found many dinosaur bones that were left behind when the dinosaurs died out.

Did you know that the name *dinosaur* came from an old Greek word that means "terrible lizard"? Actually, dinosaurs weren't really lizards, even though they were reptiles. Most of them weren't so terrible, either. Most dinosaurs were really big reptiles that ate plants. But some of the dinosaurs, like the tyrannosaurs, ate meat.

For a long time, the brachiosaur was thought to be the largest dinosaur. Many scientists believe the brachiosaur grew up to 82 feet long, but some believe they could have been even bigger. The brachiosaur had a long neck like a giraffe, and scientists believe it could raise its head more than 40 feet above the ground. But scientists believe there were dinosaurs even bigger than the brachiosaur. Bones from an enormous dinosaur called *Argentinosaurus* were recently discovered in South America. Scientists believe this dinosaur could have

grown to over 100 feet long and weighed over 100 tons. Another dinosaur, called *Sauroposeidon*, was recently discovered that may have been heavier than the brachiosaur.

Different people believe different things about where dinosaurs fit in with the creation story in Genesis 1. Some believe that God created everything in six actual 24-hour days, and that the earth is between 6,000 and 10,000 years old. That would mean that dinosaurs and people lived at the same time. Other people believe that the six days God used to create the world and all life on it weren't really actual days. Instead they believed that these "days" were really long periods of time with gaps in between them. They believe that the earth is millions or billions of years old and that dinosaurs had become extinct a long time before God created humans.

Some people even believe that dinosaurs are mentioned in the Bible. They point to names in scripture like *leviathan, behemoth, sea serpent,* and *dragon*. But the Bible doesn't say anything at all about what happened to the dinosaurs—or any other of the many creatures that at one time lived on Earth but are now extinct.

Amphibians: Animals that Live Two Lives

There are more than 6,000 species of amphibians living on Earth today. That includes frogs, toads, salamanders, newts, and strange creatures called *caecilians* (tropical amphibians that look like snakes or worms at a glance because they have no legs and a very short tail).

Some amphibians are among the strangest animals on Earth. For example, the Chinese giant (and we mean *giant*!) salamander is the world's biggest amphibian, growing up to almost six feet long. Then there's the olm, a blind salamander with transparent skin that lives in water that flows underground and can survive without food for ten years. And there is also the lungless salamander of Mexico, a species that doesn't have lungs but takes in oxygen through its skin and mouth lining.

All amphibians are vertebrates that belong to the class of animals called *Amphibia*. *Amphibia* is a Greek word that means "two lives." That's because amphibians spend their lives in two places: in water and on land.

Amphibians that live on Earth today all belong to the subclass of animals called *Lissamphibia*. This subclass includes the orders *Anura* (frogs and toads), *Caudata* (salamanders and newts), and *Apoda* (caecilians). These orders are broken down into families, with the families broken down into genera. Each genus includes one or more individual species.

Amphibians: Kind of Like Reptiles...but Different

Amphibians are a lot like reptiles in some ways. Both are cold-blooded vertebrates that can be found all over the world. And most kinds of reptiles and amphibians reproduce by laying eggs. But amphibians are also a lot different from reptiles in some very important areas.

The most important way amphibians are different from reptiles is in how they reproduce. Reptile eggs have hard, leathery shells that are designed to protect the developing babies living inside. Many reptiles lay their eggs in well-hidden nests that are protected from hot or cold weather. Amphibians, on the other hand, lay soft eggs that don't have a protective shell. They usually attach the eggs to the stems of plants growing in the water. If you were to look around pond plants during the mating season of amphibians, you would likely find clear blobs of goo with tiny frog or salamander eggs inside them.

Zap! The cricket on the leaf never saw that frog's tongue coming.

Most newly hatched reptiles look pretty much like the adults of the species. But most amphibians begin their lives in water and look nothing like their parents. This is called the *tadpole stage* of the amphibian's life. During that stage, the amphibian looks and acts more like a fish than an amphibian. It has fins and a tail and breathes using gills. Most of the time, it doesn't have legs. Most tadpoles feed on plants and algae they find in the water, but some feed on smaller tadpoles and other animals that live in water.

As the tadpole begins growing into an adult amphibian, it loses its gills as it develops lungs and forms legs so that it can begin its life on land. During that time, its mouth will also grow into the same width as its head, preparing it for feeding on what full-grown amphibians eat.

THAT'S WEIRD!

A Betic midwife toad is actually a species of frog that lives in Spain. These frogs are known for two weird things. First, they have warts on their backs that give off a strong-smelling poison when they are attacked or scared. Second, after mating, the female lays strings of fertilized eggs, which the male carries around his hind legs until they are ready to hatch. When it is time for the tadpoles to emerge from the eggs, the male deposits them in the water, where they begin the process of maturing into baby Betic midwife toads.

A frog sits in the water, surrounded by its eggs (also called "spawn").

Arthropods: Creation's Creepy Crawlers and Flyers

Can you remember the last time you came face-to-face with a kind of animal called an *arthropod*? If you're not so sure when you have, then there are a few things about arthropods you need to know.

First of all, there are millions of species of arthropods. Second, arthropods live all over the world—in saltwater, in freshwater, on land, in the air, and in the soil. Between 80 and 85 percent of animal species alive on Earth today are arthropods.

If you're still not so sure when the last time was that you saw an arthropod, then consider this: All insects are arthropods. So if you've seen an ant, a housefly, a bee, or a butterfly today, you've seen an arthropod.

Insects aren't the only animals scientists classify as arthropods. Spiders, centipedes, mites, ticks, lobsters, crabs, crayfish, scorpions, and many other animals are also arthropods—and they are all important parts in God's perfect plan of creation.

Spiders weave a web of silk to catch other spiders and bugs as food. Some large spiders can catch and eat small birds and lizards!

What Is an Arthropod?

Arthropods all share certain traits that make them arthropods. First of all, arthropods are all invertebrates. Other animals you have already read about in this book—fish, birds, mammals, reptiles, and amphibians—are vertebrates, which means they have backbones. An invertebrate, on the other hand, is an animal that has no backbone.

Instead of a backbone, or any other bones, arthropods have what *entomologists*—scientists who study insects—call an *exoskeleton*. An exoskeleton is basically a hard shell on the out-side of the body that acts like a coat of armor. The exoskeleton protects

Most millipedes eat dead leaves and live between one and ten years.

the arthropod from predators and other outside dangers. An arthropod's exoskeleton is soft when it is first born, but it hardens as the animal matures. Many young arthropods shed their exoskeletons and grow new ones as they get bigger.

Arthropod is a Greek word that mixes the words *joint* and *foot*. This means that any animal that has more than four jointed legs is an arthropod. That includes all insects, spiders, centipedes, crustaceans (like crabs and lobsters), and a long, long list of other animals. Spiders, crabs, and other species of arthropods have eight legs. Centipedes and millipedes can have anywhere from 30 to hundreds of legs.

Arthropods are also known for their *segmented bodies.* That means that their bodies are made up of more than one part. Flies and other insects have three body segments, while spiders have two. Most millipedes have 30 to 40 body segments.

Like fish, reptiles, and amphibians, arthropods are cold-blooded animals. Remember, the body temperature of all cold-blooded animals depends on the temperature of the water or air that surrounds them.

The Arthropod Family Tree

Scientists believe there are between four and six million species of arthropods living in the world today. That is more species than the rest of the animal kingdom combined! All arthropods belong to the phylum of animals called *Arthropoda*.

Scientists have placed all known arthropods into eleven different classes of animals. The class with the most known kinds of animals is called *Insecta*—you guessed it...insects! Even though scientists have identified and named just over one million species of insects, they believe there could be between six and ten million species living in the world today.

Insects all have the hard outer skeletons all arthropods have. They also have a three-part body (head, thorax, and abdomen) and three pairs of jointed legs. Insects also have what are called *compound eyes.*

Flies—like this common house fly—have large "compound eyes" made up of thousands of round lenses.

123

Compound eyes have many different lenses to see out of, instead of just one like human eyes have. Insects also have two antennae. Ants, bees, beetles, butterflies, moths, grasshoppers, and dragonflies are all insects, and there are thousands to hundreds of thousands of species of each of them.

A ruby tiger moth shows off its antennae (in white).

Another large class of arthropods that live on land is called *Arachnida*. These animals are more commonly called *arachnids*. Spiders, ticks, mites, and scorpions are all arachnids. All arachnids have eight legs—even though some arachnids' front legs are designed as claws. The best-known arachnids are spiders. There are about 38,000 known species of spiders living in the world today.

The Importance of Arthropods

Many arthropods are creepy, crawly creatures, and some of them are kind of scary looking. Most people consider some arthropods—like houseflies or grasshoppers—pests.

But, hey, even if they are a little on the scary or ugly side, and even if they are capable of causing people trouble, they're also creations of God—and they are important to humans and other animals for many different reasons.

Many species of fish, birds, and mammals often eat arthropods, and some of them eat *only* arthropods. Krill, which are shrimplike arthropods that live in the ocean, are an important part of many sea animals' diets. Many freshwater fish eat mostly insects and krill larvae. And as you read in chapter 6, some birds are specially equipped with beaks that make it easy for them to catch insects to eat.

Some crustaceans, which are all arthropods, are important parts of the human diet in many parts of the world. Crabs, lobsters, crayfish, shrimps, and prawns

This krill looks something like the shrimp you might eat at a seafood restaurant.

are all popular for food all over the world. In some cultures, insects and their *grubs* (larvae) are eaten raw and cooked. Believe it or not, tarantulas are considered a delicacy in some parts of the world!

The arthropod that plays the most important part in supplying food to humans around the world is the bee. That's not just because many people like to eat honey. Bees help in pollination, which is a process absolutely necessary in the production of many fruits and veg-

Yes, that's a bowl full of cooked tarantulas. They're a snack in the Asian nation of Cambodia.

etables. *Pollination* happens when pollen is transferred from one plant to another plant of the same species. That process allows plants to reproduce and bear fruit.

Many arthropods are important to humans because they help control populations of pests that destroy crops. Spiders and scorpions eat insects that eat plant life, including plants that produce food for humans. Ladybugs are even important this way because they eat aphids, tiny plant-eating insects that can make short work of a vegetable garden if they aren't controlled.

EXPLORING THE WORLD OF LAND ANIMALS

What kind of land animals do you find most interesting? Mammals? Reptiles? Amphibians? Arthropods? Take the time to learn about the kind of animal that is most interesting to you. Read about these kinds of animals, or visit a city zoo, wildlife center, or other place you can see the animals in person. As you read and observe, ask yourself these questions: How are these animals different from other types of land animals? How are they like other land animals? What do they eat? Where do they live in the wild? How do they benefit humans? Maybe you can use what you learn in a school report, but maybe you'll just have fun learning about the animals you think are most interesting!

One Final Step to Go!

God spent most of two days creating the millions of animals that live in the water and on dry ground—and some that split their time in both places. He made the animals that swim, animals that fly, animals that walk, animals that crawl, animals that burrow, and animals that just stay in one place most of their lives.

You probably wonder why God made many of the animals He did. Some of them don't seem to have any real purpose other than just being what they are. But every animal God made had its own special place in His wonderful plan of creation. Every animal would become part of a kingdom that would feed itself and reproduce itself until the end of time.

But God wasn't finished. Now that He had created everything you can see—and some things you can't—it was time for Him to finish His work of creation by making the one being He did it all for in the first place. That means you!

CHAPTER 8

DAY 6, PART II

HUMANS: MADE IN GOD'S IMAGE

Then God said, "Let us make human beings in our image, to be like us. They will reign over the fish in the sea, the birds in the sky, the livestock, all the wild animals on the earth, and the small animals that scurry along the ground."

So God created human beings in his own image. In the image of God he created them; male and female he created them.

Then God blessed them and said, "Be fruitful and multiply. Fill the earth and govern it. Reign over the fish in the sea, the birds in the sky, and all the animals that scurry along the ground."

GENESIS 1:26−28

After working more than five days to create the universe, the earth, and everything that lives on Earth, God did something very different from what He had been doing. The Bible tells us that when He created us humans, it was the first time He made something "in his own image" (Genesis 1:27).

You can see a lot of what God is like in everything He created. When you look outside of Earth and see the stars, planets, galaxies, and other things He placed in outer space, you can see just how big and powerful He is. When you look at the earth and how it is put together, you can see that God pays close attention to the details and that He made sure that every living thing He later created would be cared for. And when you look at the amazing number of plants and animals and other living things on Earth now, you can see that God is very creative and really likes variety.

But none of those things—as amazing and wonderful as they are—are made in God's own image like we humans are.

What Sets You Apart from Animals

What do you think it means that we humans are created in God's own image? Actually, it means a lot of things.

Dolphins raise their tails at a trainer's command—and receive a treat in return.

It doesn't mean that God has a physical body like you do. It also doesn't mean that you have the power God has, to create something out of nothing. But God created us humans to rule over the world and over all the animals that live here with us.

God made some animals to be a lot like us humans in some ways. For example, some of the world's most intelligent animals—such as primates, some water mammals (like dolphins, which are known for their amazing intelligence), and others—seem to have the ability to use their brains in ways very much like you use yours. In other words, they're just plain smarter than most animals. And some animals are very sociable, which means they live and travel in tightly knit families.

But God made people different from animals—and like Himself—in many important ways. First of all, we're made different from animals in how we think and reason. Even the most intelligent animals on Earth aren't able to use their brains the way we humans can. For example, only humans are able to read and understand the Bible and other written materials. And no animal is able to solve a complicated math equation or to figure out how to take apart and reassemble things like puzzles or car engines.

God also gave us humans the gift of creativity. Even though humans can't create on the same scale as God has, we all have the ability to use our minds and hands to create all sorts of new things—like art, music, technology, and other important human creations.

God also made us like Him in the way we communicate—both with God and with one another. While some animals have the ability to communicate using different sounds, none of them has the ability to use words like we can. God began creation with the simple words "*Let there be. . .*" and it was so.

You can dress up a chimpanzee—but you can't make him human!

From tiny computer chips to massive skyscrapers, the creativity of human beings is unmatched in the animal world.

God made us humans different from animals in that we can know the difference between good and evil and right and wrong. He also gave us the free will to choose right and wrong. Adam and Eve, the very first humans in all creation, were given the choice between right and wrong. Sadly, they chose to do the wrong thing—the one and only thing God told them *not* to do. But even though Adam and Eve messed up, we humans still reflect the image of God because we can choose to do what is right in His eyes.

The most important way God made us humans different from animals is that we have an awareness of our Creator. Not only that, we have the ability to communicate and fellowship with Him. God also gave each of us an eternal soul, the part of us that lives on after our bodies die. And God has lovingly given us the opportunity to be with Him forever after we die.

Satan, in the form of a snake, tempts Eve to disobey God by eating the "forbidden fruit."

Your Body—God's Most Amazing Creation

Before God created us humans, He put together an amazing universe and planet Earth. He created billions of galaxies, each of which contains billions of stars. He created our solar system and designed it perfectly so that our earth could support us and millions of other living things that make their home here.

But as awesome as all these creations are, they've got nothing on the human body. Your body is the most incredible, complicated living thing in the whole world. God designed your body with many different *systems* that all work together perfectly to keep you moving, thinking, talking, and growing.

These different systems include your

- nervous system (your brain, spinal cord, and nerves);
- cardiovascular system (your heart, blood, and vessels);

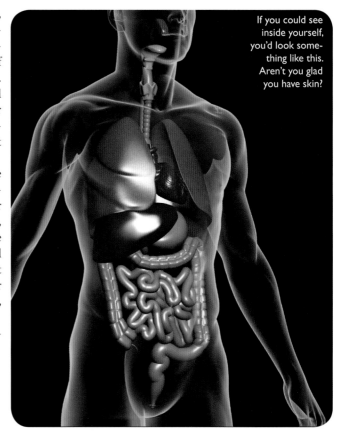

If you could see inside yourself, you'd look something like this. Aren't you glad you have skin?

- lymphatic/immune system (your lymph and lymph nodes and white blood cells);
- respiratory system (your nose, trachea, and lungs);
- digestive system (your mouth, esophagus, stomach, and intestines);
- muscular system (your muscles and tendons);
- skeletal system (your bones);
- dermal system (your hair, skin, and nails);
- excretory system (your lungs, large intestine, kidneys, and skin);
- endocrine system (your glands);
- reproductive system (your reproductive organs);

All these systems—and a few others—together make up your entire body. And by the time you are fully grown, they will account for about 100 trillion individual cells, 206 bones, 600 muscles, and 22 internal organs.

DID YOU KNOW. . . ?

There are a total of 206 bones in the bodies of adult human beings (more than half of which are in the hands and feet), but between 300 and 350 bones in the body of a baby. That's because some of the bones of babies fuse together as they grow. There are four classes of bones in the human body. There are the *long bones*, which make up the limbs. There are the *short bones*, which are grouped together to strengthen your skeleton. There are the *flat bones*, which protect your body and provide a place for the muscles to attach. Finally, there are the *irregular bones*, oddly shaped bones that don't fit into the other three classes.

No wonder that thousands of years ago, a man named David—the greatest king the nation of Israel ever had and the man who wrote many of the Old Testament psalms—declared his amazement at the design of his own body when he wrote, "You made all the delicate, inner parts of my body and knit me together in my mother's womb. Thank you for making me so wonderfully complex! Your workmanship is marvelous—how well I know it" (Psalm 139:13–14).

How We've Learned about the Human Body

One of the most important ways humans have used their God-given capacity for creativity and thought is in the study of the human body and medicine. We humans have always had a curiosity about how our bodies work, as well as a need to understand how to diagnose and treat people who are sick or injured. Over the past century, what we know about the human body has grown incredibly. So have the technology and knowledge doctors use to help people who are sick or injured.

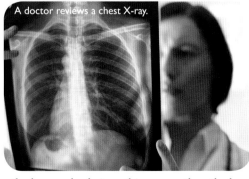
A doctor reviews a chest X-ray.

The technology scientists and doctors use on the human body is nothing more than the harnessing of what God has already created and using it in medicine. For example, the sun and other stars give off X-rays, which are used in medicine today. X-rays have also been called *Roentgen rays*, after Wilhelm Konrad Roentgen, the German scientist who discovered them and developed ways to use them in medicine. Doctors use X-rays to see images from inside the body, such as the skeleton, and also in *angiograms* (picture images of the blood vessels).

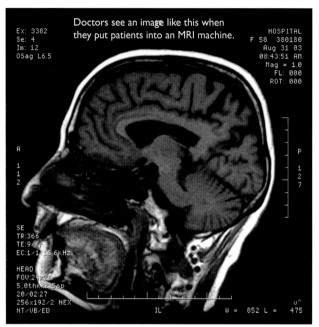

Doctors see an image like this when they put patients into an MRI machine.

While an X-ray gives doctors a *two-dimensional* (flat, like the pages of a book) look at some parts of the human body, a Computed Axial Tomography scan (or CAT scan) allows doctors to have a *three-dimensional* (height, width, and depth) look inside the human body. A CAT scan of the brain or other organs gives a lot more information than a regular X-ray. The CAT scan can allow a brain specialist to look at "slices" of the brain, which helps make finding tumors and other problems easier.

Magnetic Resonance Imaging (MRI) is a form of medical technology that gives detailed pictures of internal body parts. Unlike the X-ray or the CAT scan, the MRI doesn't use radiation or other radioactive substances of any kind. Instead, the patient is placed in a magnetic field while radio waves, which are completely harmless to the human body, are turned on and off. The body then emits its own weak radio signals, which are picked up by an antenna and fed to a computer. This produces detailed images of what is going on inside the body.

THE WAY IT USED TO BE

Today, if you were to get really sick, you would go to a doctor who would figure out what is wrong with you and then give you the medicine you need to get well. But there was a time when doctors used leeches—little creatures that look kinda like slugs and feed on blood—to treat their patients. Up until about the mid-1800s, it was believed that people got sick because of imbalances in their bodies and that one of the best ways to get rid of those imbalances was to allow leeches to take out the "bad blood" that caused those imbalances and made people sick. This procedure was called *bloodletting*.

A Perfectly Designed "Control Center"

You probably haven't given a lot of thought about just how your family's car works—other than it

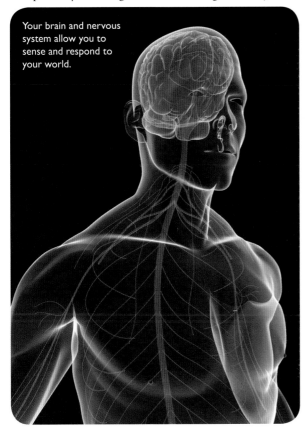

Your brain and nervous system allow you to sense and respond to your world.

needs fuel in order to take you and your family where you need to go. But today's car engines are designed to operate best through a small computer inside the dashboard that acts as a control center that keeps everything working in order.

God designed your body with a "control center" of its own that keeps every part of your body working the way He meant it to work. It's called your *brain*, and it is the key part of what is called your *nervous system*.

Your nervous system is made up of the brain, the spinal cord, and a huge arrangement of nerves that start at the top of your head and go all the way to the bottom of your feet. Your brain weighs about three pounds, and it sends messages to and receives messages from about 45 miles of nerves that run through your entire body.

Your brain is the most amazing organ in your whole body. You use your brain to store different kinds of information—like people and facts you know, things you need to remember, and what you need to do at certain times and in certain situations. You also use your brain to do things you choose to do—like eating, walking, reading, and playing ball. And, of course, you use your brain for thinking!

DID YOU KNOW...?

If you've ever been to a meat market and seen calves' brains—yes, believe it or not, some people like to eat calves' brains—then you have a general idea what your own brain looks like. Your brain will never take first place in a beauty contest. In fact, it looks kinda gross! But of all the things God created, there are few more amazing than that three-pound organ He put between your ears. Your brain is made up of more than 10 billion nerve cells and more than 50 billion other cells.

Your brain also controls every other function of your body, including the things you don't have to think about doing. You breathe because your brain tells your lungs to take in air. Your heart beats because your brain sends it signals telling it to pump blood throughout your body. And your digestive system does what it needs to do because your brain tells your mouth, your stomach, your intestines, and other parts of your digestive system what to do and when to do it.

Your brain is made up of five parts: the cerebrum, the cerebellum, the brain stem, the pituitary gland, and the hypothalamus. Each of these parts plays a vital role in how your mind and body function. The *cerebrum* is the largest part of your brain. It is the part you use for thinking, memory, and for voluntary muscle movements. The *cerebellum* is the part of the brain that controls your balance, movement, and coordination. Without your cerebellum doing its work, you couldn't walk, stand, or move around.

Your Cardiovascular System

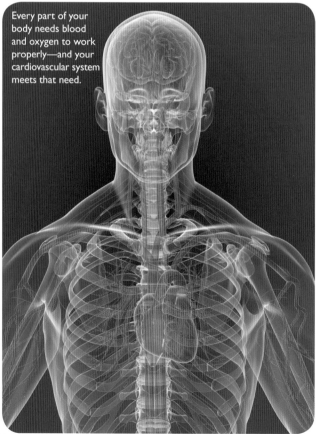

Every part of your body needs blood and oxygen to work properly—and your cardiovascular system meets that need.

If you think your nervous system is the most incredible part of your body, then you might find the *cardiovascular system*—which consists of your heart, blood, and blood vessels— a close second.

Your heart is the single largest part of your cardiovascular system. Your heart's job is to pump blood through your body. The heart of an average grown-up human beats just a little under 104,000 times a day, while a child's heart beats about 129,000 to 172,000 times a day. As the heart beats, it pumps blood through your body so that it can provide your body with the nutrients and oxygen it needs.

Your body contains an amazing 60,000 miles of *blood vessels*, which are tubes that carry blood from one part of the body to another. There are three kinds of blood vessels in your body. There are the *arteries*, which carry blood away from your heart.

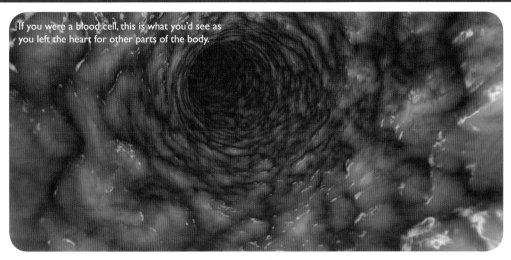

If you were a blood cell, this is what you'd see as you left the heart for other parts of the body.

There are the *veins,* which take blood back to your heart. And there are the *capillaries,* which are tiny vessels that supply your entire body with oxygen and other nutrients. The capillaries are the smallest blood vessels. Most of them are so small that blood cells have to line up single file just to pass through them.

EXPLORING THE HUMAN BODY

If you want to learn more about how your body works, you can find mountains of information in your school library and on the Internet. A good way to do your study is to investigate the systems in the human body one by one. Here they are: the circulatory system, the dermal system, the digestive system, the endocrine system, the excretory system, the lymphatic/immune system, the muscular system, the nervous system, the reproductive system, the respiratory system, and the skeletal system.

Your Respiratory System

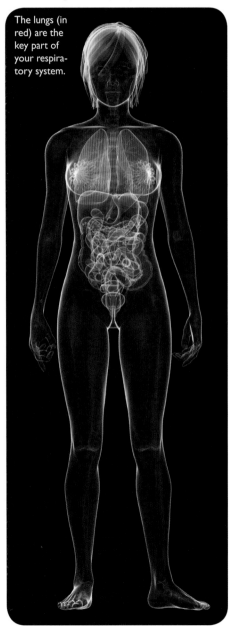

The lungs (in red) are the key part of your respiratory system.

Have you ever had a contest with your friends to see who could hold their breath the longest? If you have, then you know that it's not more than a few seconds after you stop breathing that you really want to take a breath again. That's because it's only a matter of a few seconds before your body realizes you've stopped taking in oxygen and starts screaming at your brain, *I need oxygen!*

Oxygen is one of the elements your body needs to survive. The cells in your body use oxygen to perform every one of the basic functions of life—walking, running, thinking, eating, sitting still. . .even sleeping! When the cells in your body use oxygen, they produce a gas called *carbon dioxide*. Even though there is always carbon dioxide in your body, too much of it can make a person sick or even die.

This is where your *respiratory system* comes in.

Your respiratory system serves one simple purpose: to bring oxygen into your body and to remove carbon dioxide from your body. Your lungs are the biggest and most important part of your respiratory system. They work closely with your circulatory system to bring oxygen to your cells and to remove the poisonous carbon dioxide.

Here's how it works.

When you breathe in, you fill your lungs with fresh, oxygen-filled air. At the same time, your heart pumps blood into the walls of your lungs through your blood vessels. When the blood reaches the walls of your lungs, it releases carbon dioxide into your lungs and absorbs oxygen and takes it to the rest of your body. After the oxygen-rich blood leaves your lungs, it goes back to your heart, which pumps it out through your body. When you breathe out, you release the carbon dioxide into the air around you.

Have you ever wondered why your heart beats faster and you breathe harder when you're exercising—playing basketball with your friends, hiking with your family, or running in gym class? It's because when you exercise, your body uses a lot more oxygen than it does when you're sitting still. Your lungs and heart always work together to take in the oxygen you need and then deliver it to your muscles and other parts of your body to work right, but they have to work harder when your muscles send the signal, *I need more oxygen!* So you end up breathing harder.

What Happens When You Eat— Digestion!

Can you remember the last time you started to feel hungry? Maybe it was almost lunchtime at school, and you began to feel your stomach growl—and maybe hear a few of your classmates'

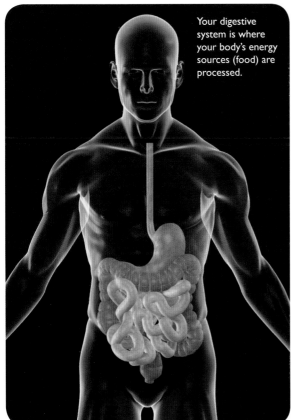

Your digestive system is where your body's energy sources (food) are processed.

stomachs doing the same thing.

As lunchtime grew closer and you began to think about eating, your mouth might have started to water a little bit. And if you started to smell the food you were about to have for lunch, then your stomach growled louder and your mouth watered even more. It seemed like all you could think about was a delicious slice of pizza or that turkey sandwich you brought to school with you for lunch.

This doesn't happen just because you like food. It's your body telling you it's time to eat!

Like all living things, you need food in order to survive. Food is the source of the energy you need to get through the day as well as the vitamins and other essential nutrients your body needs to grow, develop, heal, and function in every other way.

Your *digestive system* is an amazing system of organs that allows your body to convert food into energy. It includes your mouth, your esophagus, your stomach, and your large and small intestines. That slice of pizza or turkey sandwich wouldn't do your body a bit of good if it wasn't digested, but every part of your digestive system works together to convert the things you eat into energy and nutrients your body can use to keep it running well.

Digestion starts with the part you enjoy the most: eating! When you take a bite of food, your teeth begin crushing it into pieces small enough to swallow—and small enough for your stomach to begin breaking down. At that same time, glands in your mouth and throat produce *saliva* (you might know it better as spit), which moistens your food to make it easier to swallow and which begins breaking down your food.

After you swallow your food, it travels down your *esophagus*. The esophagus is a long, slippery tube that goes from your throat to your stomach. It has muscles inside it that force food down toward the stomach.

Your stomach has muscles it uses to grind and mix the food you have eaten. It also has glands that release the chemicals hydrochloric acid and pepsin, which together break the food down into a goopy mixture called *chyme*. The chyme then moves into your small intestine, where several chemicals break down the food even more. At that same time, your liver adds a liquid substance called *bile*, which helps neutralize the acids from your stomach. That helps move the process of digestion along.

As the chyme slowly moves along in your small intestine—aided by muscles that squeeze and roll it—the process of digestion is almost complete. Inside your small intestine, tiny folds called *villi* absorb all the nutrients from the chyme. What is left is the waste material your body can't use. Those materials enter your large intestine, which helps rid you of the leftover waste.

THAT'S WEIRD!

When you hear the word *bacteria*, you probably think of those little bugs that can make you sick. But there are lots of different kinds of bacteria in your body. Some of them can make you sick, and others are just there not really doing anything. But several kinds of bacteria working in your body help keep you healthy. Believe it or not, your body needs bacteria just to survive! Some of the good bacteria in your body help with digestion of food, with the breaking down of waste products, with cleaning out the bad stuff from your intestines, and with producing vitamins and other nutrients your body needs.

You've Got Muscles!

Remember the last time you saw a super bulked-up bodybuilder? You probably thought to yourself, *Wow! He's really got muscles!* Actually, you have the same number of muscles as even the beefiest-looking bodybuilder in the world. It's just that a bodybuilder spends a lot of time developing his muscles at the gym and making them bigger.

Any time you move, you're using one or more of the muscles your body is designed to have. You use muscles when you run, jump, throw a ball, or pick up a book. You even use your muscles when you smile or blink your eyes.

On average, about 40 percent of a human's body weight is muscle. Your body includes large muscles, like the ones in your legs, to very tiny muscles, like the ones you are using to read this book (yes, your eyes move back and forth because of tiny muscles attached to them). Each muscle in your body is designed to do different kinds of work.

Your body includes three different kinds of muscles: skeletal muscles, smooth muscles, and cardiac muscles.

Most of your *skeletal muscles* are attached to your bones with strong, flexible strands of tissue called *tendons*. These muscles are used in voluntary movements like raising your arms or scratching your leg. The largest muscles in your body are skeletal muscles.

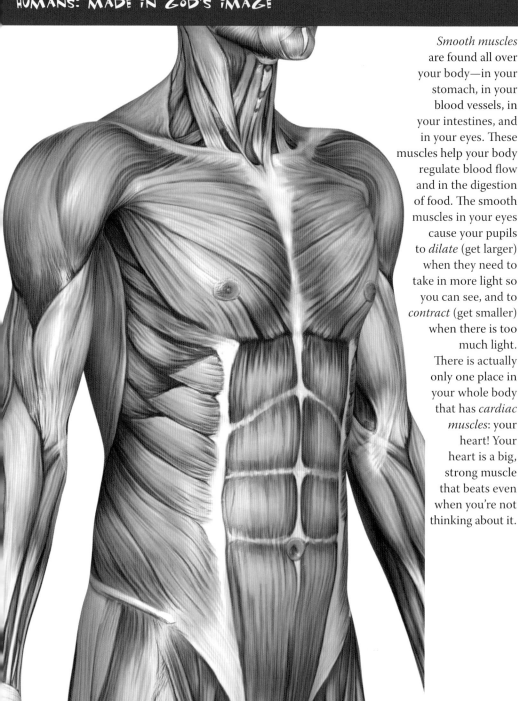

Smooth muscles are found all over your body—in your stomach, in your blood vessels, in your intestines, and in your eyes. These muscles help your body regulate blood flow and in the digestion of food. The smooth muscles in your eyes cause your pupils to *dilate* (get larger) when they need to take in more light so you can see, and to *contract* (get smaller) when there is too much light. There is actually only one place in your whole body that has *cardiac muscles*: your heart! Your heart is a big, strong muscle that beats even when you're not thinking about it.

Your Inner Frame: The Skeletal System

Have you ever gone by a building site and seen how a house is constructed? After the foundation is laid, builders assemble the house's frame—the part that will both support the rest of the house and give the builders something to build on as they work to make the house ready for people to live in.

In a way, your body is constructed very much like a house. But instead of a frame made of wood, you have one made of strong material that forms your skeleton. Without your skeleton, you couldn't run, walk, or stand upright.

Your skeleton is made up of four main types of bones. You have *long bones* in your arms and legs and *short bones* in your hands, feet, and spine. You also have *flat bones* to protect your organs. Finally, you have what are called *irregular bones*, which are bones that don't fit in with the other three types.

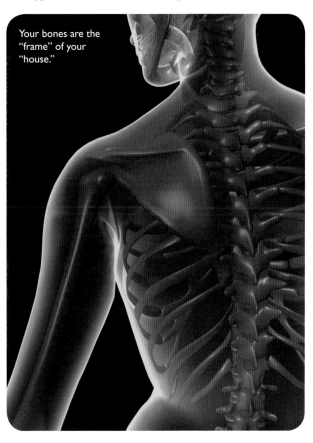

Your bones are the "frame" of your "house."

Your bones are strong enough to support your weight, hold you upright, and protect your organs, but they are also light enough to allow you to walk, run, and jump. If your bones were any weaker, they would break easily in even the lightest movement, but if they were any heavier, they would make it difficult to move around as freely and quickly as you do.

More than half of the bones in your whole body are found in your hands and feet. These bones, along with the ligaments and tendons in your hands, give your hands the flexibility they need to do things like grasp a pencil or pen or play a musical instrument. And they give your feet the flexibility they need to help you keep your balance when you walk or run.

Your bones also serve one other very important purpose. Not only do they give you strength and support and protect your internal organs, they also produce new blood for your entire body. Your blood is made up of millions and millions of microscopic cells that live for only a few months.

That means they have to be regularly replaced. In the center of your bones is a spongy material called *marrow*. The marrow is the part of your bones that creates new blood cells to replace the old ones that die or the ones you lose when you bleed.

RECORD BREAKING

Robert Wadlow was 19 years old—and 8 feet, 7 inches tall—when he was interviewed by the newspaper reporter on the ladder.

The tallest man in medical history was Robert Wadlow, who measured an amazing 8 feet, 11 inches tall at the time of his death in 1940. Wadlow weighed 490 pounds at the end of his life. He was known as the "Alton Giant," after his hometown of Alton, Illinois. The world's all-time tallest woman was Zeng Jinlian, who reached a height of 8 feet, 1 ¾ inches before she died in 1982 at the age of 17. Zeng Jinlian was the only woman among 12 people in medical history who grew to over 8 feet tall.

THAT'S WEIRD!

Here are some interesting—and really weird—facts about your skin. First, your skin is the largest organ in your whole body, with a surface area of about 21 square feet. Second, humans shed about 600,000 tiny particles of skin every hour, which accounts for about 1.5 pounds of skin a year and about 105 pounds in a lifetime for someone who reaches 70 years of age. Third, humans shed and regrow their outer skin cells about every 27 days. Finally (and this is *really* weird—and gross), most dust particles in your house are made of dead skin.

The color might vary from person to person, but our skin is always working for us!

Other Important Systems

In addition to the ones listed earlier, your body has several other important systems that work to keep your body operating and growing.

Your *integumentary system* includes the heaviest organ you have—your skin. Your skin serves a lot of important purposes. It is designed to protect your body from germs and viruses that can cause you to become sick. It also keeps your body from losing too much water and dehydrating and insulates your body and helps keep it from overheating or from cooling off too much. Finally, your skin actually produces vitamin D when it is exposed to sunlight.

Your *lymphatic/immune system* helps protect you from bad bacteria that could cause you to become ill. This system includes your lymph and lymph nodes as well as your white blood cells. Your lymph nodes produce immune cells that help the body fight infection. Your white blood cells—which are also called *leukocytes*—help defend your body against infections by feasting on bacteria and other dangerous organisms and materials that make their way into your body.

Your *excretory system* serves to rid your body of wastes and toxins that build up as a result of other bodily functions. Your lungs are part of your respiratory system, but they are also part of your excretory system because they help rid your body of the carbon dioxide your blood cells carry back from cells that have processed oxygen. Your large and small intestines are part of your digestive system, but they are also part of your excretory system because they help rid your body of waste that is left over after your body has fully digested the food you eat. And your kidneys work day and night to clean the waste and toxins out of your blood.

Your *endocrine system* is a bunch of glands that serve some very important purposes in your body. *Glands* are organs that release different kinds of chemicals called *hormones* into your body. You have more than 30 different hormones working in your body to cause all kinds of things to happen. Hormones regulate your body temperature, control your growth and physical maturity, and even help you to feel hungry when your body knows it's time to eat. They even help you to handle stressful or frightening situations you may face.

When God created us humans, He made us "male and female" (Genesis 1:27). That is so we could follow His command to "be fruitful and multiply. Fill the earth and govern it. Reign over the fish in the sea, the birds in the sky, and all the animals that scurry along the ground" (Genesis 1:28).

God made all men and women (and boys and girls) in His own image, but He also made them very different in some very important ways. He equipped women with the internal organs they would need in order to give birth to children, and He equipped men with the organs they would need to father children. These organs are all part of humankind's *reproductive system*.

CHAPTER 9
DAY 6, PART III:
CREATION COMPLETE. . .NOW WHAT?

Then God said, "Look! I have given you every seed-bearing plant throughout the earth and all the fruit trees for your food. And I have given every green plant as food for all the wild animals, the birds in the sky, and the small animals that scurry along the ground—everything that has life." And that is what happened.

Then God looked over all he had made, and he saw that it was very good! And evening passed and morning came, marking the sixth day.

GENESIS 1:29–31

If you were to go back and read the first chapter of Genesis and take a count of the times God looked at something He had created and said it was "good," you'd find that word used six different times in that part of the Bible. But as the sixth and final day of creation—the day He created us humans—drew to a close, God looked at everything He had created and saw that it was "very good" (Genesis 1:31).

What do you think it means that God saw His own finished work as "very good"? Why not just "good"? One of the reasons creation was "very good" at that point was that it was finished. God had just spent six days creating a home for all living things—as well as a universe to place that home

in—and human beings. When He had finished His work, the heavens and the earth, and everything that lived in them, were everything He had planned. They were a perfect place for God's most prized creation—you and other humans—to live and multiply.

But what does this mean to you today? Creation happened a long time ago, and some of the things that have happened since then have changed what was once a perfect planet.

Even though creation itself is no longer perfect, it is still a gift directly from God to you today. And one of the first things—if not *the* first thing—you should do when you understand that something is a gift from Him is to give thanks.

Enjoy Creation. . .and Give Thanks

One of the great things about enjoying and studying the wonders of God's creation is that doing these things can remind you of what God is really like in many important ways. For example, when you look up at the stars, planets, and galaxies that are visible from Earth, you can be reminded of just how big and powerful God really is. When you look at the beauty and variety in nature here on Earth, you can be reminded that God likes beauty and variety. And when you look at the amazing detail of your own body, you can be reminded that God made you completely ready to take your place in His carefully constructed plan of creation.

The opportunities to thank and praise God for His works of creation are unlimited. For example, when you go outside and see a beautiful day with lots of sunshine and warmth or a cloudy day with life-sustaining rain, thank God for it! When you see a beautiful woodland area or when you see a desert, a beach, or a valley, give thanks! Or when you see and hear different kinds of birds perching and singing near your home, thank Him for making such a wide array of living things for you to enjoy.

So when you step outside—whether it's light or dark, or whether the sun is shining or it's raining—don't forget to enjoy everything you see around you. And then don't forget to thank the God who made it all happen!

Many towns and cities provide recycling for plastic bottles, metal cans, and newspapers and cardboard. You can help by sorting out your throw-aways!

Taking Good Care of What God Has Given You

Do you know what the word *stewardship* means? Basically, it means taking good care of something of great value that doesn't really belong to you. It means treating something that belongs to another person the very same way you would treat it if it belonged to you.

Right after God made the first humans, He blessed them and told them, "Be fruitful and multiply. Fill the earth and govern it. Reign over the fish in the sea, the birds in the sky, and all the animals that scurry along the ground" (Genesis 1:28). So in a very real way, God created the universe and the earth for us humans. His plan from the very beginning was to put people in a higher place than all the animals and other living things. We were meant to multiply and to rule over the whole earth!

At the same time, though, the Bible teaches that even though the earth and the things that live here are for our use, they don't really belong to us. Long after God completed the creation of the earth and universe, King David wrote, "The earth is the LORD's, and everything in it. The world and all its people belong to him" (Psalm 24:1). In other words, everything God created—including your own body—belongs to Him!

How does knowing that the whole universe, the whole earth, and all living things that live here on Earth—including you and all other humans—belong to God change how you see them? Even more important, how does it affect the way you treat them?

Sadly, many Christians in the past have taken the attitude that taking care of the earth wasn't important. But that attitude went against what God specifically told us we should do (take a look at

Planting trees is a great wat to improve both the beauty and the air quality of your neighborhood.

Genesis 1:28 and 2:15). When we damage the earth by neglecting it or overusing it in certain ways, we do harm—sometimes very great harm—to something God created for us and still holds as valuable.

There are many easy but important ways you can act as a good steward, taking care of what God has given you. For example, when you go out hiking, camping, or fishing, you can make sure you pick up after yourself before you go home. Don't leave anything behind that doesn't belong there. At home, you can encourage your family members to conserve energy by turning off lights when they leave the room, and by not leaving televisions and radios running when someone isn't watching or listening. If you haven't been doing so already, you can also begin recycling the metal, glass, plastic, and paper you use, instead of throwing this material in the trash.

Remember, when you do the things that help preserve the world God created for you, you not only demonstrate good stewardship, you also show God just how much you appreciate all He's done for you—starting with creation itself!

A

Abyssal plains 62

Adam and Eve 131, 131

Africa 58, 60, 60, 95

African bush elephant 109, 109

Air 17, 40, 49, 80

Alaska 100

Aldrin, Buzz 17, 80

Alexandria, Egypt 19

Alligators 117, 118

Altitude 50

Altocumulus clouds 26

Alton, Illinois 144

Amphibians 120

Amplitude 34

Andes Mountains 61

Angiosperms 69, 69

Animal kingdom 88

Anseriformes 96

Antarctica 47, 47, 48, 58, 61, 61, 95, 117

Anteaters 116

Antennae 124, 124

Ants 124

Anura 120

Aphids 125

Arctic Ocean 54, 62

Apes 111, 111

Apoda 120

Arachnida 124

Argentinosaurus 119

Argon 40

Aristotle 20

Armstrong, Neil 17, 80

Arteries 136

Arthropoda 123

Arthropods 87, 122, 123

Artiodactyla 112

Asteroids 81, 83

Astronauts 17, 80

Asia 58, 59, 60, 60, 64, 93, 95

Astronomers 74, 81, 84

Aswan, Egypt 19

Atacama Desert, Chile 49

Atlantic Ocean 54, 56, 57

Atmosphere

earth's 40, 41, 42, 46, 50

moon lacks 80

Atmospheric pressure 41

Australia 58, 61, 61, 63, 99, 115

Axis, earth's 37, 38

Aye-aye 108, 108

Ayers Rock 61

B

Bacteria 88, 140

Barbados 63

Barometer 46

Barometric pressure 46

Bats 70, 109, 109, 110, 110, 114

Bean, Alan 80

Bears 113

Beavers 112

Bees 70, 122, 124

Beetles 124

Beginnings 14, 15

Behemoth 119

Betic midwife toad 121

Big Dipper 76, 76

Bile 140

Biologists 68

Birds 70, 87, 87, 95

aquatic 95

waterfowl 95

Bird watching 103, 104

Bishop Rock 63

Blackbirds 96

Black holes 74, 77, 77

Bladderworts 70

Blood 136, 138, 143, 144

Bloodletting 134

Blue whale 57, 108

Boas 117

Bones, human 133, 143, 143

Brachiosaurs 119

Brain, human 24, 130, 135, 135, 136

Butterflies 122, 124

Butterworts 70

C

Caimans 118

Calcium 57

Cambodia 125

Camels 65, 112

Canada 60, 95

Capillaries 137

Carbon dioxide 40, 67, 138

Cardiovascular system, human 132, 136, 136, 137, 137

Caribbean Sea 23

Carnivora 112

Carnivores 109

Carps 90

Caspian Sea 54

Cats 108, 112

CAT scan 134

Caudata 120

Cellulose 67

Centipedes 123

Cerebellum 136

Cerebrum 136

Ceres 83

Cernan, Eugene 80

Cheetahs 110, 110

Chickens 96, 100, 103

Chimpanzees 111, 111, 130

Chinese giant salamander 120

Chipmunks 112

Chloride 57

Chlorophyll 66

Chloroplasts 67

Chyme 140

Cirrus clouds 45, 45

Classes 87

Climate 47, 49, 50

Clouds 25, 26, 26, 43, 45, 45, 49,
55

Cobra lilies 70

Cockatiels 103, 103

Cold-blooded 117, 120

Colors 34, 35, 36, 40

Columbus, Christopher 57

Comets 81, 83, 83

Communication 130

Compound eyes 124

Conrad, Charles "Pete" 80

Constellations 75, 76, 76

Continental rise 62

Continental shelf 62, 62

Continental slope 62

Continents 58, 59, 62, 63

Copernicus, Nicolas 81, 81

Corona (crown) of sun 31

Cosmos 15

Coral 92

Core, earth's 21, 21

Cougars 112

Cows 112

Coyotes 113

Crab Nebula 77

Crabs 123, 124

Cranes 101

Crayfish 124

Crocodiles 117, 118

Crocodilia 118

Crows 96

Crustaceans 92, 123, 124

Crust, earth's 21, 21

Cumulonimbus clouds 45

Cumulus clouds 45, 45

Cyclones 46

D

Darkness 29

David, King 133, 152

Day 37, 38

Dead Sea 54, 54, 59

Death Valley, California 48, 48

Deer 112

Denver, Colorado 41

Deserts 65, 65

Digestive system, human 139,
139, 140

Dinosaurs 118, 119, 119

Dirty snowballs 83

Dogs 106–107, 108, 112

Dolphins 114, 114, 130, 130

Donkeys 112

Dragon 119

Dragonflies 124

Duck-billed platypus 115, 115

Ducks 95, 96, 100, 101, 103

Duke, Charles 80

Dust 18, 19, 40, 83

Dwarf planets 82

E

Eagles 96, 102

Eastern milk snake 118

Earth 19, 37, 81

    orbits sun 37, 38

    shape of 20

    size of 19, 78

    uniqueness of 23, 54, 79, 82

Earthquakes 22

Eclipse, solar 31

Eddington, Sir Arthur 31

Eels 94

Eiffel Tower 61

El 'Azizia, Libya 48

Electromagnetic energy 32, 35

Elements 21, 40

Elephants 108, 109, 109, 113, 116

Emu 99

Endocrine system, human 132, 146

Entomologists 123

Equator 20, 49, 58, 60

Eratosthenes of Cyrene 19, 19

Esophagus 139, 139, 140

Eurafrasia 59

Eurasia 59

Europe 58, 59, 61, 61, 95

Excretory system, human 132, 146

Exosphere 42

Exoskeleton 123

Eyes, human 142

F

Falconiformes 96

Falcons 96, 98, 98

Families 87

Feathers 98, 98

Finches 96

Fish 89, 90, 92, 93, 93

Flamingos 101

Flies 122, 123, 123, 124

Flowers 69

Fog 25, 26, 45

Folsom, California 44

Foxes 113

Frequency 34

Frogs 120, 121, 121

Fungi 68, 88

Fur 114

G

Galaxies 74, 81, 84, 84

Galilei, Galileo 81, 81

Galliformes 96

Gamma rays 32

Garter snakes 117

Gavials 118

Gazelle 110

Geckos 117

Geese 95, 96, 100, 102, 103

Genera 87

Gerbils 112

Gestation period 116

Gila monsters 116

Gills 93, 93

Giraffes 109

Glaciers 23, 25

Goats 115

Gobi Desert 65

God

   creator 14, 15, 29, 31, 37, 38, 57, 64, 150

   eternal 38

Gophers 112

Gorillas 111

Grasshoppers 124

Gravity 31, 41, 56, 75, 77, 80

Great Barrier Reef 57, 57

Great Britain 63

Great Plains 65

Great Salt Lake 92

Great Wall of China 60

Greenland 25, 60, 63

Groundhogs 112

Grouse 103

Grubs 124

Guinea pigs 112

Gymnosperms 69, 69

H

Hagfish 90

Hail 43, 44, 44, 45

Hair 114

Halley's Comet 83, 83

Hamsters 112, 116

Harold II, King 83, 83

Hawaii Volcanoes National Park 63

Hawks 96, 102

Heart, human 136, 136, 142

Heavens, the 15

Helium 75

Hemisphere 20

Herbivores 109

Horses 108, 112

Hubble, Edwin 84

Hubble Space Telescope 16, 18

Humidity 43

Hummingbirds 95, 97, 97, 101

Hurricanes 46

Huygens, Christiaan 32, 32

Hydrogen 18, 25, 75

I

Ice 25, 25

Ichthyologists 90

Image of God 127, 129, 130, 146

Indiana bat 110

Indian Ocean 54

Indonesia 63

Infrared light 35, 35

Insecta 123

Insectivores 110

Integumentary system, human 145, 145

Intestines 139–140, 139

Invertebrates 87, 123

Ionosphere 42

Ireland 63

Iron 21

Irwin, James 80

Islands 63, 63

J

Japan 55

Jellyfish 24, 92

Jinlian, Zeng 144

Jupiter 81, 82, 83

K

K-2 64

Kangaroo 113

Keratin 115

Killdeer 100, 100

Kingdoms 68, 88

Kitti's hog-nosed bat 114

Kiwi 99, 99

Krill 124, 124

L

Ladybugs 125

Lakes 23, 49, 57, 92

Lampreys 90

Laws, scientific 14

Leap year 38, 38

Leeches 134

Lenses 33, 33

Leviathan 119

Light 17, 29

    affected by gravity 31, 77

    essential for life 31

    properties of 31, 32, 33, 34, 35

    speed of 15

    visible 34

    white 36

Lightning 45

Light-year 15, 74

Lions 112

Little Dipper 76

Lizards 117, 118

Lobsters 124

Loons 95, 96

Lunar phases 80

Lungs, human 138, 138

Lymphatic system, human 132, 145

M

Macaws 95, 96

Madagascar 108

Magic 15

Magma 64

Magnesium 21, 57

Mammals 108, 109

Mantle, earth's 21, 21

Mariana Islands 55

Marrow 144

Mars 81, 82

Marsupialia 113

Matter 14

Mauna Kea 64, 64

Mawsynram, India 49

Mediterranean Sea 56

Mercury 81, 82

Mesosphere 42

Mexico 60

Mice 111

Migration 100, 100

Milk 115, 116

Milky Way Galaxy 81, 84

Millipedes 123, 123

Minerals 21

Minnows 90

Mississippi River 65

Mitchell, Edgar 80

Mites 124

Mojave Desert 72–73

Molecules 17, 25, 25

Moles 108, 108, 109

Monera 88

Monkeys 111

Moon 17, 17, 56, 56, 80, 80

Moths 124, 124

Mountains 49, 50, 64

Mount Evans, Colorado 41

Mount Everest 59, 59, 64

Mount Godwin-Austen 64

Mount St. Helens 65

Mouthbreeders 94

Magnetic Resonance Imaging
134, 134
Muscles, human 141, 141, 142, 142
Mushrooms 68, 68, 88

N

Namibia 58
NASA (National Aeronautics and Space Administration) 17
Nebula 18, 77
Nepal 59, 64
Neptune 81, 82
Nervous system, human 132, 135, 135, 136
Nests, bird 99, 99
New Guinea 55, 63, 117
Newton, Sir Isaac 32, 32, 36
Newts 120
New Zealand 59, 99, 100
NGC 7331 galaxy 84
Niagara Falls 60
Nickel 21
Night 37, 38
Nimbus clouds 45, 45
Nitrogen 40
North America 58, 59, 60, 60, 95, 118
Nothingness 14
Nuclear fusion 75

O

Oceania 59
Oceans 23, 49, 54, 55, 57, 62, 92

Olm 120
Olympic National Park, Washington 49
Opossums 113, 113, 116
Orangutans 111
Orders 87, 96
Ornithologists 96
Ospreys 102
Ostriches 97
Owls 102
Oxygen 21, 25, 42, 67, 75
essential for life 40, 41, 93, 138
Ozone 42

P

Pacific Ocean 54, 55, 59
Parakeets 96, 96, 103
Paris, France 61
Parrots 96, 101, 103
Particles, light 32
Passerines 96
Pelicans 102
Penguins 95, 99
Perissodactyla 112
Pheasants 103
Philippines 55
Photons 32
Photosynthesis 31, 67
Phyla 87
Pigs 112
Pitcher plants 70
Plains 65, 65
Planets 80, 81
Plankton 57, 91

Plants 43, 66, 88
as food 65, 67
vascular 68
Plates, tectonic 22
Pluto 81, 82, 82
Polar bears 109
Pollen 70
Pollination 70, 125
Porcupines 112
Potassium 57
Prairie dogs 112, 112
Prawns 124
Precipitation 43
Primates 111
Proboscidea 113
Protista 88
Protozoa 88
Psittaciformes 96
Pteridophytes 69
Python 117, 117

Q

Quails 100, 103
Quanta 32
Quasars 74

R

Raccoons 113
Radiant energy 32
Radiation 19
Radio waves 32, 34
Rain 25, 43, 55
Rainbow 35, 36, 36
Raleigh scattering 40

Rats 112

Recycling 151

Reflection 33, 36

Refraction 33

Regurgitation 100

Reproductive system, human 132, 146

Reptiles 116

Reptilia 118

Respiratory system, human 138, 138

Rio de Janeiro, Brazil 60

Rivers 23, 57, 92

Robins 97, 97

Rocky Mountains 64, 65

Rodentia 111

Roentgen, Wilhelm Konrad 133

S

Sahara Desert 47, 47, 110

Salamanders 120

Saliva 140

Salmon 94

San Andreas fault 22

Saturn 75, 81, 82

Scales 116, 117, 117

Schmitt, Harrison 80

Scorpions 124, 125

Scott, David 80

Sea anemones 92

Seals 109

Seas 23, 49, 54, 92

Seasons 79

Seismic activity 22

Sharks 90

Shepard, Alan 80

Shoemaker-Levy 9 comet 83

Shrews 114

Shrimps 124

Siamese fighting fish 93

Sierra Leone 56

Silicon 21

Sirius (Dog Star) 75, 75

Skeletal system, human 143, 143

Skin, human 145, 145

Skink 117, 117

Sky 40, 43

Sleet 43

Snakes 117, 118

Snapping turtles 118, 118

Snow 25, 43, 45, 50

Sodium 57

Solar system 81, 81, 84

Solstice 19

Soul 131

Sound 16, 17

South America 58, 59, 60, 60, 95, 118, 119

Southern Cross 76

Southern Ocean 54

Space, outer 15, 16, 17

Sparrows 96, 96

Spawning 94, 121

Species 87

Spectrum, light 34, 35, 36

Spermatophytes 68

Spiders 122, 123, 124, 125

Spinal cord, human 132, 135, 135

Spores 68, 68, 69, 70

Squamata 118

Squirrels 112

Starfish 92

Star-nosed mole 108, 108

Stars 74, 75, 75

Stewardship 151, 151, 152

Stingrays 87, 90

Stomach, human 139, 139, 140

Storks 96

Stratonimbus clouds 45

Stratosphere 42

Stratus clouds 45, 45

Sturgeon 94

Submersible 55

Sulfate 57

Sulfur 21

Sun 30, 33, 46, 81, 82

   and plant growth 30, 66–67

   size of 78, 81

   as star 74, 75, 75, 79, 84

Sundews 70

Sunrise 37

Sunset 37

Supernova 77, 77

Swallows 96, 101

Swans 95, 96, 102

Swifts 101

Syene 19

T

Tadpoles 121

Talons 102

Tanzania 60

Tarantulas 115, 125, 125
Tendons 141
Terrapins 118
Testudines 118
Thailand 114
Thermosphere 42
Thrushes 96
Thunderstorms 45
Tibet 59, 64
Ticks 124
Tides 56
Tigers 112
Time 38
Titanium 21
Toads 120
Tornado 44
Tortoises 117, 118
Tropopause 42
Troposphere 42
Turkeys 96, 96, 103
Turtles 117, 118, 118
Tyrannosaurs 119

U

Ultraviolet light 32, 35, 42
Uluru 61
United States 60, 95
Universe 15
Uranus 81, 82

V

Vapor, water 25
Veins 137
Venus 81, 82, 82

Venus flytrap 70, 70
Vertebrates 87, 92, 97, 113
Villi 140
Vipers 117
Virgin Islands 118
Volcanoes 22, 63, 65
Vostok Station, Antarctica 48
Vultures 101, 101
VY Canis Majoris 75, 75

W

Wadlow, Robert 144, 144
Walking catfish 93
Warblers 96
Warm-blooded 97, 113
Water 23, 24, 25, 26
    drinkable 24
    essential for life 24
    "glassy" 26
Waterspout 44, 44
Waves, light 32, 34, 40
Weather 43, 47, 55
Whales 114
Whale shark 91, 91
Wind 46, 70
Wolves 113
World Ocean 55
Worm lizard 118

X

X-rays 32, 133, 133, 134

Y

Year 38

Young, John 80

Z

Zebras 109, 112

ART CREDITS

Bettmann/CORBIS: Page 144

City of Hampton, Virginia/Hampton.gov: Page 62

Dominik Pasternak (MOA): Page 31

Dorling Kindersley: Page 75 (bottom), 115 (bottom)

Erich Lessing/Art Resource, NY: Page 83 (bottom), 131 (bottom)

Flickr/Jeremy Pearson: Page 63 (top)

High-Z Supernova Search Team/HST/NASA: Page 77 (bottom)

HIP/Art Resource, NY: Page 32 (bottom)

Image Plan/Corbis: Page 64 (top)

iStockphoto: Page 15, 20, 21, 23, 24 (both), 25 (both), 30, 32 (top), 33, 36, 38 (bottom), 39, 40, 42–53 (all), 54, 56–60 (all), 61 (top two), 63 (bottom), 65 (top), 66, 67 (bottom), 68 (bottom), 69 (both), 70, 74, 76, 78–79, 81 (top and bottom left), 82 (bottom), 84 (bottom), 85–87, 90, 91, 93–99 (all), 100 (top), 101 (both), 102 (bottom), 103, 104, 105, 106–107, 108 (top), 109 (both), 110 (top), 111–114 (all), 115 (top), 116–117 (all), 118 (top), 119–123 (all), 124 (top), 125 (bottom), 126–129 (all), 130 (top), 131 (top), 132–143 (all), 145, 147–152 (all)

Jack Goldfarb/Design Pics/Corbis: Page 118 (bottom)

Jan Derk/Wikimedia: Page 89 (bottom)

Kai Pfaffenbach/Reuters/Corbis: Page 35

Kristian Peters/Wikimedia: Page 67 (top)

Lunar and Planetary Institute: Page 82 (top)

Martin Camm: Page 124 (bottom)

Mick Roessler/Corbis: Page 65 (bottom)

NASA: Page 37, 72–73, 80

NASA/ESA/G. Bacon (STScI): Page 71

NASA/ESA/STScI/J. Hester and P. Scowen (Arizona State University): Page 18

NASA/Glenn Research Center Collection: Page 19 (top)

NASA/Goddard Space Flight Center/Scientific Visualization Studio: Page 100 (bottom)

NASA/Jet Propulsion Laboratory: Page 13

NASA/John W. Young: Page 17

NASA/JPL-Caltech: Page 77 (top), 83 (top)

NASA/JPL-Caltech/STScI: Page 84 (top)

NASA/Raghvendra Sahai and John Trauger (JPL)/WFPC2 science team: Page 27

NASA/STScI: Page 16

National Geographic: Page 108 (bottom)

Purestock: Page 130 (bottom)

Radius Images/Corbis: Page 125 (top)

Roger Ressmeyer/CORBIS: Page 22

Shadowlink1014/Wikimedia: Page 41

SOHO (ESA & NASA): Page 75 (top)

Somos/Veer: Page 68 (top)

Tim Pannell/Corbis: Page 102 (top)

Tristan Nitot/Wikimedia: Page 89 (top)

Usasearch.gov: Page 26, 55, 62

US Fish and Wildlife Service/Andy King: Page 110 (bottom)

Wikimedia: Page 19 (bottom), 38 (top), 61 (bottom), 64 (bottom), 81 (bottom right), 108 (center)

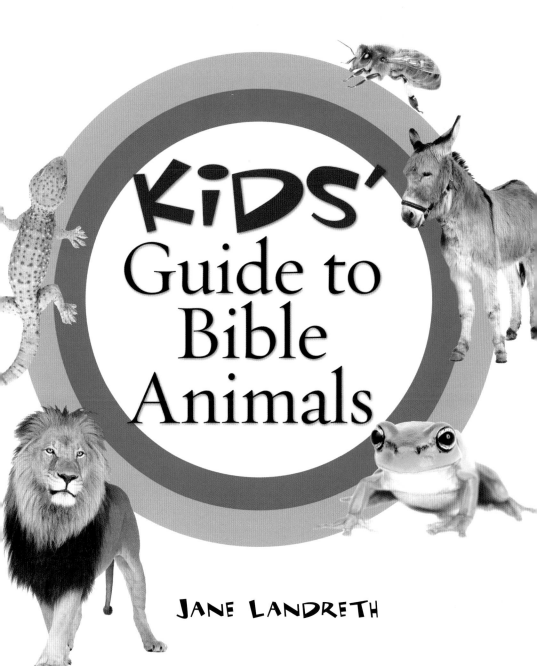

KiDS' Guide to Bible Animals

JANE LANDRETH

CONTENTS

INTRODUCTION 165

ANT 167

ANTELOPE 169

APE 170

BABOON 171

BADGER. 172

BAT 173

BEAR 174

BEE 177

BEETLE 180

BEHEMOTH 181

BITTERN. 183

CAMEL 184

CATERPILLAR 187

CATTLE 188

CHAMELEON 191

COBRA 192

CONEY 193

CORMORANT 194

CRANE 195

CRICKET. 196

CUCKOO 197

DEER 198

DOG 200

DONKEY 202

DOVE 205

DRAGON 207

EAGLE 208

FALCON. 209

FERRET 210

FISH. 211

FLEA 214

FLY 215

FOX. 217

FROG 220

GAZELLE 222

GECKO 223

GNAT 224

GOAT 226

GRASSHOPPER 229

GULL 231

HAWK 232

HEDGEHOG 233

HEN AND CHICKS 234

HERON 235

HOOPOE 236

HORNET. 237

HORSE 238

HYENA 240

IBEX 241

JACKAL. 242

KATYDID 243

CONTENTS

KITE 244

LAPWING 245

LEECH 246

LEOPARD 247

LEVIATHAN 249

LION 251

LIZARD 254

LOCUST 256

LOUSE 258

MAGGOT 259

MOLE 260

MOTH 261

MOUNTAIN SHEEP 263

MOUSE 265

MULE 266

OSPREY 267

OSSIFRAGE 268

OSTRICH 269

OWL 270

OX 271

PARTRIDGE 272

PEACOCK 273

PELICAN 274

PIG 275

PIGEON 278

PORCUPINE 280

QUAIL 281

RABBIT AND HARE 283

RAVEN 285

ROOSTER 287

SCORPION 290

SHEEP 292

SKINK 295

SNAIL 296

SNAKE 297

SPARROW 300

SPIDER 301

STORK 302

SWALLOW 303

SWAN 304

SWIFT 305

TURTLE 306

VULTURE 307

WEASEL 308

WHALE 309

WILD GOAT 312

WILD OX 313

WOLF 314

WORM 316

INTRODUCTION

Wouldn't it have been exciting to watch God create all the living creatures on the fifth and sixth days of creation week?

How much fun God must have had creating all those animals! He made creatures with eight legs, six legs, four legs, two legs, and no legs. He even made some with hundreds of legs! He shaped animals with arms and no arms. God fashioned animals with long necks, short necks, and even no necks. He formed animals with one hump, two humps, and no humps. He created fat animals and skinny animals, long and short animals.

God made some animals to live on the ground and some to live in trees. He made some to live in the cliffs of the mountains and some to burrow under the ground. He produced some to swim in the deepest oceans and some to live near the seashore. God created some animals to soar with the air currents, while others have to work hard to even get off the ground.

Wow! What an awesome God!

Our God is so powerful and mighty that He created dinosaurs that stretched up to forty feet tall, and yet He is so gentle that He made delicate insects smaller than a pinhead. And He created all the animals in between.

And when God had created all the living creatures on land and in the water, He looked over His creation and said, "It is good!"

I had fun researching these animals for you. I learned a lot of new things—just as you will as you read about these animals. I've used easy-to-read names for the different types of animals:

AMPHIBIANS: These cold-blooded creatures have backbones and skeletons and live part of their lives in water and part on land.

ANNELIDS: These are segmented worms—just like the common earthworms that burrow in the soil.

ARACHNIDS: Creepy, crawly animals with an external skeleton and eight legs, such as spiders and scorpions.

BIRDS: These warm-blooded animals have feathers and wings, though not all of them can fly. They come in many sizes, colors, shapes, and behavior patterns.

FISH: These water creatures, which come in a wide variety of shapes and colors, have fins and use gills to breathe. Most of them have scales on their bodies.

INSECTS: These hard-bodied animals have six legs and three-part bodies (the head, the thorax, and the abdomen). Some of them can fly, and some of them can't.

MAMMALS: These warm-blooded animals live on the land, in the sea, in the air, or underground. They have fur or hair, and most of them give birth to live young rather than laying eggs.

MOLLUSKS: Most of these animals live in water, and many of them have hard shells. Snails and shellfish are mollusks. So are slugs, octopuses, and squids.

REPTILES: These creatures are cold-blooded and have bodies covered with scales. Snakes, lizards, and turtles are reptiles.

INTRODUCTION

I have mentioned the Mosaic Law several times in this book. Many centuries ago, God gave His people, the Israelites, these laws through Moses. God was instructing His people in how to live, eat, and worship. God allowed the Israelites to eat many of the animals listed in this book, but He told them not to eat others.

I hope that you enjoy reading and learning about all the animals written about in the following pages. Of course, we know that God created more animals than the one hundred listed here, but I included only the ones named in the Bible.

So go ahead and enjoy reading about the animals. As you read, think about the fun God must have had as He created each one.

Sincerely,
Jane Landreth

Thank you to my husband, Jack,
who encouraged me as I researched and wrote;
he even helped gather some of the information for me.

Type of animal:
Insect

Find it in the Bible:
Proverbs 6:6

ANT

THAT'S A BIG FAMILY!

The ant is a social insect that lives in a large family called a "colony." An ant colony can be very big—sometimes numbering in the millions of individual ants. The colony is divided into a social order of queens, males, and workers. The survival of the ant colony depends on each member doing what it was designed to do.

The queen ants are the largest in the colony. The queen's job is to lay eggs, which ensures the colony's survival and growth. After a queen mates for the first time, she hunts for a crack in the soil and digs a little chamber, where she seals herself inside and lays her first batch of eggs. She guards them until they hatch. After her single mating, the queen can lay fertilized eggs for several years without mating again.

The worker ants are females that never reproduce. Their jobs are to gather food, to care for the young ants, to work on nests, to protect the colony, and to perform other duties. The male ants mate with queens and then die. Soldier ants find new places for nests.

Ants do not have ears, but they "hear" vibrations through sensory organs. They talk to one another by touching antennas. When two ants meet, they stroke antennas to feel and smell what the other ant has to say. As the feelers brush, the ants swap scents that contain messages about food, eggs, danger, and other information that has to do with the colony. The touching of antennas also helps identify strangers who may be trying to get into the nest to cause damage.

There are many species of ants, and they all behave differently from one another. Some ants eat meat, while others eat mostly vegetation. Some ants capture and hold other insects like aphids and other ants as slaves. Some conduct war on other ant colonies. Some ant colonies even have a regular army of soldiers to protect them from danger.

The larger, winged "queen ant" lays eggs deep in the ground while other "worker ants" gather food or guard the colony.

For most ants, colony life centers around the nest. The nest is a community constructed underground, in ground-level mounds, or even in trees. The nest is a maze of tunnels. It is a very busy place that can become very crowded with industrious ants working to keep the colony functioning.

Some ants live in constructed complex nests that resemble miniature cities. These ants build homes that are several stories high—sometimes five hundred times higher than the builder ant is tall. Some nests may reach twenty feet below ground, while others may be five feet tall.

WOW! WHAT A BIG HOUSE!

The nests have chambers for laying eggs, a nursery, places for food storage, resting places for workers, and rooms for mating. The many rooms, corridors, and vaulted rooms can cover an area as large as a tennis court.

The ant is mentioned twice in the Bible, both times in the book of Proverbs, which praises the ant for its wisdom in providing for itself. The ant is not lazy and does not put off the work it must do to survive. In Proverbs 30:24–25, the ant is said to have much wisdom and ability even though it is very small. This passage holds up the ant as a worthy example to us humans.

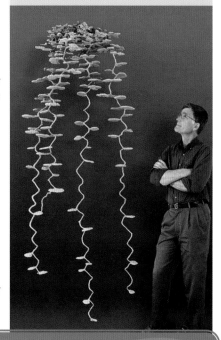

What on earth is that? Actually, it's under the earth. A man studies a plaster cast made from an underground ant colony.

DID YOU KNOW. . .

- Some ants can lift and carry up to fifty times their own weight.
- Queen ants can live up to twenty years.
- The dirt that piles up around the colony entryway is called an "anthill."
- One ant colony in Japan has forty-five thousand connected nests containing 300 million individuals, including more than 1 million queens.

ANTELOPE

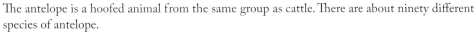

Type of animal:
Mammal

Find it in the Bible:
Deuteronomy 14:5–6 NIV

WHAT'S A CUD CHEWER?

The antelope is a hoofed animal from the same group as cattle. There are about ninety different species of antelope.

The antelope has long, bony horns that stretch backward from its head. The antelope's horns do not branch out from the central horn. Unlike most other hoofed animals, the antelope never sheds its horns. The antelope has a dense coat of brown fur with black markings and a tuft of black hair under its neck.

The antelope has keen senses of sight, smell, and hearing. Its eyes are located on the side of its head, giving it broad vision. Using its senses of smell and hearing, it can sense danger when its enemies are near.

The antelope uses its powerful legs to make spectacular leaps as high as eight feet. When the antelope leaps and kicks, the enemy is confused. Some antelope can run as fast as 60 miles per hour, making it easy for them to outrun their enemies.

The antelope can use its horns as a weapon to defend itself against a predator, but more often it uses them in competitive clashes with another antelope over a potential mate.

A CUD IS A FOOD BALL THAT IS KEPT IN A SPECIAL PART OF THE STOMACH AND BROUGHT UP LATER TO CHEW AND DIGEST.

In the Mosaic Law, antelope are listed as clean animals, so the Israelites could hunt and eat them. The Israelites were allowed to eat animals that had a split hoof and chewed the cud, which means they swallow the food and bring it back up to chew later. The antelope ate the leaves, grass, fruit, mushrooms, and twigs that grew in the grasslands of the Bible lands.

DID YOU KNOW. . .

- A group of antelope is called a "herd."

- Some antelope make warning noises that sound like a barking dog.

- The smallest antelope is about ten inches tall, and the largest is about six feet tall.

APE

YOU, EVOLVED FROM AN APE?

Type of animal:
Mammal
Find it in the Bible:
1 Kings 10:22

An ape is a large, long-haired primate with no tail. There are several kinds of apes, including gorillas, chimpanzees, orangutans, and others. Primates are a group of animals that includes lemurs, monkeys, and apes. Primates are known for their forward-facing eyes and flexible arms, legs, and fingers. Primates also have hands with five fingers, each of which has fingernails.

The ape's long, strong arms and short, weaker legs make it a great climber. Most apes have the ability to walk on two legs for short distances. Apes use their thumbs and toes for grasping objects. They also use their hands for gathering food or nesting materials and, in some cases, for using simple tools.

Most apes are intelligent animals that can learn easily. Some apes have even learned to use sign language to communicate with humans. The ape has a good memory and can perform tasks it has been taught in the past. It can also express humanlike emotions, such as happiness, fear, anxiety, and boredom.

Apes live in small family groups called "troops." The troops stay in one place until the apes have eaten most of the food, then move on to a new spot. Some male apes groan and roar to keep other males away from his family. The roar can be heard a half mile away. When courting, some male gorillas try to impress the females with a chest-beating display. The male gorilla makes a *pok-pok-pok* sound by cupping his hands together.

Apes are mentioned only twice in the Old Testament. They were not native to the Holy Land, but the Israelites were familiar with them. Some types, especially chimpanzees, were kept as pets. They were among the gifts that the ships of Hiram brought Solomon (see 1 Kings 10:22).

DID YOU KNOW. . .

- The smallest ape is the gibbon, and the largest is the gorilla.

- Some apes can live up to sixty years.

- Humans and apes are ticklish in the same body areas.

BABOON

Type of animal:
Mammal

Find it in the Bible:
1 Kings 10:22 NIV

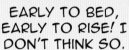

EARLY TO BED, EARLY TO RISE! I DON'T THINK SO.

DID YOU KNOW...

- Baboons have strong legs for walking long distances.

- The baboon has a bent tail that gives it a "sitting pad."

- Baboons can survive for long periods without finding water by licking the night dew from their fur.

Baboons are known for their bright red, hairless, built-in "sitting pads"!

The baboon, a large type of monkey, has a doglike muzzle, close-set eyes, powerful jaws, thick fur, a short tail, and rough spots on its overhanging buttocks. The buttocks are hairless pads of skin that provide for the sitting comfort of the baboon. And they are bright red!

The baboon is intelligent and crafty, and it interacts well with people. A group of baboons, which is called a "troop" or "congress," can be agricultural pests that destroy crops.

The baboon sleeps, travels, feeds, and socializes in its troop. There is usually one male among the family group, which may be as large as one hundred individuals. Baboons are omnivores, meaning they eat nearly everything. Sometimes the troop travels five or six miles a day looking for the berries, seedpods, blossoms, leaves, roots, and bark to eat. They also eat insects, fish, birds, and small mammals.

Baboons spend a lot of their time grooming and cleaning themselves and other baboons. When they wake up and come down from their sleeping perch, they begin grooming. Then they spend their day eating and napping. In the evening, they groom themselves and others again to get rid of the parasites they pick up during the day. They are usually in their sleeping perch by about six o'clock in the evening.

The baboon is mentioned only twice in the Bible. First Kings 10:22 and 2 Chronicles 9:21 tell us that once every three years a fleet of trading ships came to Israel and brought baboons, among other things, to King Solomon.

BADGER

HOW DOES THE BADGER KEEP ITS CLAWS SO SHARP?

Type of animal:
Mammal

Find it in the Bible:
Exodus 25:5 KJV

The badger is a short-legged, stocky carnivore with black and white stripes running down its face and over its head. Its body is more or less flattened, giving it the perfect shape for moving through the tunnels of its underground home. It has claws on its front legs, which it keeps sharp by scratching on trees.

The badger has a strong sense of smell and searches for food constantly by sniffing the ground. It catches most of its food—earthworms, mice, moles, and gophers—by digging with amazing speed. With its powerful front legs and claws, the badger can tunnel very quickly through soil to catch burrowing prey. At other times the badger captures prey by chasing it into burrows and then digging it out.

The badger does not hibernate during the winter but spends much of its time sleeping. When it becomes hungry, it searches for hibernating animals, digs them up, and eats them. Then when it is finished eating, the badger returns to its burrow for another time of sleeping.

A badger fiercely protects itself and its young. It is capable of fighting off much larger animals such as wolves, coyotes, and even bears.

Badger skins were used in making a tent or curtain for use in the tabernacle. Some sandals in biblical times were also made of badger skins (Ezekiel 16:10 KJV).

DID YOU KNOW...

- Badgers live underground in a system of burrows called "setts."
- American badgers grow to almost three feet long (head to tail) and to around twenty-five pounds.
- The badger can run or gallop for short distances at 15 to 19 miles per hour.
- The badger can eat as many as two hundred earthworms a day.

Type of animal:
Mammal
Find it in the Bible:
Leviticus 11:19

"BLIND AS A BAT"? HA!

BAT

The bat is the only mammal with the ability to fly. A bat's wings are made of thin skin stretched tightly between its legs, tail, arms, and fingers. These help some bats fly up to ten thousand feet above the ground and reach speeds of up to 60 miles per hour.

There are about eleven hundred species of bats living in the world today. Their size and appearance, what they eat, and how they behave depends on the kind of bat. Most bats eat insects, but many of them eat fruit and vegetables. Depending on the species, a bat's diet can include fruit, leaves, cacti, insects, small reptiles, or even other bats.

Many people think a bat cannot see at all. In truth, most bats can see well in dim light, but they use their sense of hearing to help them find food and navigate in the dark. The bat's big ears help it trap sounds. It finds bugs to eat by listening for their footsteps or wing beats.

Most bats sleep during the day in a cave or hollow tree, which is called a "roost." Their hooked claws on their wings and toes help them hang upside down or climb a wall or tree trunk. Like most other animals, a bat needs to drink water to survive. It slurps up water as it flies low over a stream. But if it flies too low— splash—it may go for a swim! No worry—it uses its wings to paddle through the water.

The bat is not dangerous to people, though some carry diseases that are harmful to people. Contrary to what many people think, the common vampire bat does not suck blood but laps it up after the razor-sharp teeth slices its food.

Bats are commonly seen in and around the dark caves of the Middle East. They are among the animals listed in the Mosaic Law as unclean.

BATS CAN SWIM!

DID YOU KNOW. . .

- The world's smallest bat, the Kiti's hognose bat, measures a little over one inch long and weighs less than one-tenth of an ounce.

- The world's largest bat, the flying fox, has a wingspread of up to four feet.

- Bats can catch as many as twelve hundred flying insects in one night.

BEAR

WOW!
WHAT A HUGE
BEAR!

Type of animal:
Mammal
Find it in the Bible:
2 Kings 2:24

The bear is a large, heavy animal with long, thick, shaggy hair. It has stocky legs, a long snout, paws with five claws, and a short tail. The head is large with rounded ears.

One of the most common species, the brown bear, has a shoulder hump on its back. The shoulder has superstrong muscles that help the bear roll over huge rocks and logs as it searches for food. The hump muscles and claws give the bear a powerful digging ability that lets it feast on roots, bulbs, and rodents. They also help in climbing trees and tearing apart the prey it catches.

The bear has an excellent sense of smell that helps it find food. It will eat almost anything. When it is really hungry, it may take a lamb or goat from the flock in the field.

Most bears can stand and walk on the soles of their feet, just like humans, at least for short distances. They distribute their weight toward the hind feet, which makes them look awkward when they walk. They can stand on their hind legs and sit up straight with remarkable balance. Despite their heavy build and awkward gait, most bears can run very fast. The strong muscles, powerful legs, and long claws also make the bear an excellent climber and swimmer.

Except when it is courting, the bear is typically a solitary animal. A large male will chase the younger males away from a female. Equally matched males will fight for a mate. Some bears wear scars on their heads and necks from past battles. Males may follow their

Even though bears are four-legged animals, they can stand up on their hind legs like humans.

mates around, guarding against rivals.

The bear is generally active during the day and sleeps at night. A cave or burrow in the side of a cliff is used for its den.

Before cold weather sets in, most bears forage for large amounts of food to get them ready for a long period of sleep during the winter. Some bears do not sleep all winter but come out of hibernation during warmer days to eat.

Bears were quite common in the hilly and wooded parts of Israel. The bear of the Bible has been identified, with little doubt, as the Syrian brown bear. This bear grows to as tall as six feet and weighs as much as five hundred pounds. In biblical times, the bear was a threat to vineyards and to herds of sheep and goats.

During the summer months, these bears kept to the snowy parts of Lebanon, but in the winter they traveled to villages and gardens. This bear is a large meat-eating mammal that does not hibernate because its food source lasts all year.

Shepherds guard their flocks from all dangers — including hungry bears!

DAVID AND THE BEAR

When David, the future king of Israel, was a young boy, he watched his father's sheep in the fields. He would sing to them, pour oil on their wounds, and protect them. He carried a big stick that helped fight off any animal that threatened the flock.

One day when David was watching the sheep, a bear came after one of them and started to carry it off. David went after it with his stick and beat it until it let go of the sheep.

Later, as David pleaded with King Saul to allow him to fight the giant Philistine warrior named Goliath, he told Saul how he fought off the bear that tried to steal his sheep. "I'm not afraid to fight this giant," he told the king. "I will fight for the Lord"

BEAR

A BIBLICAL BEAR ATTACK

Those forty-two youths who made fun of the prophet Elisha saw something like this coming for them!

One day, the Old Testament prophet Elisha was walking along the road toward Bethel. Suddenly some young men came out of town and began making fun of him. "Go on up! You don't even have any hair on your head!" they yelled.

Elisha turned and looked at the young men. Then he called a curse on them in the name of the Lord. Two bears came out of the woods and mauled forty-two of the young fellows. Elisha just continued walking down the road.

OTHER BIBLE VERSES THAT MENTION BEARS ARE 2 SAMUEL 17:8; PROVERBS 17:12; AND ISAIAH 11:7.

See 2 Kings 2:23–25

DID YOU KNOW. . .

- At over eight feet tall and up to fifteen hundred pounds, the polar bear is considered the largest bear in the world.
- Some bears can run as fast as 40 miles per hour.
- When a bear cub is born, it is about the size of a squirrel.
- The bear has good vision and sees in color, similar to humans.
- Bears are believed to have the best sense of smell of any animal on earth.

Type of animal:
Insect

Find it in the Bible:
Judges 14:8

THE QUEEN BEE MUST BE REALLY TIRED AFTER ALL THAT WORK!

Bees are social insects that live in structures called "hives." They are closely related to wasps and ants. They are important to humans because they provide sweet honey to eat and because they help pollinate the plants that supply us with fruits, grains, and vegetables.

The bee's body is bulky, so it needs wings large enough to keep it in the air but small enough to allow it to enter the hive. Its four wings hook together for flight. When it is not flying, the wings release and overlap, allowing it to enter a small area.

The bee lives in a colony that consists of as many as fifty thousand individuals. The colony includes the queen, the drones, and the workers. Each member has its own special job to do to meet the needs of the whole colony.

The queen bee is the mother of the drones, the workers, and the future queens. Her body is longer than the other bees, and she has a larger abdomen. Her jaws contain sharp cutting teeth. The queen bee is equipped with a curved, smooth stinger she can use repeatedly with no danger to her life. Unlike the worker bees, she has no pollen baskets on her legs or beeswax glands on her abdomen. Her job is to lay up to a thousand eggs a day in the honeycomb cells.

The worker bees perform several jobs. They are females who build and maintain the nests, using wax secreted from glands in their abdomens. They feed and care for the larvae produced from the eggs. They also gather nectar and pollen. They have pollen baskets on their legs and long tongues they use to suck up the nectar from flowers. They bring the nectar back to the colony, where it is converted to honey and placed in hexagonal cells.

The worker bee sometimes travels far to find pollen and nectar. She averages five trips each day. When a worker bee finds a source of nectar, she performs a "bee dance." This tells the other worker bees where the source of food is located. And off they go!

Worker bees hard at work making honey for their colony.

BEE

Another job of the worker bees is to protect the nests. Their only defense is to sting their enemies. Once they sting their victim they die, because the stinger remains in the victim, leaving a fatal wound in the bee's abdomen.

The hive's drones are stingless, defenseless males whose only function is to mate with the queen bee before they die.

Bees and honey are mentioned several times in the Bible. Bees abounded in Palestine, and their honey was a common food among the people.

THE OLD TESTAMENT TELLS ABOUT GOD LEADING THE ISRAELITES INTO A LAND "FLOWING WITH MILK AND HONEY."

SAMSON FINDS HONEY

One day Samson was visiting the vineyards with his parents. All of a sudden a roaring lion came after them. God gave Samson special powers, which he used to tear apart the lion with his bare hands.

Later, as Samson was traveling the same road, he noticed honeybees swarming around the lion's carcass. He reached inside and dug the honey out with his hands. He ate some of it as he walked down the road. When he saw his parents, he gave them some and they ate of it. He did not tell them that he had taken the honey from the lion's carcass.

Samson gave a feast, which was a custom for the bridegroom. He made up a riddle about the lion and the honey for the men at the feast to solve

READ THE RIDDLE AND THE SOLUTION IN JUDGES 14:14–18.

You can read the whole story in Judges 14.

A beekeeper at work harvesting honey from one of his hives.

JONATHAN EATS HONEY

The Israelites were fighting the Philistines. After winning the battle, Jonathan—the son of King Saul—and the army entered the woods and saw honey dripping out of a honeycomb. None of the soldiers ate any honey. They were afraid because Saul had made them take an oath not to eat any food before evening. If they did, they would be cursed.

Jonathan had not heard his father put the army under the oath. He had a long stick in his hand. He reached out and dipped the end of it into the honeycomb and put the honey into his mouth. It made him feel better. He told the men, "Look how much better I feel because I have eaten the honey. You would have felt better if you had eaten today."

You can read the whole story in 1 Samuel 14.

JOHN THE BAPTIST AND HONEY

John the Baptist spent time in the wilderness preparing to preach to the people about Jesus. During his time there, he ate locusts and wild honey.

See Matthew 3:1–4

DID YOU KNOW. . .

- The bee is the only insect that makes food you can eat.

- Bees sometimes travel as far as a mile to find pollen and nectar.

- When a bee flies, the wings move in a figure-eight pattern, allowing it to fly in any direction.

- The bee cleans its antenna with a piece of tissue on its front legs.

- Beeswax is used to make candles.

179

BEETLE

THOSE ARE SOME WEIRD-LOOKING INSECTS!

Type of animal: Insect

Find it in the Bible: Leviticus 11:22 KJV

Beetles make up the largest family of insects. There are hundreds of thousands of known species of beetles. Some are barely visible to human eyes, but some are as big as an adult human's hand. Beetles are mostly black or brown, but some are bright colors and patterns. They live in all types of environments. Some are even found in freshwater.

An adult beetle has an extra tough body and strong legs, but its most important feature is its hardened forewings that fit over its hind wings. When a beetle flies, the forewings open, but the hind wings are the ones that beat. The beetle has flattened legs with protective spines and silky hairlike strands. The hooked feet give the beetle a grip to hold objects. Large pincherlike structures on the front of the beetle move horizontally to grasp, crush, or cut food. The beetle also uses them to protect itself from enemies.

Beetles defend themselves in several ways. Some beetles use camouflage, hiding among surroundings that are colored like themselves. Some beetles mimic other insects that their enemies leave alone. Other beetles send out toxic substances that can poison predators. Still other beetles defend themselves with horns and spines.

According to the Mosaic Law, beetles are a clean animal and can be eaten.

DID YOU KNOW...

- The beetle uses its antennae to smell and feel its surroundings.
- There are more species of beetles than of any other animal on earth.
- The whirligig beetle, which spends much of its time on the surface of the water, has eyes that split so that it can see below and above the waterline.
- The Australian tiger beetle can run almost 6 miles per hour.

BEHEMOTH

Type of animal:
Unknown

Find it in the Bible:
Job 40:15

I WISH I COULD HAVE SEEN A BEHEMOTH!

The behemoth is a mysterious creature described in the book of Job. It is mysterious because no animal currently living on earth fits its description. Here are the biblical facts about this creature:

- The behemoth eats grass like an ox (Job 40:15).
- Its strength is in its hips and in the muscles of its belly (40:16).
- It moves its tail like a cedar (40:17).
- Its bones are like beams of bronze, and its ribs are like bars of iron (40:18).
- It is first among the works of God (40:19).
- It lies under the lotus tree and hides among the reeds in the marsh (40:21).
- It spends time in the water (40:23).

Bible scholars have debated for centuries exactly what the behemoth was. Was it an elephant? A hippopotamus? Or, perhaps, a dinosaur?

The elephant eats grass, but its strength is in its neck, head, and tusks, not in the "belly"—which happens to be the weakest part of the animal. Also, the elephant retreats to the forest in the hottest part of the day, not in the marshy areas. It also has a large trunk but a very short tail.

The hippopotamus also eats grass, but its tail is only twenty inches long and very thin—not at all like a cedar. It spends much time in the deep water because its skin will dry out if it spends much time lying under the trees in the marshland.

So could the behemoth have been a dinosaur? No other creature, living or extinct, fits the description in Job 40 better. Many dinosaurs had huge tails like a cedar tree. And it's safe to say that their bones were like beams of bronze and their limbs were like bars of iron.

BEHEMOTH

Could the behemoth mentioned in the Bible have been what is now called a hippopotamus?

- The book of Job gives some amazing details about the behemoth, so we know that it is not a mythical creature.

- Many fossils have been found to prove dinosaurs were once on the earth.

- The brachiosaurus was one of the largest animals (more then forty tons, eighty feet long, and forty feet tall) ever to walk on the earth.

- People use the word *behemoth* today to describe something of great size or power.

Some biblical experts believe the behemoth was just a mythical creature. Others believe the animal lived on the earth before God created man. But in the book of Job, God talked to Job about the animals He made along with man (Job 40:15). God asked Job to "look at the behemoth" as though the animal was there for Job to see at that very moment.

We can't know for sure what kind of animal the behemoth was. It is a mysterious beast that was apparently very large and powerful—and obviously one the people of Job's day were familiar with.

BITTERN

Type of animal:
Bird

Find it in the Bible:
Isaiah 34:11 KJV

THIS BIRD MUST BE HIDING!

The bittern is a bird from the heron family. It lives in marshy areas, where it uses its long bill to stab the frogs, small fish, snakes, and bugs it eats. Unlike most of the herons, it has a short neck, which it does not stretch out during flight.

When predators pursue the bittern, it stands very still with its beak pointing straight up and its neck vertical, which helps camouflage it. The bittern's yellow and brown markings and its striped neckband help it blend into the marsh grass. It may even wobble slowly to imitate the movement of the marsh reeds. The arrangement of the bird's eyes lets it see all around its surroundings and allows it to change positions so its chest always faces predators. The back of the bittern is not as well camouflaged.

The bittern relies more on camouflage to defend itself than on its flight, which is sluggish. It is not completely defenseless, for it has a sharp bill and claws. It can also puff up its body feathers to make it appear bigger to its enemies.

OTHER BIBLE TRANSLATIONS CALL THIS BIRD "BUSTARD" OR "OWL."

The bittern is most active at dawn and dusk. Its booming cry, "Oog-ka-chuk," which sounds like a deep foghorn, can be heard each night.

The King James Version of the Bible describes the land where the bittern lives as being marshy or swampy. It also describes the song of the bittern in Zephaniah 2:14.

DID YOU KNOW. . .

- The bittern can stand still for many hours if predators are lurking around.

- The bittern is very difficult to find among the reed beds of the marshland.

- The mating call of the bittern can be heard from up to two miles away.

CAMEL

CAMEL HAIR CLOTHING WOULD BE SCRATCHY!

Type of animal:
Mammal
Find it in the Bible:
Job 1:3

The camel is a large, humpbacked animal that has been important to people for thousands of years. There are two types of camel—the dromedary, which has one hump on its back, and the Bactrian, which has two humps. The camel has a long neck, and its eyes, ears, and nostrils are set high upon its head so it can spot threats from far away. To protect against the blowing sand in the desert, it kneels down, presses its ears flat, shuts its eyes and nostrils, and waits out the storm.

The camel's ears are small and lined with fur to filter out sand and dust. Its eyes are large and protected by a double row of long, curly lashes that also help keep out dust and sand. Its thick, bushy eyebrows help shield its eyes from the desert sun.

THAT HUMP IS NOT A WATER TANK!

Contrary to what many people think, the camel does not store water in its hump. Instead, it stores fat reserves in its hump, which it uses when food is scarce. When a camel goes without food or water, it lives off the fat reserve. When it does find water, it can drink as much as twenty gallons in ten minutes.

The camel is a cud-chewing animal. It gulps down its food without chewing it first. Later it regurgitates the undigested food and chews it in cud form. The camel eats thorny plants, leaves, twigs, and dried grasses, including some other animals will not eat.

A camel has two hoofed toes on each foot. It also has broad, flat, leathery pads on its feet that spread wide apart when it walks.

Camels are still important animals in some parts of the world, especially where there isn't much water to drink.

This helps prevent the camel's feet from sinking into the sand. When walking, a camel moves both feet on one side of its body, then both feet on the other. The gait is like a rolling boat, which explains the camel's nickname, "Ship of the Desert."

The dromedary camel was common among the nations of Palestine in biblical times. It was the primary mode of transportation for goods and people traveling across the dry, hot terrain. It could carry about four hundred pounds in addition to its rider.

The Bible mentions the camel about fifty times. It was of great importance in the lives of the people of biblical times. In addition to using the camel for transportation, the people used its milk for food and its hide to make clothes, rugs, tents, and other necessary items. Even the camel's droppings were used for fuel for their fires.

ABRAHAM AND HIS CAMELS

Abraham and Sarah were traveling through Egypt in the time of famine. Pharaoh had given Abraham camels along with other animals. Camels were a part of Abraham's wealth.

Years later Abraham sent his servant to find a wife for his son Isaac. The servant found a young maiden at the well who gave him water and also watered his camel. She and her maidens rode camels back so she could become Isaac's bride

See Genesis 24

CAMELS AND WEALTH

Animals, including camels, were a measure of a person's wealth in biblical times. Camels were included in the wealth of Abraham, Isaac, Jacob, and other biblical patriarchs. Job had much wealth, including three thousand camels along with other animals. Later many kings acquired camels as part of their own wealth. Camels not only meant wealth, but riders on camels brought wealth—gold and incense—from Sheba to the Lord.

In biblical times, owning large numbers of these animals—whether they were smiling or not—meant you were a very wealthy person.

JESUS TAUGHT USING THE CAMEL

Jesus taught that it was easier for a camel to go through the eye of a needle than for a rich man to enter heaven. Some scholars believe this was a traditional description of a camel kneeling down to creep under the low gate in the Jerusalem wall. If that is true, Jesus' words meant that if a rich man will rid himself of pride and humble himself (kneel), he can get into heaven (see Luke 18:25).

Jesus also described hypocrites as people who were very careful to strain out a gnat from a cup of drink but who swallowed a camel without notice. In other words, they gave a tithe of a small herb but omitted doing the important things.

See Matthew 23:24

DID YOU KNOW. . .

● The adult camel is about seven feet tall at the hump and weighs around fifteen hundred pounds.

● A camel can survive the scorching hot summers and harsh, severe winters in the desert.

● A young camel can walk one hundred miles in a day.

● Even though the camel spits when it is upset, it is considered a good-tempered, patient, and intelligent animal.

OTHER BIBLE VERSES THAT MENTION CAMELS ARE 1 SAMUEL 30:17; JEREMIAH 2:23; AND MARK 1:6.

CATERPILLAR

SOME CATERPILLARS ARE UGLY PESTS.

The caterpillar is the larva form of the butterfly and moth. It has a soft body that grows rapidly. It has a hard head and a strong jawbone, which it uses for chewing leaves and other vegetation. Behind the jawbone is a silk-spinning organ. The tubular body of the caterpillar has segments with many legs.

The caterpillar's body has about four thousand muscles in it. The muscles in the rear segments move the caterpillar forward.

Even though the caterpillar has six tiny eyelets on each side of the head, it does not have good vision. It judges the distances of objects by moving the head from side to side.

The caterpillar breathes through small openings along the thorax and abdominal segments. A few caterpillars are aquatic and have gills that allow them to breathe underwater.

Many animals feed on caterpillars. For defense against enemies, some caterpillars appear to look poisonous. Some actually are poisonous and shoot out acid. Some caterpillars are colored in such a way that they can hide among the plants on which they feed. Some make a silk line and drop onto the ground when disturbed. Most caterpillars have bristles on their bodies— long, fine, hairlike strands with detachable tips—that irritate the skin of those who touch them.

Destructive is how the Bible describes the caterpillar. It even caused a famine by eating the farmers' crops.

DID YOU KNOW. . .

● The caterpillar is called an "eating machine" because it eats leaves ravenously.

● Most caterpillars shed their skin four or five times as they grow to be an adult.

● The art of raising caterpillars to make silk is called "sericulture."

OTHER BIBLE VERSES WHERE CATERPILLARS (SPELLED "CATERPILLER" IN THE KING JAMES VERSION OF THE BIBLE) ARE MENTIONED ARE 1 KINGS 8:37; 2 CHRONICLES 6:28; AND ISAIAH 33:4.

187

CATTLE

DOES A BULL GET MAD WHEN HE SEES RED?

Type of animal:
Mammal

Find it in the Bible:
Exodus 9:3

Cattle are very important and useful animals to humans—from biblical times until now. Most cattle are raised for milk, meat, and hides for making items. Male cattle are called "bulls" and are usually raised for meat. Female cattle are called "cows" and are usually kept for milk and to bear young. Young cattle, both male and female, are called "calves."

Cattle are often raised by allowing herds to graze on large tracts of grassland. Depending on the breed, cattle can survive and grow by grazing on hills, marshes, and semideserts. Many farmers today add commercial grains to cattle's diets.

Cattle were important in biblical times. The term *cattle* commonly referred to all domesticated animals. In populated areas, a young boy herded the cattle, but most of the time, the cattle were left alone to forage for food in nearby pastures.

From early biblical times, herds of cattle were kept to provide milk, meat, and leather from the skins. The number of cattle and sheep a person owned revealed the person's wealth.

The land of Goshen, where the Hebrews settled during the time of Joseph, was rich in cattle. Cattle were valued for sacrifices, for food, and as work animals. They were

READ HOW BULLOCKS WERE SACRIFICED UNDER THE MOSAIC LAW IN EXODUS 29 AND LEVITICUS 1:5 AND 4:4.

For many centuries, people have allowed cattle to grow and gain weight by grazing on grass in pastures

divided into clean and unclean classifications and were covered by the law of the Sabbath. Animals, as well as their owners, were to rest on the Sabbath.

The Jews used bullocks (bulls) for sacrifices of burnt offerings to God. They had to be flawless and offered according to the Mosaic Law.

JACOB SENDS A GIFT

After Jacob had caused much trouble for his brother and family, he moved away from home. Many years later, God told Jacob and his family to go back home. Jacob sent his helpers to tell his brother Esau that he was coming home. The helpers came back and reported, "Esau is coming to meet you. He has four hundred men with him!"

Jacob was afraid. He had run away from home because he had stolen from Esau. Jacob prayed and asked God to keep him safe from his brother. Then he selected gifts to send to Esau—goats, sheep, camels, donkeys, and cattle.

Jacob and his family walked far behind the animals. When Jacob saw Esau, he bowed low over and over to show that he was sorry for the wrong things he had done. Suddenly Esau ran to him and hugged him. Jacob was forgiven.

You can read the whole story in Genesis 32–33.

ELIJAH SACRIFICES A BULL

The Old Testament prophet Elijah went to King Ahab and said, "You make the people pray to idols instead of God. Bring your people to Mount Carmel. I will show them the real God."

When Ahab and the people got to the mountain, Elijah told them to build an altar. They were to place a bull on the altar and call for their gods to burn it. Ahab and the people called and called to their gods, but nothing happened.

Elijah built his altar and laid his bull on it. Then he said to Ahab's men, "Pour water over my altar." Then Elijah prayed, "Lord, show everyone that You are the real God."

God sent fire and burned everything, even the water. The people believed and worshiped God.

You can read the whole story in 1 Kings 18:16–39.

THE PRODIGAL SON

A fatted calf is a stall-fed animal, which meant that it was forced to eat more than it wanted to eat. It was fattened and killed for special occasions, such as to feed a special guest or to make a special offering to the Lord. Jesus talked about a fatted calf in one of His parables (stories).

A father had two sons. The younger son asked the father to give him his share of the inheritance. The younger son took the money and spent it foolishly in a far-off country. Soon he had no money and was hungry. He was sorry for what he had done. He decided to go home and ask his father if he could be one of his father's servants. At least then he would have plenty to eat.

As the father looked out one day, he saw the young son coming down the road. He was filled with love for his son and ran to him and threw his arms around him. He told his servants, "Bring the fatted calf and kill it. Let's have a big dinner and celebrate my son coming home"

See Luke 15:11–31

From biblical times forward, wealthy people owned large herds of cattle.

DID YOU KNOW. . .

- There are more than one hundred different cattle breeds.
- Cattle are red-green color blind; therefore they are not angry when they see red.
- Some full-grown bulls weigh one thousand to four thousand pounds, and cows weigh eight hundred to twenty-four hundred pounds.
- Cattle have one stomach with four compartments for digesting grasses and vegetation.
- Cattle dung is used as a fertilizer for crops and for fuel.

OTHER VERSES USING CATTLE IN THE BIBLE ARE GENESIS 18:7; EXODUS 29:36; NUMBERS 15:8

CHAMELEON

LOOK! THE CHAMELEON IS BROWN. NO, IT'S GREEN. NO, IT'S RED...

The chameleon is a lizard that changes color according to its surroundings. The chameleon does not just decide to change color. Its color change is a natural and unplanned reaction to something that happens to it.

The chameleon has a long, flat body with a tail that can grasp a twig just as a human hand does. When the chameleon is not using its tail, it curls it up in a spiral.

The chameleon's forefeet have little fingerlike appendages tipped with claws. The chameleon is the only lizard with a foot designed for grasping and holding.

The chameleon's bulging eyes are able to swivel in a complete circle as it constantly watches for the insects it eats. Each eyeball moves independently, allowing the chameleon to see two ways at the same time. Its keen vision can detect the smallest fly on leaves several feet away. Those same keen eyes, combined with a quick flick of the tongue, keep the chameleon well fed.

The chameleon's tongue is usually as long as its entire body. In some species, it is twice as long. It darts out quickly to capture lunch on its sticky tip. This is a most useful tool for the chameleon, a slow-moving, hard-of-hearing reptile that lives almost its entire life in trees.

The chameleon is listed as an unclean animal because it moves on the ground. In Palestine it lives in trees and bushes and hangs on to branches with its long tail.

DID YOU KNOW. . .

- The chameleon can catch its dinner in less than one second.
- Some chameleons have hornlike ridges on their heads that make them look like tiny dinosaurs.
- Chameleons vary in size from one and a half inches to three feet long.

COBRA

WHY DOES
THE COBRA
STAND UP?

Type of animal:
Reptile
Find it in the Bible:
Psalm 91:13

The cobra is a deadly poisonous snake with loose skin on its neck that forms a hood when the cobra is excited. The cobra rears up with its hood spread when it is provoked.

This strange creature can actually throw its poison. It knows where it will do the most harm—the eyes. The snake tilts its head back, hisses loudly, and points its fangs at the face of its victim. Suddenly, it contracts the muscles around its poison glands and lets yellow liquid fly out of its fangs in two thin jets. The poison frequently causes blindness and agonizing pain.

The cobra lives where the weather is very warm. It abides in areas around human settlements or where crops grow—both places where rodents thrive. It eats rodents, lizards, frogs, and even other snakes. Most species have poor eyesight and hunt at dusk or at night when its sight is sharper. The exception is the king cobra, which is active in the daytime and can see objects more than 330 feet away.

The cobra often lay concealed in hedges and holes in the walls of biblical cities. In the Bible, it is usually a symbol of evil. The Bible likens the poison of cobras to different negative attitudes in people, such as bitterness (see Deuteronomy 32:33). The cobra was also the snake on which the serpent charmers practiced their art.

DID YOU KNOW. . .

- At up to almost nineteen feet long, the king cobra is the longest venomous snake in the world.

- The cobra can throw its poison as far as nine feet.

- The cobra can live up to twenty years.

Type of animal:

Mammal

Find it in the Bible:

Leviticus 11:5

CONEY

PEW! THOSE SMELLY FEET GIVE THE CONEY TRACTION.

The coney is a small, short-eared, burrowing creature with a squat, furry body, short, slender legs, a short tail, and rodentlike incisors. The coney is not a rodent but a member of the same family as rabbits and hares.

The small hooves on its toes, along with moist padded soles, help the coney cling to steep surfaces by suction. The coney is an excellent climber that can even scale vertical cliffs. The coney's feet perspire to give it added traction.

The coney is a slow-moving animal, making it a target for predators. But the cliffs and rocks in which it lives ensure that enemies keep their distance and also protect from rain and wind. The coney stays close to home, only going out to find food.

The greatest threat to the coney is the eagle. Circling high overhead, the eagle sees the coney on the rocks. The coney's defense against eagles is its amazing eyesight, which allows it to detect movement from up to a mile away. When a coney sees an enemy, it lets out a sharp bark to warn other conies of danger.

Conies live in colonies of up to fifty animals. This is not only for protection but for warmth. The animals cuddle, sometimes lying one on top of another, to share body heat.

The coney, which lives in the hills and deserts of Palestine, is listed in the Mosaic Law as an unclean animal.

IN PROVERBS 30:26, CONIES ARE LISTED AMONG THE FOUR THINGS ON EARTH THAT ARE SMALL AND WISE.

DID YOU KNOW. . .

- The coney is sometimes called "rock badger" or "rock rabbit."

- In extreme weather, conies may lie on top of one another four layers deep to stay warm.

- In large numbers, conies can be agricultural pests.

CORMORANT

CORMORANTS ARE "CLOWNS" OF THE WATER.

Type of animal:
Bird

Find it in the Bible:
Leviticus 11:17

The cormorant is a medium-sized to large seabird found in many parts of the world where there are fish to catch. About forty species of cormorants are known today.

The cormorant is a superb swimmer, diver, fisher, and flyer. It has a long neck and a long, hooked beak that allows it to grasp and dig into the fish it catches. Its feet are webbed between four toes, which helps the bird to propel itself underwater. Its waterproof feathers do not trap air as do the feathers of other birds. That allows the cormorant to dive more quickly and chase prey underwater.

The cormorant can locate fish while flying high in the sky. It does not dive from the air but lands first and then dives under. The cormorant can dive as deep as thirty-three feet.

Even though the cormorant performs gracefully in the air and water, its takeoff from the water is awkward. It makes a long upwind run, flapping furiously and splashing water. It then pushes off with both feet, appearing to run across the water.

The male cormorant courts his mate by spreading his wings wide and sailing along on top of the water. He performs skillful dives, popping up and down like a cork. Often he will make a deep dive to gather rockweed, which he tosses into the air, catches, and presents to his courting mate. When she accepts, the male sits in a tree and sings "okay, okay, okay."

Cormorants are listed in the Mosaic Law as unclean, meaning they were not to be eaten.

DID YOU KNOW. . .

- Fishermen in some parts of the world sometimes call the cormorant the "submarine bird."
- After swimming, cormorants often go ashore and hold out their wings for the sun to dry them.
- People have used specially trained cormorants to catch fish.

Type of animal:
Bird

Find it in the Bible:
Isaiah 38:14 KJV

CRANE

WHO DOES THE "CRANE DANCE"?

The crane is a long-necked bird that stands about four feet tall. It has long legs, long, wide wings, and a long, pointed beak. Cranes look a lot like herons, but the two are not closely related.

There are fifteen species of cranes. Most cranes are gray with some white and black on the feathers. The sandhill crane has red skin on top of its head. The African crown crane is covered with black feathers and has a fan-shaped crest of strawlike feathers on its head.

Cranes live in well-organized groups for protection against predators. Several individual birds stand off from the group to guard against danger. Cranes use their powerful voices to communicate with other cranes when predators approach.

During certain times of the year, some cranes perform a ritual dance in which adult males, females, and young birds take part. The birds walk around each other, taking stiff-legged steps with their wings half spread. They bob their heads and bow to each other. As the dance tempo becomes faster, the cranes leap into the air. Some of them use their bills to snatch up sticks and leaves, throwing them into the air and stabbing them with their bills as they fall.

As mentioned in Jeremiah 8:7, many cranes are migratory birds that travel long distances. Most cranes mate for life and return to the same nest year after year.

SOME BIBLE TRANSLATIONS USE "SWIFT" OR "THRUSH" INSTEAD OF "CRANE."

DID YOU KNOW. . .

- The windpipe of an adult crane is five feet long and is coiled inside the breastbone.

- The loud call of the crane is similar to the sound of a trombone and can be heard as far as a mile away.

- The female crane lays two eggs, and both male and female take turns sitting on the eggs until they hatch.

CRICKET

DOES THE CRICKET PLAY A FIDDLE?

Type of animal:
Insect

Find it in the Bible:
Leviticus 11:22

A cricket is an insect related to the grasshopper and even more closely related to the katydid. It has long, jointed back legs for jumping on the ground, long antennae, and forewings that bend over its sides. It finds shelter under logs, stones, and burrows, and sometimes in buildings. It eats decaying plant material, fungi, and seedling plants. When food is scarce, the cricket will eat weakened or dead crickets.

The cricket produces a well-known song or chirp that is often heard on warm summer evenings. Only the male sings, and he does it to attract females. The cricket makes this sound by a method called "stridulation," which is by the vibration of the specially shaped forewings. On the underside of the right forewing is a vein that looks like a file. The vein is rubbed rapidly against a scraper on the upper side of the left forewing, much like the bow on a fiddle. The song helps guide the female to the male.

There are about nine hundred different species of crickets. Most of them are nocturnal, meaning they move and feed at night.

The mole cricket has powerful forelegs with claws shaped like tiny shovels. It digs burrows and moves earth. It can move a load of earth weighing as much as two pounds.

The snowy tree cricket is also called the "thermometer" cricket, because the outdoor temperature can be calculated by counting the number of times it chirps in fifteen seconds and adding thirty-nine. As the temperature warms, the tree cricket chirps faster.

According to the Mosaic Law, most flying insects are unclean and are not to be eaten. But the Bible says that crickets are permitted for food.

DID YOU KNOW. . .

- Crickets have powerful jaws, and some have been known to bite humans.
- A cricket hears with "ears" on the upper part of its front legs.
- In large numbers, crickets can destroy seedlings and cause great damage to farm crops.

CUCKOO

Type of animal:	Find it in the Bible:
Bird	Deuteronomy 14:15 KJV

DOESN'T THAT HAIRY CATERPILLAR TICKLE GOING DOWN?

The cuckoo (spelled "cuckow" in the King James Version of the Bible) is a medium-sized bird that ranges in size from the little bronze cuckoo, which grows to about six inches long, to the channel-billed cuckoo, which can grow to twenty-five inches long and weigh up to a pound and a half.

The cuckoo uses its slender wings and long tail for steering and as a rudder during flights—much like the rudder on an airplane.

The cuckoo gets its name from the distinctive call of the male common cuckoo. It is heard to say, "Cuck-oo, cuck-oo," combined sometimes with an angry "Kow, kow, kow." The female cuckoo doesn't make this sound.

A female cuckoo prefers to lay her eggs in another bird's nest and let the "foster parents" raise her young. When it is time to lay eggs, she finds a nest and removes the other bird's eggs with her bill then lays an egg of her own in their place. She throws the discarded eggs to the ground or eats them.

When the baby cuckoo hatches, the first thing it does is push the other eggs out of the nest. This tiny, featherless creature has a special hollow back that helps it accomplish that task. This is essential to the young cuckoo's survival, because it is much larger than other offspring and needs all the nutrition the foster parents can give it.

According to the Mosaic Law, the cuckoo is unclean and is not to be eaten. It spends its winters in Africa but migrates to parts of Europe and Asia, including the Mediterranean area, each spring to mate.

DID YOU KNOW. . .

- The cuckoo is a shy bird and is usually heard instead of seen.

- The cuckoo will eat adult insects but prefers hairy caterpillars.

- On each cuckoo's foot are two inner toes pointing forward and two outer toes pointing backward.

SOME BIBLE TRANSLATIONS CALL THE CUCKOO BIRD A "GULL."

197

DEER

Type of animal:
Mammal
Find it in the Bible:
Psalm 42:1

The deer is an antlered animal (all males and some females, depending on the species, have antlers) with two large and two small hooves on its feet. The deer's hooves give the deer a good grip for running on hard ground.

The deer's antlers are made of dead bone and covered with a special layer of skin. During certain times of the year, the antlers are covered with a soft, fuzzy covering called "velvet." Male deer use the antlers to fight for mates—mostly shoving one another around instead of actually fighting. Deer shed their antlers each year and grow a new set.

The deer is a timid creature that can sometimes be seen near water. It is a good swimmer, which sometimes helps it escape from predators. It lives on a diet of leaves, grass, twigs, fruit, and mushrooms. A deer will spend up to twelve hours a day eating.

Deer are color blind, meaning they see everything around them in shades of gray. Their keen senses of sight, smell, and hearing alert them to movement, including that of predators.

The deer's sandy coloring sometimes makes it difficult to spot. Sometimes when a deer is

The fallow deer is known for its strange-looking antlers...kind of like a shovel!

alarmed, it will thump the ground with its front feet as if playing a drum. This warns the other deer of danger. Deer have no defense from predators other than to run from them. Wolves and cougars, along with dogs, are the deer's primary predators.

It is believed that three species of deer lived in Palestine in biblical times: the red, fallow, and roe. The red deer is the largest of the deer family and one of the most easily identifiable. It was probably the species in the list of daily provisions for Solomon's table (see 1 Kings 4:23). In the King James Bible, the hart is the male red deer, and the hind is the female.

The fallow deer has especially large, shovel-shaped antlers. It is light brown with white spots on its body. It prefers to live in herds and is valued for its meat, which is called "venison."

The roe deer is much smaller than the other two, with smaller antlers. It has a reddish body and a gray face and lives a solitary life, except during mating season.

According to Mosaic Law, the deer is considered a clean animal, which means the people of Israel could eat it. It has split hooves and chews the cud, meaning it swallows its food without chewing then brings it back up later to be chewed.

THERE'S A COOL PRAISE SONG ABOUT THE DEER PANTING!

The deer provides the Bible writers with a picture of gracefulness, swiftness, and gentleness. David wrote of the deer in many of his psalms, such as when he likens his thirsty soul longing for God to thirsty deer panting for water (Psalm 42:1). David also compares the deer to fighting men (2 Samuel 2:18 KJV).

DID YOU KNOW. . .

- A male deer is called a "buck," a female is called a "doe," and the babies are called "fawns."
- Deer tend to stay within a fairly small territory, no bigger than one square mile.
- Some deer can jump obstacles ten feet high (the height of two cars stacked on top of each other).
- In one big leap, some deer can cover the distance the length of a family van.

DOG

WOW! I DIDN'T KNOW THERE WERE SO MANY KINDS!

Type of animal:
Mammal

Find it in the Bible:
Luke 16:21

Dogs come in a variety of sizes and colors. They can be as small as a Chihuahua, which is only six to ten inches tall, and as large as the Irish wolfhound, which can grow to the height of a small pony and weigh more than 150 pounds. They come in colors ranging from white to gray to black to many shades of brown—and in a wide variation of color combinations and patterns. Their coats can be short or long, coarse or soft, straight or curly, or smooth or wool-like. It is common for most breeds to shed their coats. Dog tails can be straight, sickle-shaped, curled, or corkscrew-shaped. It is estimated that there are more than 400 million dogs living in the world today.

Domestic dogs play many important roles in people's lives. Dogs are used for hunting, for herding, for protection, for companionship, for law enforcement, and for assisting the disabled. Dogs are intelligent animals capable of learning in a number of ways, such as through reinforcement and by observation. One of the best ways for a puppy to learn is to watch an adult dog perform a task.

Even though dogs have red-green color blindness, most of them have good vision. They are able to distinguish between humans from distances of up to a mile. They are also very good at seeing moving objects.

Dogs can identify a sound's location much faster than a human can, and they can hear sounds from about four times the distance. They have highly sensitive noses, which makes them good trackers and police animals.

Wild dogs are predators and scavengers. They have powerful muscles and are strong in endurance. They use their strength and their teeth to catch and devour their prey.

Dogs are mentioned many times in the Bible, but no specific breed is identified. During biblical times, ferocious wild dogs ran in packs around fields and city streets, devouring dead bodies and other things.

Puppies are playful, curious, and energetic. They learn quickly by watching grown-up dogs.

Dogs are called man's best friend because they really make good friends!

The Bible mentions two kinds of domesticated dogs. The first is a wolflike, short-haired animal that stands guard over tents or houses and barks fiercely at strangers. These dogs ate whatever was tossed to them. At evening the dogs barked throughout the city.

The second kind of dog helped shepherds round up sheep. Dogs also served as watchdogs for herds. Job referred to the dogs as watching over his flocks. Other dogs were trained for hunting.

THE RICH MAN AND LAZARUS

Jesus used dogs to teach people important truths. He told the story of the rich man and Lazarus. The rich man dressed in purple robes and fine linen. He lived an easy life, while Lazarus was a beggar who was covered with sores, which the dogs came and licked (see Luke 16:19–31).

In biblical times, calling someone a dog was a way of insulting that person. In the Old Testament, the prophet Isaiah insulted the priests of his time by saying their sacrifices were no better than breaking a dog's neck and sacrificing it. That meant they were sacrificing in the wrong way. In the New Testament, the apostle Paul warned Christians to be watchful for those who do evil and called his enemies dogs. The Jews scornfully called Gentiles "dogs."

DID YOU KNOW. . .

- A dog's nickname is "man's best friend."
- Dogs can detect sounds from much farther distances than humans can.
- Many dog breeds have a "blaze" or "star" of white fur on their chest or underside.
- The border collie is considered one of the most intelligent dog breeds.

DONKEY

Type of animal:
Mammal

Find it in the Bible:
Luke 10:34

DONKEYS MAKE ME LAUGH WITH THEIR "HEE HAW, HEE HAW."

The donkey is a relative of the horse. It is usually gray in color and has long, pointed ears and a long tail. The tall ears pick up distant sounds and also help cool the donkey during hot weather. It is a very strong animal, which makes it ideal for doing hard work, such as pulling wagons and plows to help farmers with their crops.

The wild donkey lives in rocky places and can survive on very little water. It eats tough, spiky grass to survive in barren environments. It also grazes on herbs and even tree bark when food is scarce.

The donkey makes a good guard animal. It can look after entire herds of cattle, sheep, or goats. It defends itself with a powerful kick of its hind legs as well as by biting.

A donkey has a reputation for being stubborn. But it actually just prefers to do what is good for itself, which is not always what its human master thinks is best. This is probably because of a strong sense of self-preservation.

Donkeys were common "beasts of burden" in biblical times. They were highly valued for riding, for carrying loads, for drawing chariots or carts, and for pulling plows and doing other fieldwork. The Israelites considered donkeys unclean and unacceptable to eat.

In biblical times, donkeys were valued as pack animals. They still are today!

DONKEY

Knowing that animals, like people, needed time to rest, God included them when He gave the laws concerning rest on the Sabbath.

Abraham, Jacob, and many others are mentioned in the Bible as having large herds of donkeys. The animal is mentioned about 120 times in the Bible, so donkeys were obviously important animals in biblical times. The Bible says that donkeys were used for riding (Numbers 22:21), as beasts of burden (1 Samuel 16:20), and as helpers for agricultural work (Deuteronomy 22:10).

When the Israelites returned to Palestine from the Babylonian captivity, they brought with them more than six thousand donkeys, which was about six times the number of horses and camels they possessed.

Would you feel rich if you owned a bunch of these? In biblical times, people who owned lots of donkeys were considered rich.

THE TALKING DONKEY

Balaam saddled his donkey and went to a place God had told him not to go. God sent an angel to stand in the road. When the donkey saw the angel of the Lord, she turned off the road. Balaam beat the donkey to get her back on the road.

Later the angel of the Lord stood in a narrow path between two vineyards with walls on each side. When the donkey saw the angel, she crushed Balaam's foot against the wall. Balaam beat the donkey again. Once again the angel of the Lord moved ahead and stood in a narrow place. When the donkey saw the angel, she lay down. Balaam was very angry and beat her again. Then God opened the donkey's mouth and the donkey spoke to Balaam.

SOME OTHER BIBLE VERSES THAT MENTION THE DONKEY ARE GENESIS 22:3; NUMBERS 22:28; 1 SAMUEL 9:3; AND MATTHEW 21:2.

See Numbers 22

DONKEY

THE GOOD SAMARITAN'S DONKEY

Jesus used the donkey in His teaching when someone asked Him, "Who is my neighbor?"

The story went like this: A man was traveling from Jerusalem to Jericho when robbers jumped him, took his clothes, beat him, and left him by the side of the road. A priest and a Levite came by the man and ignored him. But when a Samaritan came by the man and saw him, he felt sorry for him. The Samaritan bandaged the poor man's wounds and put him on his own donkey and took him to an inn.

You can read the whole story in Luke 10:25–37.

JESUS RIDES A DONKEY INTO JERUSALEM

Because of its strength and usefulness to people, the donkey became a symbol for kings in the Bible. Even Jesus rode a donkey when He entered Jerusalem.

As Jesus and His disciples approached Jerusalem, He sent two of His disciples ahead to a village to find a donkey. The disciples did what Jesus told them to do. They brought the donkey and placed their coats on it. Jesus entered Jerusalem riding on the donkey through a large crowd of people who were waiting for Him. The people spread their coats and palm branches on the road and shouted, "Hosanna to the Son of David!"

You can read this whole story in Matthew 21:1–11.

DID YOU KNOW...

- Many donkeys live to be more than twenty years old.
- Donkeys can go as long as twelve hours between meals.
- A male donkey is called a "jack" and a female is called a "jenny."
- A donkey's favorite pastime is to roll.
- Donkeys are friendly and enjoy being around people.

Type of animal:
Bird

Find it in the Bible:
Leviticus 1:14

DOVE

THE TURTLEDOVE IS A SYMBOL OF LOVE.

The dove has a small, stocky body, a short neck, and a short, slender tail. It is closely related to the pigeon.

There are more than three hundred different species of doves, and each species is colored differently. The common ground dove has chestnut-colored wing patches, a drab pink chest, and a small bill that is reddish at the base and black on the tip. The mourning dove is a slender brown bird with a white-bordered tail. The turtledove has a gray head and a body that is a beige color blushed with pink.

All species of doves fly fast on powerful wings with their tails stretched behind them. They sometimes make sudden midflight ascents, descents, and dodges. When doves take off, their wings make a sharp whistling or whining sound.

The dove forages on the ground for seeds and grain to eat. Unlike most birds, it uses its bill like a straw to suck up water.

The mating display of the male dove involves strutting up and down. The male puffs up the feathers around his throat and (in some species) raises his crest. The cooing sound he makes calms the female dove.

The female dove lays only one or two eggs at a time, but she can lay eggs several times a year. When the eggs hatch, both parents feed them special milk from pouches inside their throats called "crops."

The dove is a common and important Bible bird. It was important as a sacrifice during Old Testament times. Doves alone (or sometimes with other animals) were a sacrifice called for in Mosaic Law. Those who couldn't afford a lamb or goat as a sacrifice could use two doves for sacrifices (Leviticus 5:7–11). When Mary and Joseph brought baby Jesus to the temple, Mary brought a sacrifice of two doves (Luke 2:24).

Doves have powerful wings that help them to fly very fast and make acrobatic moves in midair!

DOVE

NOAH AND THE DOVE

The first mention of the dove in the Bible was in the story of Noah and the ark. After Noah had been in the ark with the animals many days, he sent out a raven. It found no place to land. Later Noah sent out one of the doves. It came back because there was no place to land.

Noah waited seven more days. Then he let out the dove again. Noah waited and watched. Finally, the dove returned to the ark. This time it had an olive leaf in its beak.

Seven days later, Noah sent the dove out again. This time the little bird did not come back. Noah knew the waters had dried up and knew that God had kept His promise

You can read the whole story in Genesis 8:6–12.

THE DOVE AT JESUS' BAPTISM

All four Gospels in the New Testament record the appearance of a dove at Jesus' baptism. One day while John the Baptist was preaching, Jesus came to him and said, "Please baptize Me." John then led Jesus into the Jordan River and baptized Him.

As Jesus came out of the water, He saw heaven open and the Spirit descending on him like a dove. A voice from heaven said, "You are my Son, whom I love. I am well pleased with You"

See Mark 1:9–11

DID YOU KNOW. . .

- The dove is the smallest species of the pigeon family.

- The male dove can be heard in early morning singing his deep "coo, coo, coo."

- Doves are helpful to farmers, for they pick up wasted grains and weed seed.

- The white dove has become a symbol of peace.

OTHER BIBLE VERSES THAT MENTION DOVES ARE NUMBERS 6:10; PSALM 55:6; ISAIAH 38:14; AND MATTHEW 10:16

DRAGON

Type of animal:
Reptile?

Find it in the Bible:
Psalm 91:13 KJV

ARE DRAGONS ONLY IN FANTASY STORIES?

The dragon is a mythical fire-breathing animal with bat wings, sharp claws, and a barbed tail. The dragon is also described as a large dinosaur-like creature that once lived in swamps. In ancient times, coiled sea serpents were sometimes called "dragons."

What does the Bible say about dragons? It says that the dragon is a great land or sea monster, usually some type of reptile. It is powerful and deadly. Bible translations differ in what they call the dragon:

"Their wine is the poison of dragons" (Deuteronomy 32:33 KJV). Other Bible translations use the word serpents.

"Though thou hast sore broken us in the place of dragons. . ." (Psalm 44:19 KJV). Other translations used the word jackal.

"The great dragon that lieth in the midst of his rivers. . ." (Ezekiel 29:3 KJV, RSV). Other translations used the word monster.

Other Bible translations replace "dragon" with "sea monster," "whale," "snake," or "crocodile." The apostle John wrote of a mythological sea monster that symbolizes the forces of evil opposing God (see Revelation 12:3–4).

DID YOU KNOW. . .

- Lizards (some of them very large) called komodo dragons, Chinese water dragons, and bearded dragons, still exist today.

- Komodo dragons have been known to grow nearly ten feet in length.

OTHER BIBLE VERSES THAT INCLUDE THE WORD DRAGON ARE JOB 30:29 AND ISAIAH 43:20.

This is a modern-day dragon—a real one! Komodo dragons are the world's largest lizards.

EAGLE

Type of animal:
Bird

Find it in the Bible:
Isaiah 40:31

WOULD THE EAGLE BE CALLED "KING OF THE AIR"?

The eagle is a bird of prey that can be found in many parts of the world. It is powerful and majestic as it flies through the sky. Its body is small and weighs very little, allowing the eagle to soar in the air for a long period of time. It is active during the daytime rather than at night.

The eagle is an excellent hunter. It sees prey such as rabbits from as far away as two miles. It can also spot fish from several hundred feet in the air. Once the eagle has spotted its prey, it uses its strong feet with sharp talons to catch it. The powerful hooked bill tears open the flesh of the captured prey.

The nest of the American bald eagle is enormous—eight feet across and weighing as much as a ton. Eagles build their nests (which are called "eyries") in cliffs, on broad ledges, or in tall trees. They use twigs and leaves for building materials.

Though the eagle is listed in the Mosaic Law as unclean, this majestic bird has an important role in the Bible. The Old Testament writers noted the eagle's swift movements, the power of its flight, and its care for its young. In the ancient world, the eagle often was associated figuratively with God's protection and care.

Throughout history the eagle has been seen as a symbol of courage and strength. The figure of the eagle is now and has long been a favorite military emblem.

OTHER BIBLE VERSES THAT MENTION THE EAGLE ARE 2 SAMUEL 1:23; JOB 39:27; JEREMIAH 48:40; AND EZEKIEL 17:3.

DID YOU KNOW...

- The bald eagle can fly as fast as 60 miles per hour but can reach 100 miles per hour when it dives.
- The average adult golden eagle has a wingspan of more than seven feet.
- An eagle can swim by propelling itself through the water with its wings.

FALCON

IS THAT BIRD ON A CRASH COURSE?

The falcon is a bird of prey with powerful feet, talons, and a heavy, hooked beak it uses to kill and tear apart its prey. It is sometimes mistaken for a hawk, but it has longer, more pointed wings than a hawk.

The falcon eats other birds as well as small mammals. This gray-black bird hovers over the open grassland until it spots prey. Then it swoops down at amazing speeds of up to 150 miles per hour. With great accuracy, it grasps the prey in the sharp, curved, widely spread talons and at the same time kills it with a strike from one single rear talon. Sometimes the falcon will cripple the prey, return to the air, and then return later for the final kill.

Some falcons use other birds' nests instead of building their own. Some use woodpecker holes, while some take over crows' nests in trees. Some that build weak nests choose inaccessible cliff tops or just scoop out a hollow in open grassland.

Falcons tend to mate for life, which means that a pair of falcons will mate every year. The male swoops through the air displaying his flying skills while the female does most of the work looking after the eggs.

According to the Mosaic Law, the falcon is unclean and may not be eaten.

DID YOU KNOW. . .

- A falcon keeps its feathers clean by taking a bath in a stream.

- It takes a young falcon much practice and sometimes a long time to learn hunting skills.

- In a sport called "falconry," a falcon can be trained to take off from a person's wrist and hunt wild birds and small animals.

- Falcons are known as "birds of prey," also called "raptors."

FERRET

WHAT IS A "WEASEL WAR DANCE"?

Type of animal:
Mammal

Find it in the Bible:
Leviticus 11:30 KJV

The ferret is a member of the weasel family. It has a long body, short legs, and very sharp teeth. The ferret's fur is of various colors and patterns—white, black, silver, brown, albino, or mixed. It is nearsighted but has a good sense of hearing and smell.

The ferret spends fourteen to eighteen hours a day sleeping. When it is awake, it is energetic, curious, and interested in its surroundings. When a ferret gets excited, it will perform a "weasel war dance." The body becomes stiff, followed by thrashing and turning the head from side to side. The back arches, and the ferret hops from side to side and backward as it makes a soft clucking noise. During this "war dance," the ferret may bump into obstacles or trip over its own feet.

The ferret is born with scent glands, which it uses for self-defense. The glands give off a strong odor that frightens potential predators.

In years past, farmers used ferrets in their barns to help control rodents. Since a ferret has a long, lean build, it can easily slither into holes and chase rodents out of their burrows. Hunters have also used ferrets to hunt rabbits.

The ferret is listed in the Mosaic Law as an unclean animal. It is possible that people in biblical times used the animal for rodent control.

OTHER BIBLE TRANSLATIONS CALLED THIS ANIMAL "GECKO" OR "LIZARD."

DID YOU KNOW. . .

- A male ferret is called a "hob," and the female ferret is called a "jill."

- The ferret will carry small objects to secluded locations and hide them.

- A ferret makes a good pet, as it loves to play with humans.

Type of animal:
Fish
Find it in the Bible:
Luke 5:6

FISH

LET'S GO FISHING!

Fish are cold-blooded animals (those whose body temperature changes with the temperature of their surroundings) that have fins to help them swim and gills they use to take in oxygen from the water. Most fish spend their entire lives in water, but some fish are able to live on land for short periods of time.

Most fish are designed for swimming. Their sleek, slender bodies glide through the water, and they use their fins for swimming. The size, shape, and number of fins depends on the species of fish. Each of the fins serves a different purpose.

Fish also use their strong muscles to help them swim. As they wiggle their body in an S-pattern, the tail presses against the water and pushes the fish forward.

Many fish have a sac inside their bodies called a "swim bladder." The gas inside the sac helps to keep the fish upright and to stay at a certain depth as it swims. Fish that live in the deep water do not have a swim bladder.

Most fish have scales covering their skin to protect their bodies. The scales are different colors, shapes, and sizes, depending on the species. Most fish have teeth suited to what they eat. Sharks eat other fish, so they need large, sharp teeth. Other fish have smaller teeth that help them eat their favorite food, plankton. Still other fish have no teeth at all!

Fish avoid or fight off their predators in many different ways. Some fish swim very fast and can simply outrun their enemies. Some fish use

Some fish, like these tropical fish that live near a coral reef, are beautifully colored.

During biblical times, fishermen used nets to catch their fish. In some parts of the world, fisherman still use nets to catch fish.

camouflage to protect themselves. Their coloring and shape help hide them in their surroundings. Other fish are poisonous. For example, a stingray attacks predators with a poisonous whiplike tail. Others have prickly poisonous spines, while others have poisonous flesh.

Some fish have a keen sense of smell in the water. For example, the salmon smells the water to know how to return to the same stream where it was born. Others smell the water to travel to the same grounds when they migrate.

Fish are mentioned often in the Bible but not by the different species. Fish abounded in the inland waters of Palestine, as well as in the Mediterranean Sea. As the Israelites ate manna in the wilderness, they remembered eating fish in Egypt (see Numbers 11:5). According to the Mosaic Law, all fish with fins and scales were clean, but those water animals with no fins or scales were unclean (Leviticus 11:9–12).

The Bible mentions several ways to catch fish. Fishing with a line and hook, harpooning, and spear fishing are all mentioned in Job 41:1 and 7. Casting a net into the water is mentioned in Matthew 4:18, and the use of large dragnets cast from a boat is mentioned in John 21:8.

Fish caught in the Mediterranean Sea were mostly brought to the ports of Tyre and Sidon. The Sea of Galilee was also a fishing center. The fish caught there were brought to Jerusalem to be sold at the Fish Gate in the city.

During New Testament times, commercial fishing businesses were conducted on the Sea of Galilee. Many fishermen owned their ships, and fish provided food for the people along the seaport.

The most famous biblical fish story is found in the Old Testament book of Jonah. God prepared a special fish to swallow Jonah when he would not obey Him.

Some of Jesus' disciples—Simon Peter, Andrew, James, and John—were fishermen by trade. Fish was a common food for Jesus and His disciples. The New Testament gives an account of Jesus feeding more than five thousand people with a boy's five loaves of bread and two fish (John 6:1–15).

OTHER BIBLE VERSES THAT MENTION FISH ARE 2 CHRONICLES 33:14; NEHEMIAH 3:3; PSALM 8:8; LUKE 24:42; AND JOHN 21:3-13.

DID YOU KNOW. . .

- There are about twenty-eight thousand different species of fish living around the world today.

- The fastest fish in the world is the sailfish, which has been known to swim at speeds of almost 70 miles per hour.

- Fish never close their eyes because they do not have eyelids.

- Some fish travel in groups called "schools."

- The archerfish can squirt a jet of water droplets at insects on leaves above the surface, knocking them into the water.

213

FLEA

WOW! LOOK AT THAT FLEA GO!

Type of animal:
Insect
Find it in the Bible:
1 Samuel 24:14

The flea is a tiny insect less than a quarter inch long. It has a flattened body that helps it wander between the hairs of the animal it rides on and feeds from. It has no wings but has large back legs with rubbery pads. The pads are squeezed tightly by muscles and keep packed together until the flea needs to jump. Then the pads are released, allowing the flea to spring onto a passing victim. It quickly scurries between hairs and grips the skin with needle-sharp claws. When it is ready to eat, the flea cuts the skin with mouthparts that are like jagged edges of a knife blade. The sharp beak enters the skin and injects a chemical that stops the blood from clotting. The host's body pumps the blood into the flea's stomach.

Most fleas do not carry dangerous diseases. But some carry diseases that can cause death. For example, the rat flea carries the bacteria that caused a disease known as the bubonic plague, which spread through Europe during the fourteenth century. This plague killed about half of Europe's population.

The flea was a plague for people and animals during Israel's early history. Some Bible scholars believe fleas were the carriers of the disease that fell upon the Assyrians during the ministry of the prophet Isaiah (see Isaiah 37:36–37). Also, David, before he became king of Israel, humbly compared himself to a flea when he spoke to King Saul (see 1 Samuel 24:14; 26:20).

Fleas would be scary looking if they weren't so tiny!

DID YOU KNOW. . .

- The flea is about the size of a pinhead.
- Fleas have been known to jump up to two hundred times their own body length.
- A flea does not live on humans, but comes, bites, and then leaves.

Type of animal:
Insect
Find it in the Bible:
Psalm 105:31

FLY

WAITER!
THERE'S A
FLY IN MY
SOUP!

A fly has a mobile head, large compound eyes (eyes that are made up of many smaller eyes), and a single pair of wings. It has small, white knobs just behind its wings called "halters," which give it balance when it flies through the air. It also has sticky pads on its feet, which give it the ability to walk on the ceiling or hang from wires and branches. Flies are mostly inactive at night and more active during cooler rather than warm temperatures.

There are more than 120,000 species of flies, and they are found everywhere in the world except the supercold continent of Antarctica. The most common is the housefly, which is a pest that can carry disease-causing germs in its saliva and on its body.

The housefly is a scavenger that eats anything sugary or rotting that it can absorb with its spongy mouth pads. It uses its tongue, which is shaped like a straw, to suck up liquid food. The fly can easily eat liquid food, but eating solids like sugar is a little trickier for the fly because it doesn't have jaws or teeth. To eat solid food like sugar, the fly vomits saliva and digestive juices onto the meal then gives it a chance to dissolve. Then it gobbles up the liquefied meal with its tongue.

The female fly lays her eggs in rotting waste. She may lay up to five hundred eggs in several batches of seventy-five to one hundred eggs over a period of three or four days. The eggs must remain moist or they will not hatch. When the eggs hatch—usually within twenty-four hours—they produce larvae called "maggots." The maggots are active for two or three weeks, feasting on the same rotten stuff they were hatched in. Before long, the maggot becomes a pupa, which is the last step before it becomes an adult fly.

WHAT A BORING LIFE!

The fly mostly stays within one or two miles of where it was born, but it may travel as far as twenty miles to find food. One of the reasons flies are found where people are found is that they can easily find food.

Can you imagine having millions of these little pests flying around your neighborhood? That's what happened in Egypt when Pharaoh refused to let God's people go free!

A PLAGUE OF FLIES

Flies are first mentioned in the Bible in the eighth chapter of Exodus, which includes the plague of flies God sent to Egypt when Pharaoh refused to free the people of Israel from bondage.

Moses and his brother Aaron had gone to Pharaoh for the fourth time, and for the fourth time they told him, "God wants you to let His people go!" They also warned Pharaoh that God would send a plague of flies if he refused. But the stubborn Pharaoh would not let the Israelites go.

So God sent flies. Not just a few flies, but huge swarms of them. The air was literally black with the little pests. God did not allow the flies to bother the Israelites, but all of the Egyptians were swatting flies and trying to get away from them. But still Pharaoh was stubborn. "No! You may not go!" he shouted.

King David later recalled how God took care of His people when Pharaoh held them in bondage. He remembered the miraculous signs God performed in Egypt (including sending the flies!) before Pharaoh finally let the people go free

See Psalm 78:42–52

DID YOU KNOW. . .

- Houseflies have taste buds on their feet that allow them to taste sugar when they stand on it.
- A housefly can live only two or three days without food.
- Flies can beat their wings hundreds of times a second.
- The life cycle of a fly is short—an average of about twenty-one days.

Type of animal:
Mammal
Find it in the Bible:
Judges 15:4

FOX

YOU'RE A SLY OLD FOX!

The fox is the smallest member of the dog family. It has short legs, an extended narrow muzzle, erect triangular ears, thick fur, and a long, bushy tail. The red fox is the most common fox species. It has rusty red fur sprinkled with light-tipped hairs, black ears and feet, and a white-tipped tail.

The fox has a small, slender body that is designed for quickness. It can run as fast as 30 miles per hour. The fox is a shy, nervous hunter and scavenger that is most active at night. It will eat everything from insects to small mammals to berries to human garbage. Since the fox does not eat large prey, it hunts alone rather than in a pack.

When a lot of food is available, the fox will store it in shallow holes. It will make several storage places around its territory to prevent other animals from taking its food.

The fox has keen senses of smell, hearing, and sight. It can pick up low-frequency sounds, even the sound of an animal digging or scratching in an underground burrow. When the fox hears a mouse, it stands still and alert until it sees the prey. Then it launches at the prey, pinning it to the ground. If the fox is not hungry, it plays with the catch—just like cats sometimes do.

Red foxes pair for life with a mate. They make dens tucked away in rock crevices, in abandoned

The red fox is the most common species of fox in the world.

rabbit burrows, or in holes in trees. Foxes are very territorial and will defend their territory and families.

Foxes abound in Palestine and are mentioned several times in the Bible. Foxes were a threat to the vineyards, as they trampled down the fruit vines and bushes as they devoured the fruit. But foxes were also a help to the farmers because they hunted the rodents and rabbits that destroyed other crops.

NEHEMIAH BUILDS THE WALLS

Nehemiah heard that the walls of the city of Jerusalem were broken down and the gates had been burned. He was sad and asked the king if he could go help rebuild the walls. The king told Nehemiah to go help.

Nehemiah gathered some men together and said, "Let's rebuild the walls. We will make them strong."

Some men were not pleased when they heard the walls were going to be rebuilt. They did not like Nehemiah and the Jews. One of the men, named Sanballat, said, "Do these weak Jews think they can make their city strong?"

Tobiah, his servant, was with him and also made fun of the men and their work. He said, "If a fox would climb up the wall, it would break down."

The enemy tried to form an army to fight Nehemiah and keep the walls from being built. But Nehemiah prayed and asked God to help them build the wall of Jerusalem. God heard Nehemiah's prayer.

Foxes make their dens in all kinds of places. This young fox lives in a hole under an oak tree.

You can read the whole story in Nehemiah 4. Foxes are also mentioned in the New Testament, in Luke 9. One day a man came to Jesus and said that he wanted to follow Him. Jesus told the man, "Foxes have holes and birds of the air have nests, but the Son of Man has no place to lay his head" (Luke 9:58 NIV).

THE FIERY FOXES

Samson went to see his wife, but her father would not let him into the house to see her. Samson became angry. "I will get even with them," Samson said to himself.

Samson went out and caught three hundred foxes and tied them together in pairs by their tails. Then he tied a piece of wood between the tails. When the Philistine's grain was ready to harvest, Samson lit the wood and let the foxes loose. They ran into the fields of grain and burned up the shocks and grain, along with the vineyards and olive groves (see Judges 15:1–8).

Some Bible scholars believe that the foxes mentioned in this story were actually jackals. That's because foxes are solitary animals while jackals run in packs and hide in caves, which would have made them easier for Samson to catch. But most of the translations of the Bible use the word foxes in the story.

DID YOU KNOW...

- The red fox is about the size of a large cat.

- A fox's hearing is so good that it can hear a watch ticking forty yards away.

- The gray fox is the only fox species that can climb trees.

- The fox's average lifespan is about twelve years.

Samson was tough, but dumb...even though he burned the Philistines' fields with flaming foxes, he fell in love with a Philistine woman, Delilah—who led to his death in a Philistine temple.

FROG

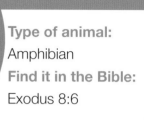

Type of animal:
Amphibian
Find it in the Bible:
Exodus 8:6

IS IT TRUE THAT FROGS HAVE TEETH?

Frogs are known for their short bodies, long hind legs, webbed toes, bulgy eyes, and by the fact that they don't have a tail. Frogs have very strong hind legs, which give them amazing jumping ability. Most frogs spend the majority of their time in water, but they can also move easily on land by jumping, crawling, or climbing.

A frog must be able to move quickly to catch prey and to escape predators. Some frogs use their sticky tongues to catch their food. All frogs are carnivorous, which means that they eat other animals. Most of them eat small prey such as insects and other bugs. But some frogs eat small fish, reptiles, and animals. Some frogs like to eat. . .other frogs!

The frog has a ridge of very small teeth around the upper edge of the jaw and teeth on the roof of its mouth. It doesn't use its teeth to chew but to keep a good grip on its prey, which it swallows whole. When the frog swallows a meal, it closes its bulgy eyeballs as it pushes its food down its throat.

A frog begins its life as an egg its mother laid in a pond, puddle, or lake. When the baby frog hatches, it isn't yet a frog but a tadpole, which looks like a little fish and breathes with gills like a fish. As the tadpole feasts on algae and other plant life, it undergoes some big changes. It begins to grow back legs then front legs. The gills are replaced by lungs, and the digestive system changes so that the adult frog can begin life as a meat eater. The last step toward maturity is the disappearance of the tail, which is absorbed into the frog's body.

There are thousands of species of frogs living wherever it's warm enough and wet enough for frogs to live. They come in many different colors and sizes.

This animal is mentioned several times in the Old Testament, including the account of Moses and the ten plagues on Egypt.

From tadpole to frog. . .the transformation is almost complete!

THE PLAGUE OF THE FROGS

Moses had returned to Pharaoh when he would not let the Israelites go after the first plague—when the water in Egypt turned to blood (Exodus 7:19). "God will cover the land with frogs if you will not let the people go," Moses warned Pharaoh.

But Pharaoh would not let the people go. So, just as God had promised, swarms of frogs entered the houses and the land. They were everywhere!

Then Pharaoh said, "Tell God to take the frogs away. I will let the people go."

Moses told Pharaoh the frogs would go away. But do you think that sly old pharaoh let the Israelites go? Read the whole story in Exodus 8 and find out!

CAN YOU IMAGINE FINDING A FROG ON YOUR BED?

DID YOU KNOW. . .

- Some frogs can jump more than twenty times their length, which is about like you jumping one hundred feet.

- The Goliath frog is nearly a foot long with legs that long, too.

- The adult gold frog is only three-eighths of an inch long.

- In captivity, some frogs have been known to live as long as forty years.

Other Bible verses that mention frogs are Psalm 78:45 and 105:30.

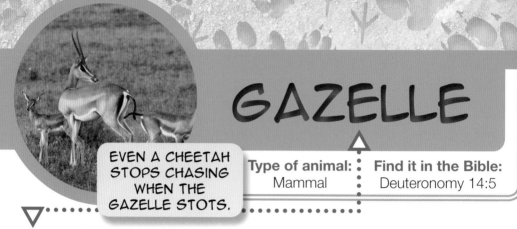

GAZELLE

EVEN A CHEETAH STOPS CHASING WHEN THE GAZELLE STOTS.

Type of animal:
Mammal

Find it in the Bible:
Deuteronomy 14:5

The graceful, speedy gazelle is a species of antelope. It is light brown in color with a white underbelly. It has black and white markings on its face with a horizontal dark band along each side. It has long, pointed ears, large eyes, and V-shaped antlers that extend backward from its head.

Some gazelles live in the mountainous regions, but most graze on grassy plains with very few places to hide. Life on the plains exposes the gazelle to predators such as lions, leopards, and wild dogs. Its antlers offer no protection, so it relies on its speed to elude its enemies. Gazelles are very fast.

The gazelle has a clever way of dealing with its enemies. It is called "stotting." The gazelle leaps high in the air with all four legs stiff and back arched as if to say, "I see you! Don't sneak up on me!" It sometimes does this while an enemy is chasing it. It often works as the enemy breaks off the chase.

Gazelles live in herds, and that offers them some protection against predators. When one gazelle in the herd senses danger, it wiggles its white rump to tell the other gazelles of the threat.

According to Mosaic Law, the gazelle is considered clean, which means it was permitted as food for the people of Israel. The gazelle has divided hooves and chews the cud.

DID YOU KNOW. . .

- The gazelle can run as fast as 50 miles per hour.
- To reach leaves on a tree to eat, the gazelle stands on its hind legs and stretches its long neck.
- The gazelle has little need for drinking water, because it gets most of its moisture from plants.

Type of animal:
Reptile
Find it in the Bible:
Leviticus 11:30

GECKO

OH, WHAT BIG EYES YOU HAVE!

The gecko is a lizard that comes in a variety of colors and patterns. Some are delicately patterned and rubbery looking, while others are brightly colored. Some species even change colors to blend in with their surroundings. The different color patterns help camouflage the gecko from its enemies.

The gecko has a triangular head and a large tail where it stores fat. It can break off its tail when threatened, leaving a predator with nothing but a tail in its mouth as the lizard scurries away to safety. Its skin is bumpy. It has huge eyes and sees very well—especially at night, when it is most active. The gecko's toes have brushlike foot pads on them that hold them to most surfaces. This makes it easy for them to climb walls and walk across ceilings.

The gecko is harmless to humans and is in fact welcomed in homes in some parts of the world because it feeds on annoying insects such as mosquitoes, which it swallows whole.

The gecko is the only reptile that has the ability to use its voice (other than the hissing sounds some reptiles make). It often makes barking, chirping, and clicking noises when it interacts with fellow geckoes.

The gecko mentioned in the Bible is probably the fan-foot gecko, which is common in Egypt and in parts of Arabia, and might also be found in Palestine. It is reddish brown with white spots. It is considered unclean according to Mosaic Law.

SOME VERSIONS OF THE BIBLE CALL THIS ANIMAL A FERRET, BUT LATER SCHOLARS BELIEVE "GECKO" IS THE CORRECT TRANSLATION.

DID YOU KNOW...

- The gecko gets its name from the peculiar sound it makes: "geck-oh, geck-oh, geck-oh."
- The gecko's feet are self-cleaning and will usually remove clogged dirt within a few steps.
- The gecko makes a good pet—if you like lizards, that is!

The design of the gecko's toes allows the lizard to cling to nearly any surface.

GNAT

Type of animal:
Insect
Find it in the Bible:
Matthew 23:24

WHAT'S THAT CLOUD OF SMOKE COMING AT ME?

A gnat is a tiny flying insect with two wings, jointed legs, large eyes, and long hairlike antennae. The body is often covered with soft hairlike strands. There are several species of gnats. Some gnats use their snout for piercing and sucking. The female gnat will bite and suck a tiny bit of blood, which she uses to feed her eggs.

Gnats are barely visible to the human eye, but some kinds of gnats leave a bite that stings and burns. The buffalo gnat, with its humpbacked appearance, can inflict painful bites on humans. Swarms of buffalo gnats have been known to kill farm animals with their bites. Most gnats are pests and cause damage to plants, especially flowering plants. Some gnat larva feed on the roots of potted flowering plants.

Gnats often come together in large groups called "swarms." They hang in the air like a cloud of smoke. The gnat usually lives alone, but during mating season, the males gather, especially at dusk, in large swarms called "ghosts." If a female approaches the ghost, one of the males will quickly approach her, and they will fly away together to mate. If the weather changes or a breeze blows, the ghost breaks up.

Some species of gnats fly at night, while others fly in the day, mainly in shaded areas. Still others attack in the bright sunlight.

The Old Testament writers knew about gnats and considered them pests. Because of the disease and damage the tiny insects can cause, many scholars identified the Egyptian plague as being gnats instead of lice, as is used in the King James Version (Exodus 8:16–19). David also wrote about the swarm of gnats God sent as a plague on Pharaoh and the Egyptian people (Psalm 105:31).

The fungus gnat is a pest because its larvae feed on plant roots and mushrooms.

THE THIRD PLAGUE

God had earlier sent Moses to ask Pharaoh to let His people, the Israelites, go free from slavery. He had sent the plague that changed the water into blood, but Pharaoh would not let the people go. God had sent the frogs that covered the land. Still Pharaoh said, "No!"

Again God sent Moses to Pharaoh. "If you do not let the people go, God will send a swarm of gnats," Moses warned Pharaoh.

So God sent the swarm of gnats to cover the land, the people, and the animals. But Pharaoh's heart was hardened and he would not listen to Moses.

See Exodus 8:16–19

Can you imagine being surrounded by millions of insects like this one that wanted to bite you? The people of Egypt found out just how that felt!

DID YOU KNOW. . .

- A swarm of gnats can include as many as a million individuals.
- The larvae of some species of gnats live in the water and provide food for aquatic life.
- A gnat flies in circles because its right and left wings are different sizes.
- Several tiny species of gnats are called "midges."

GOAT

A GOAT WILL NOT EAT A TIN CAN!

Type of animal:
Mammal

Find it in the Bible:
2 Chronicles 29:23

The goat is one of the oldest domesticated animals. The most common goat has long, floppy ears and is usually covered with long black hair. Some goats don't have horns, but different species have horns of various shapes and sizes. Both male and female have a wattle, a flap of skin that hangs from under their necks.

The goat is useful to humans in several ways. Goat's milk is used for drinking and for making butter and cheese. In some parts of the world, goat's meat is eaten. Also, the goat's intestines are used to make the strings on music instruments, and its horns are carved into spoons. Once or twice a year, farmers shear goats for the wool. Angora goats produce long, curling, glistening locks of

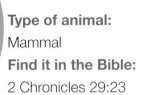

A WATTLE IS A FLAP OF SKIN HANGING FROM UNDER THE NECK.

mohair. Cashmere goats produce cashmere wool, which is a valuable natural fiber. Both are used to make clothing.

This pygmy goat has found the grass greener on the other side of the fence. And, no, he isn't looking for tin cans to eat!

Contrary to what many people think, goats don't like to eat tin cans, clothing, or garbage. They are actually very picky eaters when they are provided a well-balanced diet. The goat's four-chamber stomach breaks down any organic substance, providing the animal with the nutrients it needs.

Goats prefer to eat the tips of woody shrubs and trees. Sometimes they stand on their back feet to reach leaves on low tree branches. They also browse on grass and weeds, including certain plants that are poisonous to other animals. Goats can be very destructive to vegetation because they tear plants out of the soil by the roots when they eat. This can contribute to erosion.

A goat is a social animal. It is lively, curious, and independent. It explores anything new in its surroundings.

Sometimes it nibbles with its tongue and upper lip to check out items such as buttons or clothing made with plant or wood fibers.

The goat can easily be trained to pull carts and walk on a leash, but it is a great "escape artist." It can open gates and push down or climb over any weak fence. It can jump as high as five feet, so it is difficult to keep a goat in a penned area.

When the male goat, which is called a "buck," is ready to mate, he goes through a period called "rut." During this time, he has a decreased appetite, fights with other bucks, is obsessive with does, and gives off a strong, musky odor.

PEW! WHAT IS THAT STRONG SMELL?

The Bible mentions goats as being a hardy animal that can live nearly anywhere, even in the hot deserts of the Holy Land where there is very little plant life. A shepherd in biblical times treasured the goat because each doe provided him and his family with a gallon or more of milk each day. The goat's milk was also used to make cheese, yogurt, and butter. Each spring the shepherd cut the hair from their goats so it could be woven into water-resistant tents, cloaks, carpets, sacks, and even ropes. The hide was dried in the sun and then sewed into sandals and sturdy bags to hold water or wine. Goat meat was a source of food for the herder and his family.

Goats and sheep grazed in the same field. Many times the shepherd had to separate the herds because the male goats were sometimes hostile toward the sheep. The shepherd also kept the herd of goats moving so they wouldn't gobble up all the plants and pull the roots from the

If you ever get close enough to a goat, you might find he's more curious about you than you are about him!

ground. Vegetation would not grow back when the roots were destroyed. Since goats were sometimes stubborn and troublesome, the shepherd had to keep them from wandering away from the herd.

Male goats were used for sacrifices in the Old Testament. When Abraham received a covenant from God, the goat was among the animals he sacrificed to God (see Genesis 15:9). Samson's

GOAT

Like sheep, goats were important animals to people living in biblical times. Shepherds often cared for both sheep and goats.

parents sacrificed a goat to God as an angel talked to them about raising their son (see Judges 13:19).

In the Mosaic Law, a male goat without defect (meaning it was perfect in every way) was among the burnt offerings that Israelites were to sacrifice for their sins (Leviticus 4:24 and 16:15). The priests under King Hezekiah offered goats at the temple as a sin offering (2 Chronicles 29:23).

During Old Testament times, two goats were brought to the altar of God once a year on the Day of Atonement. One goat was dedicated and sacrificed to God. The priest laid his hands on the second goat and spoke the sins of the people. This goat was sent into the wilderness as a symbol of sending sin away from the people of God. That goat was called the "scapegoat."

DID YOU KNOW. . .

- The male goat is called a "billy" or "buck," the female is called a "doe" or "nanny," and the baby goat is called a "kid."
- A goat can go as long as two weeks without water.
- In certain circumstances, the goat has the ability to climb trees.
- A goat does not like to get wet and will seek shelter when it is raining.
- A goat's hooves are used to make gelatin.

GRASSHOPPER

Type of animal:	Find it in the Bible:
Insect	Numbers 13:33

HOW ABOUT
A CRUNCHY
CHOCOLATE
GRASSHOPPER?

The grasshopper is a common insect that feeds on plants. It has a slender body, powerful hind legs, short antennae, and two pairs of well-developed wings. Its narrow, leathery forewings have markings that help camouflage this insect. Its large hind wings are much thinner and can open out like fans, which help propel the grasshopper into flight. The grasshopper usually moves by jumping, but it flies when it needs to get somewhere fast or when it needs to escape predators.

The grasshopper uses its long, slender hind legs for jumping. If a predator grabs the grasshopper by a leg, it can shed its leg rather than being caught and eaten. A special lining quickly seals the wound so not much blood is lost. The grasshopper can still jump with only one hind leg.

WITH
LEGS LIKE
THOSE, THIS
GRASSHOPPER
SHOULD BE A
WORLD-CLASS
JUMPER!

The grasshopper has three ways to survive attacks from predators. It will hop or fly away when possible. Also, with its green or brown coloring, it can blend into its surroundings. Finally, it spits a smelly brown juice when it is threatened.

In some grasshopper species, the process of mating begins when the male attracts the female by rubbing his legs against his wings to make music. After mating, the female grasshopper drills a hole in the ground and lays her eggs, using a tube-like appendage called an "ovipositor." The eggs, which are laid in small pods that contain several dozen, stay in the ground during the winter and hatch in the spring.

When the young grasshoppers begin to hatch, they tunnel out of the ground and then begin to develop into adult grasshoppers. Grasshoppers live only a few months after they hatch. During their short lifetime, they eat, grow, reproduce, and then die. Since so many animals—including birds, reptiles, fish, and mammals—like to eat grasshoppers, many of them end up being someone else's dinner and never have the chance to reproduce.

Grasshoppers can be found just about anywhere they can find enough green plants to eat.

Can you see the green grasshopper hiding in the grass? Maybe a predator won't see him either!

DID YOU KNOW...

- The grasshopper can jump twenty times the length of its body.

- The young grasshopper does not have wings but develops them later as an adult.

- The grasshopper is of great value because it provides food for many people.

Grasshoppers are eating machines! In large numbers, they have been known to destroy entire crops of grass, alfalfa, clover, cotton, corn, and other valuable crops.

According to the Mosaic Law, grasshoppers are clean and can be eaten (Leviticus 11:21–22). Grasshoppers are also mentioned in the Bible in reference to their size. Ten of the twelve spies who went to check out Canaan saw themselves as grasshoppers when compared to the giant inhabitants of Canaan (see Numbers 13:26–33).

Type of animal:
Bird

Find it in the Bible:
Deuteronomy 14:15

GULL

WOW! LOOK AT THOSE BRIGHT PINK LEGS!

The gull, which is most often called a "seagull," is a seabird found along coasts. There are many kinds of gulls, but most of them have mainly white plumage with gray or black markings on the wings. The gull's wings, which help the bird soar through the air, are narrow and long, and its feet are webbed like a duck's for swimming. The gull has a bright orange spot on the lower part of its beak. The beak is powerful and has a hooked tip used for tearing up pieces of food and defending the bird against attackers. When a gull is resting, it folds its wings over its back.

While gulls are seabirds in nature, they are now often found inland, where they can scavenge through garbage dumps and other places to find leftover food that people discard. Gulls also often follow large ships at sea so they can find food by picking through waste thrown overboard.

Gulls will eat a wide variety of foods, but they prefer meat and fish. In the wild, they catch fish and other marine creatures—such as crustaceans and shellfish—that live in the water and along the shoreline.

Some gulls have learned a trick that helps them to eat the best tidbits from the marine creatures they catch. They drop hard-shelled clams and sea urchins onto hard surfaces to crack them open. In the winter, they drop mussels onto the ice to crack them.

Most gulls nest once a year in large, noisy colonies. After mating, the female lays two or three speckled eggs in her nest, which is built on the ground out of vegetation. The young are born with dark, mottled down instead of feathers. Mother gulls are known to be very protective of their eggs and babies.

The gull is listed in the Mosaic Law as an unclean bird, meaning the Israelites were not to eat it.

DID YOU KNOW. . .

- Some gulls build their nests on inland rooftops.

- Herring gulls have bright pink legs!

- Food gulls cannot digest, such as fish bones and crab claws, is spit out in pellets.

HAWK

WHAT WAS THAT STREAKING ACROSS THE SKY?

Type of animal:
Bird
Find it in the Bible:
Job 39:26

The hawk is a bird of prey (a meat eater that catches its own food) with short, rounded wings and a long tail—both of which it uses to fly swiftly. It has a hooked beak and sharp talon feet. It captures and kills its prey with its claws and then tears it apart with its beak.

There are many species of hawks, and they vary in their hunting habits. The marsh hawk uses its sense of hearing to listen for snakes and rodents as it silently flies low over marshlands. The crane hawk has double-jointed legs that can bend both backward and forward to catch small mammals sheltering in cracks of cliffs.

Seeing prey from the air, the northern goshawk folds its wings to its side, maneuvers with its long tail, and follows the prey through the trees and bushes. The red-shouldered hawk sits quietly on a low-lying perch, waiting and watching for prey, and then swoops down on it.

Different species of hawks have different mating habits. Red-tailed hawks, which mate for life, fly at great heights during courtship—up to two hundred feet. The male then does a steep dive toward the ground. He repeats this several times before he approaches the female from above to touch her or grasp her in midair.

The hawk is listed in the Mosaic Law as an unclean animal, which means Israelites were forbidden to eat it (Leviticus 11:16).

WHAT A CLOWN!

DID YOU KNOW. . .

- Some hawks can fly as fast as 150 miles per hour.
- A hawk's eyesight is eight times better than a human's eyesight.
- The male hawk brings food to the female while she sits on her nest, but she must catch it as he drops it from the air.

HEDGEHOG

Type of animal: Mammal

Find it in the Bible: Isaiah 14:23 RSV

WHAT A PRICKLY BALL!

The hedgehog has a sharp narrow snout, small eyes, and short legs. It has weak eyesight but has excellent hearing and smell. Its face, legs, tail, and belly are covered with fur, but its back and sides are covered with smooth spines.

The hedgehog's spines are hollow but not barbed like the porcupine's spines. The adult hedgehog loses its spines only when it is stressed or sick. Young hedgehogs shed their baby spines and grow adult spines in their place. This is called "quilling." The adult male hedgehog may have as many as five hundred spines.

Other than running away, the hedgehog's spines are its primary defense against predators. After first trying to run from a predator, the hedgehog rolls its body into a tight ball, causing the spines to point outward. That leaves the predator no place to catch hold or attack.

The hedgehog sleeps a large portion of the day under a bush, rock, or hole in the ground. It curls up in a ball as it sleeps. It awakens at night to hunt for frogs, lizards, bird eggs, worms, snails, and insects. It will also eat mushrooms, as well as berries and other fruit.

Hedgehogs aren't found in the wild in the United States, but people sometimes keep them as pets. They live in the wild in Europe, Asia, Africa, and New Zealand. They are valuable to humans because they eat large numbers of pests that are harmful to gardens.

The Bible mentions hedgehogs only twice. The prophets Isaiah (14:23) and Zephaniah (2:14 RSV) wrote of the hedgehog as living in a desolate place.

DID YOU KNOW. . .

- The hedgehog sometimes performs a ritual known as "anointing." When it comes upon a new scent, it will lick the source. Then the hedgehog will form a scented froth in its mouth and paste it on its spines with its long tongue.

- The baby hedgehog begins developing quills within an hour after it is born.

- The hedgehog gets its name "hedge" because it moves through hedges and "hog" because of its piglike snout.

233

HEN & CHICKS

THOSE LITTLE CHICKS ARE SO SOFT AND FLUFFY.

Type of animal:
Bird

Find it in the Bible:
Luke 13:34

The hen—the name for a female chicken—has a solid body, sturdy legs, soft feet, and a short, pointed beak. Her short wings are not useful for continuous flight, but smaller, lighter hens can fly (or glide) short distances over a fence or into a tree. The hen has a fleshy red growth on her head called a "comb."

If a hen is allowed to run free, she will eat grains, insects, worms, and other sources of food she finds. Domesticated hens, which are important sources of meat and eggs for humans, are usually fed prepared chicken feed.

Even though domesticated hens lay eggs just like any other hen, most of them won't sit on them until they hatch. Once they have laid their eggs, they leave them behind to be gathered up for food for people.

Hens that sit on their eggs until they hatch usually lay one egg a day until there are ten to twelve eggs in the nest. The hen then stops laying eggs and begins spending most of her time on the nest until the chicks are ready to hatch—usually three weeks.

Before an egg hatches, the hen hears the chick peeping from inside the egg. She will gently cluck to the chick, encouraging it to break out of the shell. The chick first pecks a breathing hole in the egg's shell. After resting a few hours, the chick pecks open the egg and crawls out. The chick is wet when it first hatches, but it dries quickly in the warmth of the nest.

The hen guards her chicks from predators and leads them to places where they can find water and food. She also takes them under her wings at night to keep them warm.

The hen and chicks are mentioned just two times in the Bible, but the birds must have been common in Palestine. In the New Testament, Jesus compared Himself to a mother hen as He grieved over the wayward city of Jerusalem. Just as a mother hen gathers her chicks under her wing to protect them, Jesus wanted to gather His people in Jerusalem and care for them and protect them (see Matthew 23:37).

DID YOU KNOW. . .

- The hen is a female chicken.
- A hen will usually live five to eleven years, depending on the breed.
- The world's oldest hen died of heart failure when she was sixteen years old.

Type of animal:

Bird

Find it in the Bible:

Deuteronomy 14:18

HERON

WHAT IS POWDER DOWN?

The heron is a medium- to large-sized wading bird with a long neck and legs. It has long, thin toes—three of which point forward and one backward—on its feet. It is a meat-eating bird that feeds around water, catching fish, amphibians, reptiles, crustaceans, mollusks, small birds, and aquatic insects.

The heron hunts by standing by the water and waiting to ambush unsuspecting prey. When a fish or frog comes along, the heron spears the victim with its long, sharp bill. It usually swallows the prey whole.

Some species of herons gather in groups or colonies and build bulky stick nests in trees, while others tend to nest in reed beds by the water.

The heron has a strangely shaped sixth vertebra in its neck, which allows it to kink its neck into an S-shape. Unlike other long-necked birds, such as the stork or ibis, the heron flies with its neck retracted instead of stretched out. It also holds its legs and feet backward when it flies.

The heron is the only species of wading bird that has powder down on its body. Powder down is a layer of fine feathers found under tougher exterior feathers. The young birds are clad in all down.

There are more than sixty species of herons, each with different feathers and plumage. The egret is a small member of the heron family with mainly white feathers and some decorative plumes. The great blue heron is a large bluish gray bird with a black plume extending from behind the eye to the back of the neck. The black night heron is small with a shorter neck than most herons. It has a black crown and back with a white or gray body and red eyes.

Nearly all known species of herons are found in the vicinity of Palestine. They are listed in the Mosaic Law as unclean birds.

DID YOU KNOW. . .

- The gray (or grey) heron has a wingspan of up to six feet.

- Pillows are sometimes made from the "powder down" of a heron.

- The heron makes a harsh croak and is quite vocal during mating season.

235

HOOPOE

WHAT IS THAT AWFUL SMELL?

Type of animal:
Bird

Find it in the Bible:
Leviticus 11:19 NIV

The hoopoe is a colorful bird found across Africa and Asia. It has a cinnamon-colored body and black and white wings. It has a crown of feathers on its head that rises when it eats. When the hoopoe is not feeding, the feathered crest is flat and tilted back. The adult hoopoe stands ten to twelve inches tall.

The hoopoe forages on the ground, looking for insects, small reptiles, and frogs to eat. When it finds an insect, it inserts its bill into the ground. The muscles of the head allow the hoopoe to open its long, thin, tapering black bill. The hoopoe uses its bill to pull the insect out of the ground, but it sometimes uses its strong feet to dig it out. Sometimes the hoopoe beats larger prey against the ground or a rock in order to kill it and to remove uneatable parts such as wings and legs. Occasionally it feeds in the air on swarming insects.

This bird builds its nest in hidden hollows and cracks of trees and rock crevices. The hoopoe is known for its terrible housekeeping. The nests are filthy and smell very bad. That is because the bird doesn't remove its dung from the nest and because the female releases a musty-smelling substance from her preen gland when she is disturbed. The smell helps keep predators away. When an enemy approaches the nest, even the young birds will lift their rears and shoot a load of stinking droppings into the enemy's face.

Mosaic Law lists the hoopoe as an unclean bird that is not to be eaten. Even though the bird is called a "hoopoe" in modern Bible translations, the name is uncertain. It is called a "lapwing" in the King James Bible and a "waterhen" and "woodcock" in other translations.

DID YOU KNOW...

- The hoopoe is an excellent runner.
- The hoopoe calls out, "Oop-oop-oop," during the mating season.
- The hoopoe enjoys taking dust and sand baths.

HORNET

Type of animal:
Insect

Find it in the Bible:
Exodus 23:28

OUCH! THAT STING HURTS!

The hornet is a type of wasp, a social insect (one that lives in colonies with others of its kind) known best for its ability to dish out painful stings. Depending on the species, a hornet can measure from half an inch long to over two inches long. The hornet has deeply indented, C-shaped eyes. The wings are reddish orange, and the abdomen is orange with a brown strip across its middle.

In spring, the queen hornet, who has already mated, builds a nest of chewed tree bark. She selects a dark sheltered place and builds a nest of individual hexagonal (six-sided) cells. The queen lays an egg in each cell. After five to eight days, the eggs hatch and become larvae. This first generation is made up of female workers who take over the queen's job of building nests and feeding the larvae.

At the end of the summer, the queen produces the first individuals capable of reproducing—both female and male. The males don't take part in nest building or repair or in the care of the larvae. Their only purpose is to mate with the queens during what are called "nuptial flights" and then die. The workers and the queens survive until late autumn when the workers die. Only the fertilized queens survive the winter. In the spring, they perform the same tasks their mothers did the year before.

Though the hornet's sting is painful—and sometimes dangerous—this insect is actually beneficial to humans because it helps keep the populations of some kinds of pests under control. Hornets hunt flies, wasps, bees, beetles, grasshoppers, caterpillars, and spiders.

Hornets are mentioned in the Old Testament as one of God's instruments for driving Israel's enemies out of Canaan (see Exodus 23:28).

DID YOU KNOW. . .

- Late in the summer, a hornet colony may include seven hundred workers.

- A hornet's sting is painful to humans, but some stings can cause dangerous allergic reactions.

- At more than two inches long, the Asian giant hornet, which has a dangerous sting, is the largest hornet species.

237

HORSE

Type of animal:
Mammal
Find it in the Bible:
Exodus 14:9

HOW MANY NAMES DOES A HORSE HAVE?

The horse is a solid-hoofed animal that is important to people in many ways. People use horses for pleasure riding, sports competitions, entertainment, police work, agriculture, and several other purposes. In the past, horses were a primary source of transportation and were also used in warfare.

With its well-developed sense of balance, the horse can walk, trot, canter, and gallop. The horse walks at about 4 miles per hour and gallops at average speeds of between 25 and 30 miles per hour.

The horse is a very intelligent, trainable animal that has five highly developed senses. The eyes are larger than any other land animal, giving the horse the ability to see in nearly all directions. It has excellent day-night vision. Horses can also see color, even though they distinguish colors differently than humans. The horse also has a keen sense of smell.

A young foal relaxes in the grass, knowing mom is nearby. Mother horses are very tender and very protective of their young.

The horse's tail is important for several reasons. Not only is it used to swat flies, but also to keep the horse's "behind" warm during cold weather. Horses also use their tails to signal each other about how they are feeling.

Horses are plant eaters with digestive systems designed to handle grasses and grains. Horses have relatively small stomachs, so they must eat steadily throughout the day. A horse weighing around 950 pounds eats around 24 pounds of food and drinks about eight gallons of water each day. Horses do not "chew the cud" like cattle.

A male horse is called a "stallion," and a female is called a "mare." A father horse is called a "sire," and a mother horse is called a "dam." A horse just born is called a "foal." A boy foal is a "colt," and a girl foal is called a "filly."

There are currently about three hundred different breeds of horses. The different breeds of horses are identified through the color of their hair and skin, through their size, and through their physical abilities, such as strength and speed.

The average life span of a horse is about twenty-five to thirty years. "Old Billy," a horse that lived in England, was the oldest recorded horse on record—sixty-two years!

Horses are mentioned many times in the Bible. In Old Testament times, horses pulled chariots. Pharaoh and his men rode in chariots as they pursued the Israelites during the time of the Exodus. In later years, Egypt was the main source for the supply of horses used by the kings of Israel.

In biblical times, the horse was a "weapon" of war and stood for power. David made reference to using horses in battle. In his victory over the king of Zobah, David captured the chariots and let the horses go free. He kept a hundred of the horses for use in battle on the flat ground of his country (see 2 Samuel 8:1–4).

King Solomon gained a great supply of horses through his trade with Egypt. He built stables with stalls for the horses. Solomon established a very active trade in horses he imported from Egypt and resold to make a profit. An imported chariot cost six hundred shekels of silver, and a horse cost one hundred fifty shekels (see 1 Kings 10:29).

Kings or men of wealth or position were the main users of horse-drawn chariots. They rode in chariots covered with embroidered trappings or paraded around in royal robes on their decorated horses.

Though horses and chariots were used for war in biblical times, today they are used for sport and recreation.

DID YOU KNOW. . .

- A horse can sleep both standing up and lying down.
- Most foals are born at night when there is less activity.
- When a horse is born, its legs are almost their full adult length.
- Horses like calm or cheerful music, but loud music makes them uneasy.

HYENA

WHO IS THAT LAUGHING?

Type of animal:
Mammal
Find it in the Bible:
1 Samuel 13:18 MSG

The hyena is a hunter and scavenger with a broad head, large eyes, and pointed ears. The hyena's front legs are longer than the rear ones, so it walks and runs awkwardly. The mane on the back of its neck is long and stands erect when the animal is frightened.

The hyena's coat coloring depends on the species. The aardwolf, striped hyena, and brown hyena all have striped pelts. The spotted hyena's fur is shorter and spotted instead of striped.

The hyena uses its bushy tail to communicate with other hyenas. The hyena holds its tail high when it is ready to attack. It holds its tail over its back when it is excited but tucks it between its back legs when it is frightened.

Hyenas also communicate with wailing calls and howling screams. The spotted hyena makes a haunting laughterlike call much like the laughter of a human. This call can be heard from as far away as three miles.

INSTEAD OF "VALLEY OF HYENAS," THE KING JAMES VERSION AND NEW INTERNATIONAL VERSION OF THE BIBLE USE THE TITLE "VALLEY OF ZEBOIM" IN 1 SAMUEL 13:18.

Most hyenas hunt in packs and run their prey down by exhaustion. Hyenas also eat the "leftovers" of dead animals killed by other predators.

The hyena's jaws are very strong. The animal's amazing digestive system allows it to eat and digest the entire prey—skin, teeth, horns, hooves, and bones. The only part it cannot digest is the hair. It coughs up the hair, which is known as a "hyena hair ball."

Hyenas are mentioned several times in The Message paraphrase of the Bible. First Samuel 13:18 mentions the Valley of Hyenas. It is assumed the valley was named for the animal that resided there. Hyenas are also mentioned in the same paraphrase in Isaiah 13:22 and 34:14 and in Jeremiah 15:3.

The hyena was regarded as a repulsive creature because it sometimes dug up dead bodies in Palestine.

DID YOU KNOW...

- The spotted hyena, which is mostly a predator, is also known as the "laughing hyena."

- The hyena can go for several days without water.

- The hyena can be dangerous to people and very destructive.

Type of animal:
Mammal

Find it in the Bible:
Deuteronomy 14:5

IBEX

THOSE HORNS ARE BIGGER THAN THE IBEX!

The ibex is a type of wild mountain goat. It has a heavy, stocky body and short, sturdy legs. The male ibex has a long pointed beard and a dark brown coat with a black stripe down its back and up the front of each foreleg. It has extremely large horns for its size. The horns sweep upward and backward in a semicircular direction and have knobby ridges across the outer surface of the curve. The female has a tan coat and smaller, thinner, straighter horns.

The ibex has a unique hoof structure that makes it an excellent climber on steep rocks and rocky ledges. Its even-toed hooves have hard edges and soft rubbery centers, which give the ibex a good grip on slippery rocks. Being able to climb to great heights helps protect the ibex from predators, because it can't be followed by other animals.

With keen sight and smell, the ibex is alert to any danger. It uses its horns as defense against predators. If the ibex senses danger, it raises its hind legs and points its horns toward the predator.

The Nubian ibex is the only species that adapts to the desert conditions of Bible lands. In fact, this animal is still found in the mountainous areas of Israel, Jordan, Saudi Arabia, Egypt, Yemen, and Sudan. The adult Nubian ibex stands about two feet tall at the shoulder and weights about 110 pounds. Its pale, shiny coat reflects sun rays and keeps it cool, even in the hot afternoon sun. It is active during the day and rests at night in the high sloping areas.

IN SOME BIBLE TRANSLATIONS, "WILD GOAT" IS USED INSTEAD OF "IBEX." BIBLE VERSES IN WHICH "WILD GOAT" IS USED ARE 1 SAMUEL 24:2 AND PSALM 104:18. IN THE KING JAMES VERSION, DEUTERONOMY 14:5 USES "PYGARG" INSTEAD OF "IBEX."

DID YOU KNOW. . .

- When it rains, the ibex does all it can to avoid getting wet.

- The ibex stands on its hind legs to reach leaves in trees.

- The ibex receives help in grooming from the birds called "grackles," which pick parasites from its fur coat.

JACKAL

THE JACKAL IS A HOWLER!

Type of animal:
Mammal

Find it in the Bible:
Psalm 63:10

The jackal is a cunning and resourceful animal that belongs to the same family of animals that includes wolves, foxes, coyotes, and domestic dogs. In fact, the jackal looks a little like a coyote and a little like a fox.

The jackal has long, slender legs, a pointed muzzle, and big feet that give it the ability to run very fast—up to 10 miles per hour for an extended period of time. The most common coat is sandy yellow to pale gold with brown-tipped hair.

The common jackal lives in the open deserts and grasslands of Africa, Asia, and southeastern Europe. It lives in a social unit, which usually consists of a family. They work together to defend their territory against enemies—including other jackal families. They spend the day in holes or hidden brush and hunt at night.

Jackals usually hunt alone or in pairs. They are perfectly designed to hunt small mammals, birds, and reptiles. Occasionally they assemble in packs to bring down larger animals, such as antelope. Sometimes they feed from carcasses other predators leave behind after they have eaten their fill.

The jackal is a noisy animal, especially at night. Each family has a distinct howl. It starts as a high-pitched, long, drawn-out cry that is repeated several times. Each time the howl is moved to a higher pitch than before. Then there are several short, loud, yelping barks. Often when one jackal raises the cry, others join in.

Most of the biblical references to jackals connect them with desert ruins. For a city or nation to be made a "den of jackals" is for it to be destroyed (see Jeremiah 9:11, 10:22 NKJV). Farmers and herdsmen found the jackal to be a pest, as it destroyed crops and vineyards and often attacked livestock.

DID YOU KNOW. . .

- The golden jackal is the largest and most common of all jackal species.

- Jackal family members communicate with each other by screaming yells.

- The jackal can hunt prey four to five times its own body weight.

KATYDID

Type of animal:
Insect

Find it in the Bible:
Leviticus 11:22 NIV

THAT KATYDID LOOKS LIKE A HALF-EATEN LEAF!

The katydid is a large, winged insect that is often referred to as the long-horned grasshopper because of the length of its antennae. But the katydid is more closely related to the cricket than the grasshopper. It has long, powerful hind legs, which it uses for jumping. The wings are filmy and extend past the body. It has long threadlike antennae that run above its back and curl under its bottom.

There are about sixty-four hundred known species of katydids living in the world today. Most have two pairs of long wings, but some are wingless. Those with wings are poor flyers. Many do not fly but flutter their wings during long leaps.

The katydid can be heard on a warm summer night as the male courts the female with a song, "Katydid-katydidn't-katydid." The female responds with her own call. To make the musical sound, the insect rubs its forewings, one of which is ridged, together. It sounds much like a violin and bow playing. Each species of katydid has its own distinctive call.

Katydids are usually green, but a few are brown. Some are even pink! The green coloring helps hide them from birds and other predators during the day. They can also match the appearance of their surroundings. The leaf katydid can look like a partially eaten or disfigured leaf. The angle-winged katydid has a flattened, humped back with wings that resemble large leaves.

Most katydids feed on leaves, flowers, bark, and seeds, which makes them pests to commercial farmers. Some katydids, however, feed on other insects, snails, and small reptiles.

The katydid is listed in the Mosaic Law as a clean animal because it is an animal that jumps on the ground.

DID YOU KNOW. . .

- The katydid hears through organs on its legs called "tympana."
- Both male and female katydids can produce sounds when they feel stressed.
- The fork-tailed bush katydid often licks its feet to clean its adhesive pads.

KITE

LOOK! A KITE. . .NO IT'S A BIRD!

Type of animal:
Bird
Find it in the Bible:
Leviticus 11:14

The kite is a keen-sighted bird of prey belonging to the same family of birds as the hawk and eagle. It has a small head, short beak, narrow wings, and a forked tail. There are two species of kites—the red kite and the black kite. The difference between these two birds is, obviously, the color, as well as the tail. The red kite's fork is more deeply split than that of its black cousin.

The kite is a graceful flyer with amazing maneuverability. To gain height, the kite flexes its wings and twists its long tail from side to side to use air currents to their fullest. It is capable of fast swoops and twisting dives. In flight the kite flaps once, and then it glides for a long distance before flapping again. While gliding, it tucks its wings behind it to create minimal air resistance so that it seems to float in midair.

The kite is both a predator and a scavenger. It eats mostly small mammals, such as mice, shrews, and young hares and rabbits. It will also occasionally eat reptiles, amphibians, and other birds. This bird is useful as a scavenger because it cleans up dead carcasses left by other predators. The black kite is attracted to fires and smoke, where it swoops down on escaping prey.

MY, WHAT YOU'LL FIND IN A KITE'S NEST!

A kite builds a large, sloppy-looking nest, usually in a fork high in a tree. It is quite a hoarder. It picks up artifacts along its travels and adds them to the nest—anything from cellophane bags to keys. It lines its nest with grass or other vegetation and sometimes sheep's wool.

The Mosaic Law forbade the eating of kites by the Israelites. In the King James Version, the word glede—another name for the kite—is used (see Deuteronomy 14:13).

DID YOU KNOW. . .

- The kite's cry sounds like a high-pitched mewing.

- The kite's tail looks almost like streamers or the tail of a child's kite when the bird is in motion.

- The kite can be a hazard to airplanes taking off at airports.

LAPWING

Type of animal:
Bird

Find it in the Bible:
Deuteronomy 14:18 KJV

WHAT'S THAT NOISE I HEAR?

The lapwing is a medium-sized inland shore bird with a body mainly of black and white coloring. A long, greenish black wispy crest extends from the back of the head, turning up at the end.

The lapwing gets its name from the lapping sound of the wings as it flies. The rounded wings have a slow wing beat and give the bird an uneven, flopping flight.

The lapwing is found in wetlands and coastal pastures with short grass. During mating season, the male lapwing announces his presence to potential mates by wobbling, zigzagging, rolling, and diving in flight.

The lapwing builds its nest and lays its eggs on the ground in shallow hollows of open meadows. The nest needs to be close to bare, damp ground where young birds can feed. It also needs to be in rough or well-planted ground to help hide it from predators. The female lays four eggs, which hatch in three or four weeks. The chicks are covered in down when they hatch, and the parents quickly lead them to places where they can find food.

The lapwing is very protective of its young. When a predator is near, the bird will pretend to have a broken wing, drawing the predators away from the young birds.

The lapwing has a shrill, catlike cry, "Pee-wit, wit, wit-eeze, wit." The call can be heard along the shores and meadows, especially during mating season and when the bird defends its young against predators.

The lapwing is listed in the Mosaic Law as an unclean bird, which means the Israelites were not to eat it. The bird is called a "hoopoe" in some modern Bible translations.

DID YOU KNOW. . .

- Other names for the northern lapwing are "peewit" and "green plover."
- The lapwing's throat is black in the summer and white in winter.
- The lapwing's eggs were once prized and were gathered and sold as food.

LEECH

YUCK! A BLOODSUCKER!

Type of animal:
Annelid
Find it in the Bible:
Proverbs 30:15

The leech is an annelid, a type of worm that lives in wet places. It has a long, flattened body that is soft but tough and is usually black or brown. One end contains a head with two to ten eyes and a mouth. The leech's body is made up of thirty-four segments with a large disk-shaped sucker on the last few segments.

There are hundreds of species of leeches. Some live in freshwater, some in saltwater, and some in moist ground. All leeches are carnivorous. Some eat prey such as worms, insects, and snails, which they swallow whole. Other leeches feed on blood from animals and sometimes from humans. These blood eaters have suckers they use to attach themselves to a host (the source of the blood they eat). They use mucus and suction to stay attached to the host, and they squirt an anti-clotting enzyme called "hirudin" into the host's bloodstream. They stay attached until they are full and then fall off to begin digesting their meal.

The leech is equipped with a "crop," which is a type of stomach it uses to store its food. The crop allows the leech to store blood in volumes up to five times its body size.

Many kinds of animals—including several species of fish—like to eat leeches. The leech hides from predators in thick plant growth or mud. If attacked, it tries to swim away fast or go limp and play dead. The leech may also curl into a ball and sink to the bottom of the water.

The leech is mentioned only once in the Bible. Perhaps the writer of Proverbs 30 referred to the leech as having a greedy appetite when he wrote, "The leech has two daughters 'Give! Give!' they cry" (Proverbs 30:15 NIV).

DID YOU KNOW. . .

- The smallest leech is about one-half inch long, and the largest leech is about twelve inches long.
- Some nonsucking leeches can swallow an earthworm whole.
- Most leeches live in the sea, but some live in freshwater and some on land.

LEOPARD

Type of animal:	Find it in the Bible:
Mammal	Jeremiah 13:23

IS THAT A PURR I HEAR FROM THE LEOPARD?

The leopard is a member of the cat family. Leopards are found in Africa and parts of Asia. They live in forests, mountains, and flat grasslands.

The leopard has short legs, a long body, and a large skull. The animal comes in a variety of coat colors, from light buff or yellowish brown to darker shades, even black. The patterned spots, which are called "rosettes," are circular or square depending on the region where the leopard lives. Even the long tail has rosettes. The spots help it hide from other animals and help camouflage it when stalking its prey.

The fully grown leopard stands up to two and a half feet tall at the shoulder and measures three to six feet long. The tail is two to three and a half feet long. Male leopards weigh up to two hundred pounds, but the females are slightly smaller.

The leopard has a keen sense of smell that helps it in hunting for food. It stalks its prey by slinking through the grass or bush. It keeps its head low, legs bent, and belly nearly touching the ground until it is close enough to pounce on the prey. When it does pounce, it bites through the back of the neck, damaging the spinal cord of the prey. Then it strangles the victim.

The leopard's coat is partly made up of patterned spots. . . and no two leopards' spots are exactly the same!

The leopard is not a picky eater. If a deer, antelope, wildebeest, or other large animal can't be found, the leopard will make due with a meal of small animals— even as small as birds or rodents. The cat is a powerful swimmer and is at home in and near the water. It sometimes eats fish or crabs.

The leopard has an amazing method of protecting its food from other animals. Rather than let a hungry lion or other animal steal its meal, the leopard will carry its prey up into the branches of a tree. A leopard's jaws are strong. It can carry animals up to three times its own weight.

The leopard will announce its presence with a raspy cough that sounds like a buzz saw. It also growls and spits with a screaming roar of fury when angry, but it

This leopard is taking a nap in one of its favorite places to be: up a tree!

purrs like a kitten when it is content.

The leopard spends much of its day sleeping in trees, underneath rocks, or in the tall grass. In the evening, it descends from the tree headfirst to hunt until dawn.

The word *leopard* appears several times in the Bible, which means the writers must have been familiar with the cat. Leopards would have lived in biblical lands in the surrounding forests, grasslands, and even deserts. Since leopards are meat-eating animals, herdsmen of sheep, cattle, and goats would have been fearful of them. When the Bible refers to a leopard, it's mostly as a symbol to help teach a lesson.

Jeremiah used the leopard in his preaching. He asked the people, "Can. . .the leopard [change] its spots?" (13:23 NIV). This was to remind them that they had done wrong things for so long that it would be hard for them to change.

Hosea reminded the people of Israel that God was angry with them because they had forgotten Him: "I will come upon them like a lion, like a leopard I will lurk by the path" (Hosea 13:7 NIV).

In another Bible passage, the leopard is used to show what God's kingdom will be like once Christ returns to earth. The prophet Isaiah wrote that wolves will live with lambs, and leopards will lie down to rest with goats. Cows and oxen will eat with bears and lions. All will be at peace with one another (see Isaiah 11:6).

WOW! THERE WILL BE ANIMALS IN HEAVEN!

DID YOU KNOW. . .

- Leopards are solitary animals that like to live and hunt alone.
- Like human fingerprints, no two leopards' markings, spots, or coloring are alike.
- Leopards can run up to 35 miles per hour.
- Leopards are the only "big cats" that carry their prey up a tree.

LEVIATHAN

WHAT A SEA MONSTER!

Type of animal:
Reptile?

Find it in the Bible:
Job 41:1

The leviathan is a mysterious biblical creature, because no animal currently living on earth fits its description. Scholars have debated whether the animal is a crocodile or a whale—or perhaps some type of dinosaur. The facts about the leviathan are written in Job 41:

- The leviathan cannot be caught with a fishhook (vv. 1–2).
- Its mouth has a ring of fierce teeth (v. 14).
- Its back has rows of shields (v. 15).
- Sparks of fire shoot out of its mouth, and its eyes glow like the morning sun (vv. 18–19).
- Smoke comes out of its nostrils like steam (v. 20).
- Its strength is in its neck, and the chest is hard as rock (vv. 22, 24).
- It rises up and causes fear (v. 25).
- It cannot be killed with a spear (v. 26).
- Its underside is sharp and leaves a trail in the mud (v. 30).
- It is a powerful and ferocious creature without fear (v. 33).

Could the leviathan have been a large crocodile? The crocodile has fierce teeth and scales, but an arrow can do much damage to it. Its eyes rise out of the water before the rest of the head, which could fit the description in Job 41:19. The crocodile cannot rise far from the water or ground. The underside of the crocodile is smooth, not sharp, leaving a trail in the mud. The crocodile does not swim deep in the water, stirring it up. No fire shoots from its mouth. Even though many fear the crocodile, this creature does not completely fit the description of the leviathan given in the Bible.

The whale is even less likely to fit the description, even though it can sink deep into the water and surface shooting a stream of water. A spear or harpoon can certainly kill or injure the whale.

Was the leviathan a crocodile or whale, or was it some mythical sea creature—as some

LEVIATHAN

scholars think? God's description of the leviathan seems to describe a dinosaur-like, water-living reptile that terrorized the waters during Job's lifetime. The leviathan was among the "real" creatures that Job knew about and that God spoke about as being made along with man.

One sea creature that might match the description of the leviathan is the kronosaurus, an animal from the family of the plesiosaurs. This sea monster was not a true dinosaur (meaning an animal that lived only on land) but a marine reptile. It could reach lengths of thirty feet and had a head six to ten feet long. It had a short, stocky neck with a large head with powerful jaws and a mouthful of sharp teeth. The teeth are believed to have been able to crack the shells of animals such as turtles.

The leviathan could have been any number of creatures—some of which are now extinct. But what exactly it was remains a mystery.

DID YOU KNOW...

- The leviathan was the greatest creature in the sea, and nothing on earth was its equal.

- Job 41 includes amazing details about a creature called the "leviathan."

- Scientists have found pieces of turtle shells inside the stomach cavities of a fossilized kronosaurus, proving the power of the jaws and sharp teeth.

This is an artist's drawing of an extinct sea creature called a kronosaurus. Could this be the leviathan mentioned in the Book of Job?

Type of animal:
Mammal
Find it in the Bible:
Daniel 6:22

LION

MY, WHAT
BIG TEETH
YOU HAVE!

The lion is the tallest and most powerful of the "big cats." It is covered with yellowish brown fur and has a long tail ending with a tuft of black hair.

You can tell a male and female lion apart just by looking at their physical differences. The male has a large, flowing mane that gives him a regal appearance and makes him look bigger, which is helpful during confrontations with other male lions. The female, which is called a "lioness," is much smaller than the male. A full-grown male lion usually weighs between 350 and 550 pounds, while the lioness weighs between 260 and 400 pounds.

Lions live in groups called "prides." There are usually one to four males in a pride, but there are many lionesses and cubs. A lioness stays in one pride all her life, but a male lion stays for just a few years. Eventually a younger, stronger male lion will drive it out of the pride. The male lions usually stay on the fringes of the pride's area, keeping an eye out for intruders.

The pride normally hunts at night. The lionesses do most of the hunting. Lions have powerful forelegs, strong jaws, and long canine teeth that help them hunt and kill their prey.

Lions don't usually do much during the day. . . other than lying around napping and waiting until it gets dark outside.

They prefer to hunt larger animals so the whole pride can eat.

The lion spends much of its time resting and is inactive for about sixteen to twenty hours of the day. Its peak activity is after dusk, with a period of socializing and grooming. The lion communicates by head rubbing—nuzzling its forehead, face, and neck against another lion. This appears to be a form of greeting.

Lions are now found in the wild in sub-Saharan Africa, in parts of Asia, and in northwest India. They used to be found in North Africa, the Middle East, and Western Asia but have disappeared from those areas in recent decades.

During biblical times, lions made their lairs in the forests, mountain caves, and canebrakes on the banks of the Jordan River. The lions were not only a danger to shepherds watching their sheep in the fields, but they often lay along roadsides waiting to attack people.

Several biblical stories mention lions. Here are a few of them:

DANIEL IN THE LIONS' DEN

This is an artist's painting of the prophet Daniel in the lion's den. Even with all those hungry lions around him, Daniel was safe!

In Old Testament times, lions were used as punishment for disobeying the orders of kings. Daniel 6 tells the story of King Darius being tricked into throwing Daniel into a den of lions because he refused to worship the king. But the following morning, Darius ran to the mouth of the den to find that Daniel's God had kept him safe—even though he had just spent the night in a pit filled with hungry lions!

DAVID'S BATTLE WITH A LION

A lion also played a part in the story of David's historic battle with the giant Philistine warrior named Goliath. When David was a young boy, he watched the sheep in his father's fields. He carried a stick to protect his sheep from wild animals. On more than one occasion, he had to kill a lion with the stick when it tried to steal one of his sheep.

Later, as David tried to persuade King Saul to let him fight Goliath, he said to the king, "Your servant has been keeping his father's sheep. When a lion or a bear came and carried off a sheep from the flock, I went after it, struck it and rescued the sheep from its mouth. When it turned on me, I seized it by its hair, struck it and killed it. . . . The Lord who delivered me from the paw of the lion and the paw of the bear will deliver me from the hand of this Philistine"

See 1 Samuel 17:34–35, 37 NIV

OTHER BIBLE PASSAGES THAT MENTION LIONS INCLUDE JUDGES 14; 2 SAMUEL 17:10; PSALM 17:12; AND 1 PETER 5:8.

DID YOU KNOW. . .

- Even though the lion is called "king of the jungle," lions don't actually live in jungles.
- A lion can run as fast as 50 miles per hour.
- A lion's roar can be heard from up to five miles away.
- A large male lion can eat sixty-six pounds of food at one time.
- Male lions are the only members of the cat family with a mane.
- "Lion tamers"—people who train lions to perform in shows—usually have a college education in zoology or veterinary medicine.

LIZARD

Type of animal:
Reptile
Find it in the Bible:
Proverbs 30:28 NIV

WOW! LOOK AT THAT DRAGON!

The lizard is a long-bodied reptile that lives everywhere in the world except Antarctica. There are nearly thirty-eight hundred known species of lizards. Most lizards have two sets of short legs and long tails. A few species, however, don't have legs and look more like snakes than lizards. Some lizards have short tails. The lizard's skin is covered in scales, which helps protect the animal from injury.

Like other reptiles, the lizard is a cold-blooded animal. That means it cannot control its body temperature like warm-blooded creatures (birds and mammals) can. Because lizards are cold-blooded, most of them live in warm climates. Because lizards are unable to produce their own body heat, they need the sun's heat to warm their bodies. On very hot days, lizards must sometimes find shade, because most of them can't survive if their body temperature goes too high. To escape the scorching midday sun of the desert, lizards burrow below the surface of the sun-baked sand where the temperatures are cooler.

Lizards can be found in almost every color, from black to bright orange to metallic blue to a mixture of colors and patterns. Some species can turn many different colors and patterns according to their emotions and surroundings. Lizards use colors to blend into their surroundings for protection from their enemies. They also rely on body language, using specific postures and movements to protect their territory.

The lizard's tail is one of its most interesting and useful features. For some lizards, the tail almost

This animal looks like a snake, but it's actually a lizard—a California legless lizard. No kidding!

The emerald basilisk is sometimes called the "Jesus lizard" because it can walk on water!

serves as a fifth leg. It aids in balance and helps those that run upright on their hind legs to attain great speed. One type of lizard—the basilisk lizard—uses its hind legs and tail to skim over water so quickly that it never gets wet! Some lizards have the ability to wind their tails around tree branches when climbing. And others can scale walls and ceilings of buildings.

The lizard's tail is also important in self-defense. Some lizards have sharp, spine-covered tails, which they use as weapons to lash at their enemies. Others can shed their tails when a predator tries to catch and eat them. The severed tail continues to jump around, distracting the enemy while the lizard makes its escape. The lizard then grows a new tail within a few months. When food is scarce, the lizard will sometimes eat its own tail!

Most lizards are meat eaters that like to dine on insects and other prey. They use their small, sharp teeth to grab and hold the catch while the jaws make a series of quick snapping movements over the animal. Many lizards swallow their prey whole.

Most lizards spend their time on land, but some are strong swimmers. For example, the marine iguana spends nearly all its time in the water, where it feeds on saltwater algae. Also, the Nile monitor lizard spends a lot of its time in the water, where it feeds on fish, snails, frogs, crocodile eggs, baby crocodiles, snakes, and other foods it can find.

There are several different kinds of lizards mentioned in the Bible. All of them are listed in the Mosaic Law as unclean.

FIND THE DIFFERENT KINDS OF LIZARDS IN LEVITICUS 11:30.

255

LOCUST

WOW—AN ARMY OF LOCUSTS!

Type of animal:
Insect

Find it in the Bible:
Deuteronomy 28:38

The locust is a kind of grasshopper that gathers in swarms—sometimes huge ones—and travels great distances and causes terrible damage to crops. There are several species of locusts. The desert locust has caused awful damage to crops to the Middle East, Asia, and Africa for centuries. The adult brown locust is about three inches long and has powerful hind legs that help it jump great lengths.

When this powerful jumper is ready to leap, it folds its hind legs up and tucks its feet underneath its body. The legs are held in this position by a special catch inside the knee joint. As the leg muscles contract, the catch on the knee is opened. The leg straightens out with a kick and launches the locust into the air.

Young locusts cannot fly but can hop long distances in search of food. As a locust grows, it sheds its skin. It clings to a twig, and the old skin splits down the back. The locust pulls free, leaving the empty skin. It hops around the ground with millions of other locusts, molting and searching for food. As it grows, it sheds its skin six times. At the final molting of the skin, the locust has fully working wings and can fly well.

Locusts gather together in swarms in search of food. The swarms are sometimes so dense that the sky is darkened. The swarm can strip a field bare of green vegetation in a couple of hours.

According to Mosaic Law, locusts are considered a clean food for the Israelites to eat. The eating of locusts is mentioned in the New Testament—John the Baptist ate locusts and wild honey in the wilderness (see Mark 1:6).

One locust isn't a problem, but when they get together in swarms, look out!

A PLAGUE OF LOCUSTS

The Old Testament book of Exodus tells how a swarm of locusts devastated the nation of Egypt when Pharaoh refused to let the Israelites leave their lives of slavery and travel to their own land.

God had sent Moses to Pharaoh to tell him to free the Israelites, but Pharaoh refused. God had sent seven plagues, but still Pharaoh would not let the Israelites go. So God told Moses, "Go to Pharaoh and tell him that I will send locusts to cover the ground." Again, the stubborn Pharaoh said, "No, I will not let the people go."

So God told Moses to stretch out his staff. When he did so, the wind blew in the swarm of locusts and they covered the ground. They ate everything that was left after the other plagues. They even moved into the Egyptians' houses and ate the food there.

This locust was photographed in 1915, during a locust plague in the Bible lands.

Pharaoh sent for Moses and then told him, "Tell your God to take the locusts away."

Read Exodus 10:18–20 to see what happened.

DID YOU KNOW. . .

- A locust can jump more than forty times its body length.
- A single locust can eat its own weight in grass and leaves each day.
- In 1874 a swarm of locusts estimated to cover 198,000 square miles and numbering 12.5 trillion insects was recorded.
- The desert locust can fly as fast as 20 miles per hour.

LOUSE

Type of animal:
Insect
Find it in the Bible:
Exodus 8:17 KJV

> I WANT TO SCRATCH WHEN I THINK ABOUT LICE!

Lice (the plural for louse) are tiny wingless insects with short legs, flattened bodies, and antennae on their heads. Lice are no larger than a sesame seed.

There are more than three thousand known species of lice, and they make their homes on the bodies of nearly every bird and mammal known to man. Most of them are scavengers that feed on dead skin and other debris found on their hosts' bodies, but some of them feed on blood and other bodily fluids.

Some lice have hook-shaped claws and six strong legs that cling to the hair of the animals they live on and feed from. They use three slender needlelike mouthparts to pierce the skin. These lice feed on blood several times a day.

Most lice are not dangerous to human health, but they can spread from person to person quickly and can be very annoying. They cannot jump or fly. They are spread through close contact with a person or through shared items such as a hat or hairbrush. Lice attach themselves to hair and snuggle close to the scalp where it is dark and warm. When they get hungry, they crawl down, poke a hole in the skin, and take a sip of blood. The bite usually causes the skin to itch.

Female lice lay eggs on strands of hair. They fasten the eggs in place with a liquid that sets like superhard glue. When the young lice are ready to hatch, the top of the eggs come off and the baby lice squeeze their way out.

Lice are mentioned in the King James Bible in two places. Exodus 8:17 recounts the third Egyptian plague, when God sent lice to Pharaoh and the people of Egypt. In Psalm 105:31, David recounts the story of Moses and the plague of lice. Many newer Bible translations use the word gnats in place of lice.

DID YOU KNOW...

- Lice cannot jump or fly.
- The egg of the louse is called a "nit."
- Some biting lice feed on the feathers and skin of poultry, pigeons, and other birds.

MAGGOT

Type of animal: Insect (Larvae)

Find it in the Bible: Exodus 16:20

IT'S HARD TO BELIEVE THESE ARE USEFUL!

Maggots are the larvae of insects, especially those of flies. They are the soft-bodied, legless grubs that are the middle stage in the lives of some insects. Their parents lay their eggs in rotting organic matter—and that's what they feed on!

Although maggots are repulsive, both in looks and in what they eat and where they grow, they are very useful in the medical world. Believe it or not, many doctors use them today to treat flesh wounds that are stubborn to heal. The maggots eat away the damaged tissue, which helps the wound heal.

Maggots are mentioned in the Bible in reference to death (see Isaiah 14:11) and to the low place of humans when compared with God (see Job 25:6).

MANNA-EATING MAGGOTS

After God set the Israelites free from Egyptian bondage and slavery, Moses led them into the wilderness. After their food and water were gone, they began to complain because they were hungry. Moses prayed and asked God to provide food for the people.

God sent the people manna, which was small round flakes, each morning with the dew. His only limitation on eating the manna was, "Gather only what you will need for the day. Don't save any for future days."

The next day, God left manna for the people. Some of the people did not believe God would supply their needs for later days, so they saved more than they needed for the day. The following morning, the saved manna was full of maggots and smelled very bad.

See Exodus 16:11–20

DID YOU KNOW. . .

- Maggots hatch from eggs within twenty-four hours after the female fly lays them.

- Maggots are usually found near or in garbage, dead animals, and rotting food.

- Some fishermen use maggots as bait.

259

MOLE

DOES A MOLE HAVE EYES?

Type of animal:
Mammal
Find it in the Bible:
Leviticus 11:30 KJV

A mole is an animal that looks like it is closely related to rodents like mice. But moles aren't rodents at all but part of a family of animals known for eating large numbers of insects.

The mole's round body is covered with gray-black fur. It has a short tail, a long snout, and tiny eyes that are hard to see because they are obscured by hair on the animal's face. Moles burrow through soft, sandy soil with their long, sharp front claws. They eat bugs and earthworms that live underground.

The mole's tunnel includes a special underground compartment called a "mole larder," which it uses to store food to eat later. Since the mole's saliva contains a toxin that paralyzes earthworms, it can store the prey for later eating.

Most moles burrow underground. A few species spend part of their lives in water. The star-nosed mole is a good swimmer and forages along the bottom of streams for food. It has water-resistant fur and scaled feet. This mole has a strange-looking circle of twenty-two pink fleshy tentacles at the end of its snout, which it uses to identify food by touch.

Several animals are similar to the mole in appearance and behavior. One is an animal often called a "golden mole," sometimes called a "mole rat." Though it is called a "mole rat," it is not considered a true mole. It is much larger than the true mole, feeds on vegetables, and burrows on a larger scale.

This animal burrowed among the ruins of ancient cities and is found in abundance on the plains of Palestine today. It might be the "mole" mentioned in the Bible. In some Bible translations, the word mole is replaced with the words rat or lizard.

DID YOU KNOW...

- The mole can eat three times its body weight in one day.

- The star-nosed mole can detect, catch, and eat food faster than the human eye can follow it.

- Some moles are considered pests because they burrow through the soil, raising molehills and killing plant roots.

Type of animal:
Insect

Find it in the Bible:
Matthew 6:19

MOTH

WHAT ATE A
HOLE IN MY
SWEATER?

The moth is an insect closely related to the butterfly, but there are several differences between the two. While most butterflies have thin antennae, the moth has feathery antennae. Most butterflies have smooth, slender bodies, while most moths have fatter, furrier bodies. And while most butterflies tend to be active during the day, most moths are active during the night. These are just a few examples of the differences between moths and butterflies.

The moth uses its antennae, which are also called "feelers" and "smellers," to find food and, when the time is right, a mate. When a moth lands, it folds its wings against its body or points them out flat from its sides.

The moth's tongue is long and curled up inside itself like a spring. It unrolls the hollow tongue to sip nectar—like sipping soda through a straw.

Some moths are unattractive pests. Their caterpillars, such as those of the hawk moth, do great damage to plants. The caterpillars of some moths even eat holes in clothing.

Not all moths are pests. Some are helpful to humans. During the night, some moths are active pollinating night-flowering plants. Moths are also a source of food for other animals.

Many moths are very colorful and pretty to look at. The tiger moth uses its bright colors to warn predators of danger. It tastes disgusting and can be slightly poisonous if eaten. It produces a high-frequency sound that jams the sonar system of bats that find moths delicious.

The giant silkworm moth does not have a mouth and cannot eat. All the energy it needs is stored in its body from the food it ate while

Many moths aren't very colorful, but some, like this scarlet tiger moth, are beautiful to look at.

MOTH

a caterpillar. Because of this, the silkworm moth sometimes lives only a day or two.

The male robin moth has huge antennae that he uses to detect a female's scent from a great distance away. After the robin moths mate, the female does not fly far, because she is loaded down with eggs. She usually lays hundreds of eggs on the nearest tree. After a week or so, the larvae hatch and start feeding on the leaves of the trees.

When the moth breaks out of its cocoon, it is wrinkled and wet. It pumps body fluid into its wings until they unfold and dry. Then it is ready to fly.

Job 13:28 makes reference to the destructive habits of the clothes moth. The moth must have been a well-known insect, which in its caterpillar state was destructive. This destructive power is used to illustrate the result of sin in Psalm 39:11.

STORE UP YOUR TREASURES IN HEAVEN

Jesus used moths as part of a lesson He taught His followers on the mountainside. He had been teaching His followers about many important things. He warned them not to store up treasures on earth where moths would destroy them and thieves would break in and steal them. Jesus told the followers to store treasures in heaven instead, where moths could not reach them.

See Matthew 6:19–20

Having learned this important lesson that Jesus had taught, the apostle James later warned rich people not to be so concerned with their wealth. He told them that their wealth would rot and moths would eat their clothes.

See James 5:2

DID YOU KNOW...

- The hawk moth can fly up to 30 miles per hour.

- The Atlas moth is the largest known moth, with a wingspan of up to twelve inches.

- The larva of the hawk moth, called a "hornworm," is an eating machine, chomping up both poisonous and nonpoisonous (to people) plants.

MOUNTAIN SHEEP

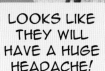

Type of animal:
Mammal

Find it in the Bible:
Deuteronomy 14:5

LOOKS LIKE THEY WILL HAVE A HUGE HEADACHE!

A mountain sheep is one and a half times bigger than its domesticated cousin. Its coat coloring is from light tan to chocolate brown, and it has a white rump. Under the sheep's outer wool are "guard hairs"—long, coarse hairs that shed water and snow. Under the "guard hair" is a layer of wool that traps the animal's body heat to help keep it warm. When a mountain sheep sleeps, it folds its legs under its body to help keep them warm, too.

The mountain sheep's amber yellow eyes can spot things a mile away. This sharp eyesight is the animal's best defense against predators. The mountain sheep also has sharp senses of smell and hearing.

Male mountain sheep are called "rams" and females are called "ewes." The rams have thick, curved horns that can weigh up to thirty pounds. The horns sometimes form a complete circle on each side of the head. The ewes have smaller horns that are not quite as curved.

Mountain sheep eat only plants. They graze on grasses and shrubs, but they will seek minerals at natural salt licks. In winter, when the snow covers the ground, the mountain

Mountain sheep aren't afraid of heights. In fact, they're built to live in places that most other animals wouldn't dare go!

MOUNTAIN SHEEP

sheep sometimes dig in the snow with their hooves to find grass and plants to eat.

These sheep live high in the mountains, where they find protection from predators. Most predators are not sure-footed enough to chase them along the narrow mountain trails. Only the cougar hunts in the high mountains. The parents must protect the young sheep, called "lambs," from golden eagles, which can swoop down and snatch them up.

The mountain sheep can leap a 150-foot cliff and land safely. Their hooves have a hard, sharp outer edge that cuts into the earth, gravel, and ice. The center of their hooves is made of spongy material that provides traction. The split hooves can pinch and hold on to rocks. Two smaller claws high up on the foot serve as brakes if they begin to slip. Even sheep as young as two or three weeks old can jump and climb in rugged, dangerous mountain areas.

Mountain sheep live in "bands" of ten to one hundred animals. During mating season, horn clashing between the males takes place. Two rams will circle each other at a distance of about thirty feet apart. They approach one another and rear up on their hind legs and charge head down at full speed. Their heads crash together, making a cracking sound that can be heard from a mile away. They keep the horn clashing up until one of the rams wears down or gives up. Sometimes the clashing lasts for several days and nights.

Mountain sheep were listed in Mosaic Law as animals the Israelites could eat. Not only were the mountain sheep hunted for meat, but also their horns were used as trumpets (Joshua 6:4) and as oil containers (1 Samuel 16:1).

DID YOU KNOW. . .

- The mountain sheep never sheds its horns, which only grow larger every year.
- The mountain sheep sheds its thick winter coat in spring and grows a new coat by the following winter.
- The mountain sheep can run as fast as 35 miles per hour.
- A mountain sheep can leap seven feet into the air.

Type of animal:
Mammal
Find it in the Bible:
Leviticus 11:29 KJV

MOUSE

MICE WILL EAT ANYTHING THAT DOESN'T EAT THEM FIRST!

Mice are small rodents with pointed noses, whiskers, beady black eyes, round ears, and long hairless tails. Five toes on each of their four feet help them grip when climbing. Mice use their sharp teeth for gnawing on food and, as a last resort, biting predators.

Mice run, walk, and stand on all four legs. But when they eat, they stand on their hind legs, using their tails for support.

Mice have a long list of enemies. Many different kinds of birds, reptiles, mammals, and even fish love having fresh mouse for dinner. Their only defenses are to blend into their surroundings or to run to safety. Since they are small, mice can fit into tight places predators can't reach.

In the wild, mice live near open fields and forests, but they commonly make their homes in houses and other manmade structures. They dig burrows near food supplies because they like to eat fifteen to twenty times per day. They make paths connecting their homes to food sources. They also store food in several hiding places.

Mice are considered pests. They eat seed stored by people, damage crops, and carry disease. The best known of the mice species—the common house mouse—has been domesticated and is a popular pet, but it is also a pest in the home.

The Mosaic Law lists mice as unclean and forbids eating them. As a guilt offering for stealing the ark of the covenant, the Philistines were advised to send "five golden mice" to the Israelites when they returned the ark to them (1 Samuel 6:4–5).

SOME BIBLE TRANSLATIONS USE THE WORD RATS INSTEAD OF MICE.

DID YOU KNOW. . .

- Mice stay in one place all their lives unless food runs out or their homes get too hot or cold.

- Instead of sleeping at night, mice take several short naps in the day.

- Mice rely on their size, speed, and cleverness to survive.

- It is believed that the domestication of cats was first done with the purpose of controlling mouse and rat populations.

265

MULE

STUBBORN AS A MULE, REALLY?

Type of animal:
Mammal

Find it in the Bible:
1 Kings 1:33

A mule is the offspring of a male donkey and a female horse. It has a short, thick head, long ears, thin limbs, small, narrow hooves, and a short mane like a donkey. But it has the height, shape of neck, coat, and teeth of a horse. It comes in all sizes, shapes, and characteristics of both donkey and horse.

The mule is more patient, sure-footed, hardy, and longer-lived than a horse. It is less stubborn, faster, and more intelligent than a donkey. The mule may appear to be stubborn, but it is actually just a cautious animal that does not want to be put in a dangerous position.

Every mule has a unique bray. Its sound is similar to the bray of a donkey but also similar to the "whinnying" of a horse. It often sounds like this: "Whinee-aw-ah-aw."

The mule's hooves are harder than a horse's, and they work well in clay soil. For that reason, farmers for centuries have plowed their clay-soiled fields using mules.

Like many "hybrids" (animals that result from crossbreeding), all male mules and most female mules are infertile, meaning they can't produce offspring.

Since the Mosaic Law outlawed crossbreeding of animals, the Israelites of biblical times imported mules. They were used as war animals, for riding, and for carrying burdens. They were also used for moving heavy burdens, being better than a horse, donkey, or camel.

It is likely that only kings and the wealthy rode on mules in Old Testament times. David chose a mule to symbolize royalty for Solomon's coronation as the king (see 1 Kings 1:33).

DID YOU KNOW. . .

- The average mule can carry about two hundred pounds.
- A mule is a very curious animal.
- The mule is sure-footed and can live and work in much rougher country than a horse can.

OSPREY

Type of animal:
Bird

Find it in the Bible:
Leviticus 11:13 NIV

IS THAT A SPEEDING BULLET IN THE SKY?

The osprey is a fish-eating bird of prey that is sometimes called a "fish hawk," though it is not really a hawk. This bird can be found on every continent in the world except Antarctica.

The osprey differs from other birds of prey, as its toes are equal in length. The outer toe is reversible, allowing it to grasp prey with two toes curved forward and two curved backward. The talons are also rounded rather than grooved.

The osprey, with its narrow wings edged with four long, fingerlike feathers and a short fifth feather, circles the water searching for food. When the bird's sharp eyes spot a fish, it plunges toward the water with its wings bent back and legs bent. It reaches its legs forward as it nears the water. The feet break the surface of the water as the osprey snatches up the fish. It takes the fish back to its perch to eat it. An osprey's diet consists of about 99 percent fish, but if fish are not available, it will catch and eat small mammals, amphibians, or reptiles.

The male osprey displays courtship for a mate by soaring high and diving with fantastic spins. Sometimes the male will carry a fish as a gift to the female. The two build a bulky nest of sticks and seaweed in a tree or rocky cliff. Ospreys sometimes build their nests on top of telephone poles and other manmade structures. The female lays two to four white eggs then begins incubating them. The male feeds the female while she sits on the eggs.

The osprey is listed in the Bible as an unclean bird. It is still found around the lakes and the coasts of the Mediterranean Sea.

THE IDENTITY OF THE BIRD IN THE BIBLE IS QUESTIONABLE. SOME TRANSLATIONS CALL IT A "BLACK VULTURE," SOME A "BLACK EAGLE," AND OTHERS A "BUZZARD."

DID YOU KNOW. . .

- The osprey is sometimes called a "fish hawk," as it is closely related to a hawk and feeds on fish.

- The osprey has a black "eye patch" that runs back to its neckline.

- The osprey flies with its wings held in an M-shape.

- A pair of ospreys will mate for life.

267

OSSIFRAGE

THAT'S A STRANGE NAME FOR A BIRD!

Type of animal:
Bird

Find it in the Bible:
Deuteronomy 14:12 KJV

The bird referred to as the ossifrage in the King James Bible has been identified by some Bible scholars as what is now called the "bearded vulture." This bird gets its name from the black "beard" of feathers on its chin. This bearded vulture has large, narrow wings with a span of about nine feet and a long, wedge-shaped tail. It also has deep red eyes, which are not found in any other vulture species.

The underparts of the bearded vulture are usually colored deep orange. It acquires this color by rubbing against rocks containing iron oxides.

The bearded vulture is found in high mountainous areas above tree lines. A pair of these birds builds an enormous nest in a rocky crevice where the female deposits one or two pinkish or yellowish eggs. After they hatch, the young spend 106 to 130 days in the nest before venturing out to fly on their own.

The bearded vulture does very little hunting for food. Instead, it waits until other vultures have eaten the fleshy parts of the carrion and then picks the bones to eat the marrow, which makes up about 90 percent of its diet. Sometimes the bird carries large bones high into the sky then drops them. When they fall on the rocks below, they crack open, making it easier for the bearded vulture to get to the marrow. Occasionally the bearded vulture does the same thing to a tortoise, which it also likes to eat.

WHAT A WAY TO EAT!

The ossifrage is mentioned in Mosaic Law in a list of birds that are unclean. Eating carrion makes it unclean. The Hebrew word for ossifrage means to "crush" or "break," making it a fitting name for the bearded vulture!

DID YOU KNOW. . .

- Unlike most other vulture species, the ossifrage does not have a bald head.

- The ossifrage can live up to forty years in captivity.

- It takes a young ossifrage up to two years to develop red eyes.

OSTRICH

Type of animal:
Bird

Find it in the Bible:
Job 39:13

JUST HOW TALL ARE YOU?

The ostrich is the largest of all birds. It has wings, but it can't fly. Ostriches stand between six and nine feet tall and weigh between 140 and 290 pounds when they are fully grown. The males have black and white plumage, while the females are brownish gray. The ostrich has a long neck and a small head with large eyes. The eyelids have long lashes made up of fringes of hairlike feathers. The ostrich has very good eyesight and can see danger from a long way off.

Although the ostrich cannot fly, it can walk or run fast enough to escape any of its enemies. It has two long, enormously powerful legs with large, hooflike, two-toed feet that allow it to run as fast as 45 miles per hour, making it the fastest runner of any bird. An ostrich can cover up to sixteen feet (the size of a family car) in one step.

JOB 39:13-18 TELLS THE CHARACTERISTICS OF THE OSTRICH.

Ostriches use their speed to outrun predators, but if they have to, they can defend themselves by kicking their enemies with their powerful legs. The female ostrich lays the biggest eggs of any known animal—up to three pounds each. She lays her eggs in depressions in the sand and incubates them during the day. The male ostrich sits on them at night.

Ostriches are now found in the wild only in Africa, but they once lived in the Middle East. The Bible lists the ostrich as unclean, meaning the Israelites were not to eat it. This could be because of its eating habits. It has been known to swallow substances such as iron, stones, and, in modern times, bullets.

DID YOU KNOW. . .

- The ostrich can go without water several days but enjoys taking a bath.
- A wild ostrich can live to be thirty to thirty-four years old.
- Contrary to what many people believe, ostriches don't really bury their heads in the sand.
- Ostriches are now raised on farms and are prized for their plumes, their meat, and their hides.

OWL

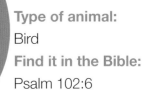

WHAT BIG EYES YOU HAVE!

Type of animal:
Bird
Find it in the Bible:
Psalm 102:6

The owl is a bird of prey that usually lives and hunts alone. Most often hunting during the nighttime, it flies on nearly silent wings and swoops down on the small creatures it eats, grabbing them with its huge talons. Some owls can carry off prey larger than themselves.

Depending on the species, an owl feeds on anything from insects to mammals as large as rabbits. Most owls swallow their prey whole. The parts of the meal they can't digest—fur, bones, scales, and feathers—they cough up in the form of pellets.

An owl has big eyes, a short, hooked bill, and a round face. It cannot move its eyes but turns its head to look to the side. Owls have excellent vision and depth perception, but most owls don't see well close up.

There are more than a hundred species of owls. The largest is the great eagle owl, which grows to twenty-eight inches long and has a wingspan of more than six feet. The smallest is the elf owl, which grows to only five inches long. Not all owls make the hoot sound. Different species make different sounds.

How an owl mates and nests depends on the species. Some owls nest in trees, sometimes using the old nests of other birds. Some nest on the ground in marshy or open grasslands. Some owls even nest underground in the abandoned burrows of other animals.

The Bible mentions several different kinds of owls, all of which are listed in the Mosaic Law as unclean. Some of the species were common in Palestine and were often found inhabiting the ruins of cities. Deuteronomy 14:15–17 (NIV) lists a number of owl species—the horned owl, the screech owl, the little owl, the great owl, the white owl, and the desert owl.

DID YOU KNOW. . .

- The owl's soft wing feathers allow it to fly silently.
- The owl has a keen sense of sight and hearing.
- The female owl is much larger than the male owl.
- Though owls tend to be solitary birds, a group of owls is called a "parliament."

Type of animal:
Mammal
Find it in the Bible:
Deuteronomy 22:10

OX

TWELVE YOKE OF OXEN EQUALS TWENTY-FOUR!

The ox is a heavy-bodied bovine (in the same family of animals as cattle) animal with short legs and sliced hooves. It chews cud, meaning it consumes its food then brings it back up from its four-part stomach to chew it again later. The ox isn't really an individual species of animal. It is commonly an adult bull that has been neutered and trained to perform certain tasks for its owners.

In Old Testament times, oxen were extremely valuable as work animals. Farmers depended on their oxen for all the ordinary operations on the farm. Oxen were commonly used for plowing, for treading out corn, for pulling, and for transporting people and materials. They were also sometimes eaten.

Oxen were usually yoked in pairs to do the work their owners needed them to do. A specially designed wooden yoke was fastened around the neck of each pair. The oxen were trained to respond to the ox driver's signals. Sometimes, depending on the work, oxen worked in teams of as many as twenty animals.

READ HOW ELISHA PLOWED WITH TWELVE YOKE OF OXEN IN 1 KINGS 19:19.

Oxen were also used in several methods of threshing. They were driven over the grain lying on the threshing floor. Their hooves did the work of threshing. Another method was having the oxen pull a threshing board over the grain while the thresher stood on the board.

God gave the Jews a strict code of laws regarding the treatment of their oxen. The oxen that threshed the corn were not to be muzzled. They (along with their masters) were also to be rested on the Sabbath.

OTHER BIBLE VERSES THAT MENTION OXEN ARE EXODUS 23:12; NUMBERS 7:3; AND DEUTERONOMY 25:4.

DID YOU KNOW. . .

● The word oxen, as the Hebrews used it, meant both male and female.

● Both male and female oxen have horns.

● Oxen can pull harder and longer than horses, which make them better with heavier loads.

● A person who drives a team of oxen is sometimes referred to as a "teamster."

PARTRIDGE

THAT BIRD MUST BE TIRED AFTER LAYING THAT MANY EGGS!

Type of animal:
Bird

Find it in the Bible:
1 Samuel 26:20

The partridge is a medium-sized game bird belonging to the pheasant family. It has a plump body with a deep chest, a feathered tail, round wings, and a short, thick bill. It is smaller than most pheasants but larger than most quail. It is ten to fourteen inches long and weighs less than a pound.

Partridges are found in the wild in Europe, Asia, Africa, and the Middle East, which includes biblical lands. They live in groups called "coveys," which consist of a male, a female, the young, plus a few other birds. The partridge feeds on grain, seeds, and insects.

During the mating season, a pair of partridges builds a shallow, grass-lined nest on the ground, where tall grass conceals them from predators. The female is a very nervous mom when sitting on the eggs. Sometimes, if she is disturbed, she will abandon the nest.

To avoid predators, the partridge uses its deep chest to propel it quickly across the ground to safety. The partridge prefers to run rather than fly, but if pursued it will fly a short distance.

The Bible refers to the partridge as the hunting bird upon the mountain. The Greek partridge somewhat resembles the chukar or rock partridge but is much larger. It has a brown back with black and white bars on the sides, a black outlined head with a white throat, and red legs and bill. It lives in the hill country of Judea. Its ringing call, "Kar-wit, kar-wit," is heard in early morning.

DID YOU KNOW. . .

- The gray partridge lays the largest cluster of eggs of any bird—nineteen to twenty eggs.
- Most species of partridges do not migrate but stay in the area where they were raised.
- The partridge is sometimes associated with the grouse, bobwhite, and quail.
- Two species—the chukar and the gray partridge—have been successfully introduced to North America.

PEACOCK

Type of animal:
Bird

Find it in the Bible:
1 Kings 10:22 KJV

BEAUTIFUL, PROUD—BUT A BIT TOO NOISY!

The peacock is one of the most beautiful birds in the world. The peacock—the male of a bird called "peafowl"—spreads his long, beautiful tail, which is colored with markings of gold, green, and purple. He has a blue-green or blue head, neck, and breast. The female, called a "peahen," is mostly brown with a shiny green neck and shorter tail feathers.

The peacock, which is native to India and is India's national bird, spends much time grooming his tail. Every feather must be in place. The peacock uses his tail to show off to the peahen. He begins his ritual with a few shivers and shakes. Then there is a sound like rustling silk as the layers of feathers seem to open and float upward. The shivers get stronger, and soon the whole tail is spread. He prances back and forth in front of the peahen with his tail spread and his head held high. He announces his act with an ear-splitting yell: "EEEooo. . .LOOoww. . .EEEonn. . .LEEow!"

The peacock often spends the night in a tree, on a fence, or on a rooftop. He doesn't fly very well, and sometimes he lands on the ground in the morning with an undignified *kwwammp*! He eats insects, plants, and even small reptiles. The peacock really likes eating small cobras, which are dangerous to humans. He uses his long legs and sharp spurs to protect himself against enemies.

The peacock is mentioned in the Old Testament. When King Solomon's fleet of ships arrived in Jerusalem, they brought many valuable items, including peacocks. Solomon kept peacocks around the royal palace because they showed his wealth and majesty.

SOME BIBLE TRANSLATIONS REPLACE "PEACOCK" WITH "OSTRICH." OTHER KING JAMES BIBLE VERSES MENTIONING THE PEACOCK ARE 2 CHRONICLES 9:21 AND JOB 39:13.

DID YOU KNOW. . .

- When you combine the length of his tail and his wingspread, the peacock is one of the largest flying birds in the world.

- The peacock is from the same family of birds as the pheasant.

- The peacock's tail can be more than six feet long.

- A group of peafowl is called a "pride" and usually includes one peacock and several peahens.

273

PELICAN

THAT'S QUITE A FISHING NET YOU HAVE THERE!

Type of animal:
Bird

Find it in the Bible:
Psalm 102:6 KJV

The pelican is a large seabird. It has a huge bill with a huge pouch that hangs from the lower part of the bill. There are more than six species of pelicans. They live on coastlines and also near lakes and rivers. They live and travel in flocks and breed in groups called "colonies."

The pelican's pouch is made of skin and stretches to hold up to three gallons of fish and water. Most pelicans feed by scooping up water and fish in the shallows then lifting their heads and forcing the water out. All that's left in the pouch is the pelican's food, which it swallows whole.

Like other species of pelicans, the brown pelican lives in large colonies. But it is the only pelican species that feeds by diving. It flies over the water from as high as sixty or seventy feet in the air, looking for fish to eat. When it spots its prey, it dives under the water, making a big splash.

Special air sacs under the brown pelican's skin and bones hold pockets of air. The air sacs cushion the impact as the pelican hits the water. Then all the air in the body makes it bounce back to the surface like a cork.

The pelican's nest is made of twigs and seaweed and is usually close to water. Both parents feed and care for the young. The parents feed the youngsters on partly digested fish. When the mother or father pelican arrives at the nest, the babies put their heads into the adult's throat and feed.

Pelicans are found in Palestine. In the King James Bible, Leviticus 11:18 and Deuteronomy 14:17 forbid the people of Israel to eat the pelican's meat. In Psalm 102, David compares his sad mood to a pelican, probably because the pelican looks sad as it rests its bill on its breast.

DID YOU KNOW. . .

- A group of pelicans is called a "pod."

- A pelican must eat four pounds of fish a day to survive.

- A pelican never carries water or food around in its beak.

274

Type of animal:
Mammal
Find it in the Bible:
Mark 5:11

PIG

THAT PIG IS
TAKING A
BATH—IN MUD!

A pig has short legs, a thick, heavy body, and a small tail that is either curly or straight. It has a thick, coarse coat of brown or gray fur. The pig has four toes on each foot with the two large toes in the middle used for walking. The pig's snout, which it uses to root around in the dirt for food, includes very sensitive smell organs.

Pigs are omnivores, meaning they eat meat, plants, and other foods. The pig eats plants, bugs, and insects, along with grains the farmer feeds it.

The pig is most active early in the morning and just before dark. It spends much of the time sleeping, only waking to eat and drink. When a pig sleeps alone, it usually lies on one side with its legs sticking straight out.

A pig is a social animal. It enjoys close contact with other pigs and with other animals. Pigs often cuddle together when they sleep so they can keep warm. They grunt and squeal to communicate with one another.

A female pig is called a "sow" and a male pig a "boar." Baby pigs are called "piglets" and can walk soon after they are born. Before they are ready to eat solid food, the piglets feed on milk

When it's time for lunch, baby pigs go where they know they can get something to eat. . . straight to mom!

275

from their mother. The sow grunts when she calls the piglets to tell them it is time to eat. The sow can feed twelve piglets at once. If she has more than twelve babies (which she sometimes does), the extras are given to another sow to feed.

Wild pigs are called "wild boars." They are smaller than farm pigs and have more hair. They also have tusks for digging and fighting other boars. They can destroy a farmer's crop with their digging for food.

A pig is used for meat as well as for leather. Pigskin can be used to make purses, wallets, and gloves. Some paintbrushes are made from pig bristles. Some baseball gloves are stuffed with hair from pigs.

The pigs of the Bible were probably wild pigs, which are still common in Palestine. While the Canaanite pagans kept herds of pigs, the Mosaic Law listed them as unclean animals and forbade the eating of their meat. Even those who tended the pigs were not allowed to enter the temple.

Many ancient people ate pigs and used them as animal sacrifices to their idols. The pigs were pests to farmers because they dug up crops in the fields.

THE PRODIGAL SON

One of Jesus' most famous stories (called "parables") mentioned pigs.

When the religious leaders of Jesus' time—the scribes and Pharisees—complained that He spent time with "sinful" people, Jesus told the parable of the prodigal son. It was the story of a young man who wanted to leave home so badly that he asked for his inheritance before his father died. The man gave his son the money, and the boy ran off to party. He had lots of friends, until the money ran out—and when a famine struck the land, the only job he could find was feeding pigs.

The Jews hated pigs, since they were an "unclean" animal according to Moses' law. When the boy realized what a mistake he'd made—that he was wishing to eat the pigs' food when his father's servants were better fed—he decided to go home and ask his father if he could serve him as a slave.

But the father was so thrilled to see his boy coming home, he threw a party. The point of the story? God loves it when sinners "come home."

See the whole story in Luke 15:11-32.

JESUS AND THE DEMON-POSSESSED MEN

Pigs played an important part in one account of Jesus healing two demon-possessed men He and His disciples encountered one day. They were passing through the area called the Gadarenes when they met two men coming from the tombs where they lived. The men were controlled by evil spirits and were so wild that people stayed away from the area because they were afraid.

The men shouted, "Son of God, what do You want with us? Have You come to punish us?"

Not very far from the men was a herd of pigs that were eating. "If You drive us out of the men, send us into the herd of pigs," the demons begged Jesus.

Jesus said to the demons, "Go!"

The demons came out of the men and went into the pigs. Then the entire herd ran down the steep cliff into the lake and drowned.

You can read this whole story in Matthew 8:28–34.

A herd of pigs played an important part in the story of Jesus healing a man who was tormented by evil spirits.

DID YOU KNOW. . .

- Pigs are also called "hogs" or "swine."
- A pig likes to wallow in wet mud to keep it cool on a hot day.
- Pigs are very intelligent and learn quickly.
- An adult pig can weigh as much as a piano!
- A pot-bellied pig makes a good pet.

PIGEON

Type of animal:
Bird

Find it in the Bible:
Leviticus 5:7

The pigeon is a plump bird with a small head, a short, slender bill, and large wings. With its strong wing muscles, the bird can make low wing landings. A soft swelling that plays an important role in breathing is found on the pigeon's beak.

Most pigeons have a blue-gray body with two dark wing bars. There are twenty-eight pigeon color types with a variety of patterns. Pigeons come in an assortment of sizes, too. The smallest, a ground pigeon, is the size of a sparrow. The crowned pigeon, the largest species of pigeon, is nearly the size of a turkey—four to eight pounds.

Pigeons mate for life and can nest at any time of the year—though the peak times are in the spring and summer. They build their nests from sticks and other debris. In the wild, they nest in cliffs, but they will nest on building or bridge ledges that resemble cliffs. Some pigeons prefer to build on the flat ground.

The female pigeon lays one or two eggs, and both male and female care for the young, which are called "squabs." Both parents produce and feed their young "crop milk," sometimes called "pigeon milk." They keep the crop milk in a saclike food storage chamber that shoots outward from the bottom of the esophagus.

Pigeons are a common sight in nearly every city around the world.

PIGEON

Pigeons were the first animals to carry messages for people. The Romans trained pigeons to carry news of battles back and forth to the generals. During World War I and World War II, pigeons saved many lives by carrying messages across enemy lines. Pigeons are easily trained and seem to have a built-in "homing" device within them that allows them to return home after flying long distances.

In the Bible, pigeons are named as birds used for sacrificial offerings. Sometimes the dove and pigeon, which are closely related, were interchanged with each other. They were used for both burnt offerings and sin offerings. They were also used as an offering for a healed leper. Pigeons were one of the least expensive animal offerings. People who could not afford to sacrifice a sheep or goat would offer two pigeons, which they could buy in the temple courts.

GOD'S COVENANT WITH ABRAM

One day God and Abram were talking together. "Look at the stars, Abram," said God. "Count them if you can. That is how many descendants you will have."

Abram believed God and built an altar. God told him to bring a heifer, a goat, and a ram, along with a dove and a young pigeon. Abram brought all of those animals and put them on the altar. Then God made a covenant, or agreement, with Abram.

You can read the whole story in Genesis 15.

DID YOU KNOW. . .

- **The pigeon is one of the strongest fliers of any bird.**
- **The pigeon sucks up water using its beak like a straw.**
- **Some pigeons can fly 40 to 50 miles per hour and can fly as far as six hundred miles in one day.**
- **Many pigeons have received military awards and medals for their service during wartime.**

PORCUPINE

BALLOONS WOULDN'T BE A GOOD IDEA AT A PORCUPINE PARTY!

Type of animal:
Mammal

Find it in the Bible:
Isaiah 34:11 ASV

The porcupine is a large rodent (in the same family as mice and rats) with a short, rounded body. There are about twenty-four species of porcupines around the world. They are found in Asia, Africa, America, and Europe.

The porcupine's best-known feature is the coat of sharp spines or quills that defend it from predators. The porcupine has soft hair, but the hair on its back, side, and tail is mixed with the quills.

The porcupine keeps its quills flat against its body—at least until the animal is threatened. Then the quills spring upward. The quills are hollow and have sharp tips with overlapping scales or barbs. The barbs make the quills difficult—and very painful!—to remove once they are stuck in a predator's skin.

Contrary to what many people believe, the porcupine can't throw its quills at attackers. The quills are released when a predator comes in contact with them. They may also be dropped when a porcupine shakes its body. The porcupine grows new quills to replace the lost ones.

Porcupines are plant-eating animals that like to dine on bark and twigs. They are fond of hemlock, fir, pine, maple, beech, birch, oak, elm, cherry, and willow. Some porcupines can climb trees and have been known to do damage to trees by stripping them of their bark. They will also eat fruit and springtime buds.

Porcupines also crave salt. They will eat just about anything that has salt on it, including plywood, tool handles, shoes, clothes, and tires. The porcupine is attracted to roads where rock salt has been used to melt ice and snow.

Porcupines mate in the fall and give birth in the spring. Baby porcupines are called "porcupettes." The mother porcupine gives birth to between one and three babies. Porcupines are born with spines, but they are soft and flexible.

The porcupine lives in a wide range of places—forests, grasslands, deserts, and rocky hillsides. Palestine still has porcupines, as it did during biblical times.

DID YOU KNOW. . .

- A group of porcupines is called a "prickle."

- A porcupine may have thirty thousand or more quills.

- The African crested porcupine's quills are nearly a foot long.

Type of animal:
Bird
Find it in the Bible:
Numbers 11:31

QUAIL

WHO
IS BOB
WHITE?

The quail, which is a member of the pheasant family, is a small, plump ground bird that lives in the tall grasses and brushy borders of the plains and farmlands. It has sturdy legs, head plumage curling forward, and a curved bill. Its feathers are usually brown, speckled with white, black, or chestnut. These colors blend with the grassy surroundings, camouflaging the bird from predators. The quail is mostly a seedeater but will also eat insects and other small creatures, some of which are harmful to farmers' crops.

The quail spends most of its life on the ground, running and zigzagging through the grass. The quail is not a strong flying bird, but when necessary, it can fly short distances.

The female quail, which is called a "hen," is larger and stronger than the male, which is called a "rooster." She does the nest building. She builds her nest in a scratched hollow of the ground, usually concealing it under shrubs, logs, or rocks and lining it with leaves or grass. In the spring, she lays eggs, which the male helps incubate. Both female and male quail care for the young.

One of the daily activities of the quail family is the dust bath. They select an area where the ground is soft. Using their underbellies, the quail burrow downward for one or two inches. Then they wiggle about, flapping their wings and ruffling feathers, causing dust to fly into the air.

The male quail is designated as the family guard. He perches on a high place to keep watch over the clan. When he sees danger approaching, he uses a variety of calls to warn his family. The best-known quail call is "bob-white, bob-bob-white," which comes from a species called the "bobwhite."

The quail the people of Israel gathered in the wilderness probably looked more like this bird—the common quail—than the bobwhite quail we see in America.

The quails mentioned in the Old Testament differ from the "bobwhite" quails we see in America today. Besides being migratory, which American quails are not, the quails of the Bible are shorter, stockier, and spotted brown in color. The bill is smooth and the legs are spurred.

The quail is mentioned in the Bible only in connection with God's provision of food for Israel in the wilderness. It is probable that these quail, which visited the Hebrew camp, were a migrating flock. Enormous numbers of quail migrate north during the spring. When the birds stop to rest, they can be easily caught—even by hand. It has also been noted that quail migrate at night. In God's timing, the birds came to provide for the needs of His people. (You can read the whole story in Exodus 16.)

Like chickens, quails provide food for humans in two ways—by their meat and by their eggs, considered a delicacy in many countries.

DID YOU KNOW. . .

- Young quails leave the nest as soon as they have hatched but stay with their parents during the first summer.
- The quail (or family of quail) lives individually but forms flocks to migrate.
- Because the quail's wings are short, it must beat them rapidly to fly.
- The quail is considered a game bird and is hunted by humans.

RABBIT & HARE

WHAT BIG TEETH YOU HAVE!

A rabbit is a furry animal with long ears, short tail, and powerful hind legs for speedy running. It has big front teeth, which never stop growing. It prefers to nibble on grass and other plants at dusk or during the night. The rabbit lives in meadows, woods, thickets, and grasslands in many parts of the world. Some rabbit species are also found in deserts and wetlands.

The rabbit is a sociable animal that lives in family groups. Several rabbits dig a group of connected burrows called a "warren." There are many separate entrances into the burrow and some quick escape routes.

The hare, sometimes called "jackrabbit," is often mistaken for the common rabbit, simply because the two animals look so much alike. It is closely related to the rabbit, but there are several differences between the two animals.

First, the hare is larger and heavier than the rabbit, and it has longer ears. It also has black markings on its legs. The hare has powerful back legs that enable it to jump high and fast.

Unlike the rabbit, the hare is not a social animal but lives and moves around individually. Instead of living in underground burrows, the hare lives in the open countryside. When it needs shelter or rest, it goes to a shallow trench in the long grass called a "form," which it makes itself. Because of its color, the hare is well camouflaged as long as it stays still.

Hares and rabbits are closely related, but there are differences between the two animals. How does this hare look different from the rabbits pictured above?

Hares put on an amazing display during mating season. They chase each other, leap in the air, and "box" each other. Scientists used to believe that the two "sparring partners" were male hares (called "jacks") fighting for the right to mate with certain females (called "jills"). But recently it has been observed that it is usually a female rabbit hitting a male. That could be because she is not quite ready to mate, but it could

RABBIT & HARE

also be to test the male to see how much he really wants to mate.

Unlike baby rabbits, which are born blind, naked, and helpless, baby hares are born with a full coat of fur and with their eyes open.

There are also several similarities between the rabbit and the hare. They are both fond of all green growing things and have earned a reputation for doing damage to gardens and field crops. In the winter, both feed on the bark of trees and shrubs, which damages the plants.

The rabbit and hare are both well equipped to detect enemies. Their long ears are very sensitive. When the animal is at ease, the ears lie quietly along its back. But at the slightest sound, the ears stand upright, waving backward and forward, as they try to locate the danger.

The nose of both animals is also very sensitive. As they try to pick up scent, the nostrils twitch and the head moves up and down. The two eyes also see in every direction, even scanning overhead. The tail is used to alert others of a predator.

The rabbit and hare are hunted by many different predators and are constantly on guard against them. When threatened, they will freeze and observe. The five toes on the forefeet and four on the hind feet give the animal the ability to make a fast getaway.

The Bible lists rabbits and hares among the unclean even though the animal does not have a split hoof.

The rabbit and hare were valued by hunters for their meat and fur. They were pests to the farmer because they often damaged crops.

IN SEVERAL BIBLE TRANSLATIONS, SUCH AS THE KING JAMES VERSION, THE WORD HARE IS USED INSTEAD OF RABBIT.

DID YOU KNOW. . .

- A rabbit can run 25 miles per hour and jump ten feet.
- Some hares can run up to 45 miles per hour and jump fifteen feet.
- The rabbit or hare can see behind itself without moving its head.
- The rabbit and hare can hop, jump, leap, and zigzag every which way as they streak forward, with lightning-fast movements.

Type of animal:
Bird

Find it in the Bible:
Luke 12:24

RAVEN

LOOK OUT FOR THE THIEF!

The raven is a member of the crow family, but it is much larger than the common crow, sometimes weighing more than three pounds. It has black, glistening plumage, a large beak, shaggy throat, and a wedge-shaped tail. The raven is known for its intelligence and for its remarkable ability to solve problems.

Though the raven is omnivorous—meaning it eats plants and meat alike—its diet varies with its location. In some areas, it is mainly a scavenger that feeds on food waste and animal carcasses. In other areas, it feeds on insects and other bugs, small amphibians and reptiles, and small mammals and birds. It becomes a pest to a farmer when it eats grains, berries, and fruit and damages crops.

The raven's wide and complex vocabulary consists of much cawing and croaking. It has an alarm call, a chase call, a flight call, and many others. The raven even has a few nonvocal sounds, such as the whistling of wings and the snapping of the beak.

Young ravens travel in flocks, but later they mate for life and defend their territory against other pairs of ravens. Only when they have obtained a territory are a pair of ravens ready to build a nest. The nest is a deep bowl made of large sticks and twigs and bound with an inner layer of roots, mud, and bark. It is lined with soft material such as deer fur. The nest is built in a high tree or in a cliff ledge.

Raven chicks look out of their nest to see who's coming. Is it mom with something to eat?

RAVEN

OTHER BIBLE VERSES THAT MENTION THE RAVEN ARE DEUTERONOMY 14:14; PSALM 147:9; AND ISAIAH 34:11.

Ravens are very protective of their nests and are even known to drop stones on predators that get too close.

The raven is listed in the Mosaic Law as an unclean bird. But it is also listed as an example of God's care for His people. The raven was the first bird Noah sent out from the ark following the flood (see Genesis 8:1–7). Noah may have chosen the raven for several reasons. It can fly without rest for long spans of time. Also, it makes its home in the rocky crags and would probably scout out mountain peaks emerging from the flooded earth. Finally, the raven is a resourceful bird with a remarkable memory.

In another biblical account, ravens served as symbols of God's love for His servant Elijah. After Elijah told the wicked King Ahab that it would not rain, God sent him to the brook. God told Elijah, "You will drink from the brook, and I will send ravens to feed you."

Elijah did what God told him to do. He drank from the brook, and the ravens brought him bread and meat in the evening (see 1 Kings 17:1–5).

DID YOU KNOW. . .

- A raven calls other ravens to share its food bonanza, usually a carcass.

- A raven steals shiny objects, such as pebbles, metal, and golf balls.

- Ravens like to have fun and have been seen sliding down snowbanks.

- A raven may hide surplus food out of sight from other ravens.

- In the 1840s, Edgar Allen Poe wrote a famous poem called "The Raven." In the poem, a bird taps on the window of a man who's sad about a girl he loved. The raven makes him even sadder by saying "Nevermore, nevermore"!

ROOSTER

Type of animal:
Bird

Find it in the Bible:
John 13:38

DOES A ROOSTER REALLY DANCE?

The rooster, which is an adult male chicken, has a solid body, strong feet, spurs on his legs, and a short pointed beak. Unlike the hen, he has long, flowing tail feathers and shiny hackles (long, pointed feathers) on his neck and back. The large, fleshy, red growth on his head is called a "comb," and the flap of red skin hanging under his beak is called a "waddle."

The rooster is well known for its crowing, especially just before dawn. In past years, before there were alarm clocks, farmers relied on roosters to wake them in the mornings. Roosters also crow at other times of the day.

There are many theories about why roosters crow. One of them is that the rooster is sounding an alarm of danger or disturbance to the other chickens. Another is that the rooster is simply "announcing his presence" to potential predators or other roosters. Some believe the crowing is part of the rooster's mating ritual.

At night, the rooster (as well as the hen) perches on a roost to sleep. The rooster guards the hens while they are nesting. The rooster is territorial and will attack other roosters who try to enter his territory. During the day, the rooster sits on a high perch and guards the flock.

Two colorful roosters fighting to settle their differences over territory

287

ROOSTER

PETER DENIES JESUS. . . BEFORE THE ROOSTER CROWS

At the Last Supper, hours before the crucifixion, Jesus told His disciples that He would be leaving them soon and they would not be able to follow. Peter told Jesus, "I will lay my life down for You."

Jesus answered Peter, "Before the rooster crows, you will disown Me three time."

When Jesus said that Peter would deny Him "before the rooster crows," He may have meant before dawn. Some roosters crowed at other hours. The Roman soldiers used one late-night crowing as a signal to change the guards.

Later, when the soldiers took Jesus, Peter followed him but had to wait outside in the courtyard. A servant girl asked Peter, "Are you one of the disciples?"

Peter answered, "No, I am not."

As Peter stood warming himself by the fire, he was asked again. "Are you one of the disciples?"

Again Peter answered, "No, I am not."

Then one of the servants who had been with the soldiers who arrested Jesus asked Peter, "Didn't I see you with Jesus?"

Just as Peter denied it, a rooster began to crow. The crowing reminded Peter of what Jesus had said. He was sorry for his actions and words

See Matthew 26:31–35, 69–75

When Peter heard the rooster crow, he remembered what Jesus had told him.

THE ROOSTER IS POLITE AND HAS GOOD MANNERS.

Like the hen, the rooster scratches and claws the ground looking for food—grains, worms, insects, and other kinds. When the rooster finds food, he calls other chickens to enjoy a meal with him. He does this by clucking with a high-pitched call, as well as by picking up and dropping the food.

When the rooster wants to court a hen, he will drag one wing on the ground while circling around her. This courting ritual "dance" lets the hen know he wants to mate with her.

The Bible says little about roosters, but the people of Israel were apparently familiar with them. In the Old Testament, King Solomon compares the king parading before the people to a "strutting rooster" (Proverbs 30:31 NIV).

DID YOU KNOW . . .

- The male chicken is called a "rooster," but males less than a year old are called "cockerels."

- Some breeds of rooster crow almost constantly, while others crow only a few times during the day.

- A rooster begins to crow when he is only four months old.

- A bold, red rooster makes up the flag of Wallonia, a French-speaking region in the south of Belgium. The flag was designed in 1913.

SCORPION

Type of animal:
Arachnid

Find it in the Bible:
Deuteronomy 8:15

The scorpion is a small crawling animal that looks a little like a flat lobster. It has a thick body with a "head" consisting of eyes, mouthparts, claws (or pincers), and four pairs of legs. There are two eyes on top of the head and two to five pairs along the front corners of the head. The narrow, segmented tail ends with a poisonous stinger. The scorpion moves along in a threatening stance with its tail in the air. It feeds on spiders and insects, crushing them in its pincers or injecting venom to kill or paralyze them.

Though it might be easy to mistake the scorpion for some kind of insect, it is actually what is called an "arachnid." Arachnids are a lot like insects in some ways. They both have shells around their bodies called "exoskeletons." But arachnids have eight legs instead of six. Also, the scorpion's body is divided into two parts, while the bodies of insects are divided into three parts.

Scorpions also have a pair of organs called "pectines," which they use to sense the

Some scorpion moms take care of their babies until they are mature enough to take care of themselves.

smallest movements around them. This helps them in hunting down prey and in sensing the presence of potential predators.

During the daytime heat, the scorpion spends its time in dry, dark places, such as under rocks and logs or in the ruins of buildings. It comes out at night to hunt and eat.

During courtship, the scorpion pair performs a "dance." The male grasps the female's claws and leads her around. He even gives her a kiss! After the young scorpions are born, the female carries them on her back until they molt once.

The inhabitants of biblical lands feared scorpions. They were a danger when Moses led the children of Israel through the hot, rocky wilderness. God told the prophet Ezekiel not to be afraid of his enemies, whom He referred to as "scorpions" (Ezekiel 2:6).

Jesus taught of the perfect love of God when He pointed out that a good earthly father would never give his child a scorpion instead of an egg. His point was that even the best fathers are imperfect but still do good things for their children. And if an imperfect man does good things for his children, how much more will God do good things for His children? (See Luke 11:12)

DID YOU KNOW. . .

- The scorpion's sting is seldom fatal but can be very painful.

- There are about two thousand different species of scorpions.

- Most scorpions are about two or three inches long, but the emperor scorpion, which is found in Africa, can grow up to eight inches long.

- The scorpion's thick body helps protect it from predators.

SHEEP

Type of animal:
Mammal
Find it in the Bible:
John 10:3

> I'VE HEARD OF SMELLY FEET BUT NOT OF SMELLING WITH YOUR FEET!

Sheep have always been important to humans—from biblical times all the way to the present. For many centuries, people have raised sheep for their meat, milk, and wool. Sheep fleece is sheared and sent to a factory to be cleaned and spun into wool. Special cheeses and yogurts are made from sheep's milk.

A sheep's thick coat—also called its "fleece"—may be long and curly or short and smooth. It keeps the sheep warm in the winter but is shed in the summer. Most sheep's coats are white, but some are black or dark brown.

The sheep has a good sense of hearing and can be very sensitive to noise. It also has an excellent sense of vision. The sheep can see behind itself without turning its head. It has scent glands in front of its eyes and on its feet.

The sheep's hooves are divided into two toes with scent glands between the toes. Some scientists think the sheep can smell its way back to the flock if lost.

A sheep's mouth is made for grazing on short grass. It bites off grass between its bottom front teeth and upper pad and swallows it. The sheep is a ruminant, meaning an animal that chews the cud. Like other ruminants, sheep have stomachs made up of four chambers, each of which has special functions in the digestion of the sheep's food. The cud chewing allows the sheep to graze more quickly in the morning and chew later. When grazing, the sheep lowers its head, leaving it exposed to predators.

Male sheep are called "rams." Many

Two little lambs snuggling up to their mother for warmth and security.

A shepherd working in traditional clothing in Israel. In some parts of the world, people still make their living working as shepherds.

rams have at least one pair of horns. The horns curve outward on the sides of the head. The horns are used to protect the female sheep and to fight off other rams. Some female sheep have horns, too, but they are smaller than a ram's horns.

The female sheep is called a "ewe." She usually gives birth to twins. The baby sheep are called "lambs." The lamb can walk within an hour of birth. Sheep make a high-pitched noise called "bleating." A lamb can identify its mother by her bleat.

As the day turns to night, the sheep gather together to sleep. They find a sheltered area and lie down with their backs to the wind.

In biblical times, sheep wool was spun and woven into warm cloaks and tunics. Tents were made from sheepskins. Rams' horns were used as trumpets (Joshua 6:4) and as oil containers (1 Samuel 16:1).

Sheep skins were used in the construction of the tabernacle. Ram skins were dyed red and used as a covering for the tabernacle (see Exodus 25:5). Sheep were also important

SHEEP

animals for temple sacrifices. They were also used as sacrifices at altars built by people who worshiped God. Abel was the first keeper of sheep and brought his firstborn from his flock as an offering to God. Abram made an altar and sacrificed a ram, among other animals, when God made His covenant with him (Genesis 15:9).

The sheep raised and kept during biblical times were hardy animals that were well-suited to the rough hill pasture. Shepherds often protected flocks of sheep from wild animals and lead them to fresh grazing land and watering places. King David was a shepherd when he was a boy. He protected the sheep from bears and lions (see 1 Samuel 17:34–37).

Having a lot of sheep was a sign of wealth in biblical times. God blessed Abraham with many sheep. He also blessed Solomon, who gave 120,000 sheep at the dedication of the temple (see 2 Chronicles 7:5).

THE NEW INTERNATIONAL VERSION MENTIONS SHEEP 205 TIMES, RAMS 101 TIMES, AND LAMBS 103 TIMES.

The Bible contains hundreds of references to sheep. Jesus made reference to sheep when He taught His followers during His time on earth. He told the parable (story) of the lost sheep. In this story, the shepherd left the ninety-nine sheep still in his flock to go look for one lost sheep. Jesus told this story to teach people about the love of God for His people (You can read the whole story in Luke 15:1–7.)

Jesus also called Himself the "Good Shepherd" who knows His sheep, and His sheep know Him. Jesus cares for us, His sheep (John 10:1–18)!

DID YOU KNOW...

- A group of sheep is called a "flock."
- Sheep are social animals and prefer being together in a flock.
- Sheep's wool is the most widely used of any animal.
- A shepherd, sometimes with the help of a sheepdog, takes care of the sheep.
- There are about 150 yards of wool yarn inside a baseball.

Type of animal:
Reptile

Find it in the Bible:
Leviticus 11:30 NIV

SKINK

LOOK AT THAT BLUE TONGUE!

The skink is part of a family of more than one thousand different kinds of lizards. Most skinks are fairly small with cone-shaped heads and very long tails—usually as long as their bodies. The skink looks like other lizards but has no distinct neck and has small legs. Several species have no limbs at all and look more like snakes than lizards.

Most skinks are carnivores (meat eaters) that like to dine on insects, earthworms, snails, slugs, other lizards, and small rodents.

The skink, like many other lizards, can shed its tail and grow a new one. If a predator takes hold of the tail, the skink twitches a muscle and the tail snaps off. The tail wiggles and keeps the predator busy while the skink escapes.

THAT'S WHEN STICKING OUT YOUR TONGUE IS PERMITTED!

The blue-tongued skink is colored to blend in with its surroundings, which keeps predators from finding it. But when the male wants to attract a mate or to frighten off a rival or enemy, he opens his mouth and sticks out his bright blue tongue.

Most skinks burrow under rocks or logs. Those species that live in the hot climate swim through the sand where it is cooler than above ground.

The skink is listed in Mosaic Law with several other lizards that are unclean and not to be eaten. Some Bible translations call the animal a "snail" (King James Version) or a "sand lizard" (New Revised Standard Version).

DID YOU KNOW. . .

- The largest skink can grow to thirty inches long, but most of them are around eight inches long.
- Most skinks are striped, but a few are spotted or one color.
- The skink sends out a foul-smelling musk to keep enemies away.

SNAIL

Type of animal:
Mollusk
Find it in the Bible:
Leviticus 11:30 KJV

WHERE'S THAT SLIME COMING FROM?

Snails are mollusks that have coiled shells on their backs when they are fully grown. Most snails live in freshwater or saltwater, but there are also many species of land snails. Land snails have thinner shells than the aquatic snails. As snails grow, so do their shells.

The snail's body is made up of two parts. The main part is attached to the inside of the shell. It contains the snail's vital organs. The mantle, a layer of tissue, covers the internal organs. It extends outward in flaps that reach to the edge of the shell.

The soft part of the body that comes out of the shell is mainly muscle. The snail uses this part of its body, which is called the "foot," to move about. The snail's body produces thick, slimy mucus that helps it move along on its muscular foot. The mucus also helps keep the snail safe from injury when it moves over sharp objects.

The snail breaks up its food using a hook called a "radula." In a quiet setting, some land snails can be heard "crunching" their food.

The snail has two eyes on the end of flexible tentacles. Below the eyes, there are two tentacles that aid in smelling food.

The snail is listed in the Mosaic Law as an unclean animal. In Psalm 58:8, the psalmist refers to the slimy track left by the snail, which seemed to be wasting itself away.

DID YOU KNOW. . .

- The snail can withdraw into the shell and close a doorlike structure for protection from predators.
- Some snails have lungs and some have gills.
- The world's biggest snail, the Australian trumpet, a marine species, can grow up to thirty inches in length and weigh as much as forty pounds.

Type of animal:
Reptile
Find it in the Bible:
Deuteronomy 8:15

SNAKE

VENOMOUS
MEANS
POISONOUS!

Snakes are long-bodied, meat-eating reptiles that don't have legs. Snakes are found in every continent of the world except Antarctica. Many islands around the world don't have snakes living on them.

The snake's body is covered with scales, which help it move on the ground. Snakes also have plates on their bellies that work the same way as a bulldozer track. The muscles attached to ribs drive the plates into the ground and move the snake forward. Contrary to what many people think, the snake's scales are smooth and satiny, not slimy.

There are many thousands of snake species, and most of them are not venomous. Venomous snakes have long, hollow fangs that are folded back against the roof of the mouth when not in use. When the snake strikes, the fangs unfold and shoot directly forward and stab the victim and inject it with venom. The venom either kills or paralyzes the prey. The venom of some snakes can be deadly to people.

Venomous snakes come in a variety of sizes and colors. The different colors help to camouflage the snake for better concealment in hunting and for protection. Smaller venomous snakes eat smaller animals like insects and frogs while larger snakes eat fish, birds, mice, rabbits, and other larger prey.

Snakes have limited detailed vision at a distance, but they see movements around them immediately. Their "hearing" is limited to ground vibrations that travel through the jawbone to the brain. The snake's sense of touch is sharp. Smell is the snake's most powerful sense. It smells through its nasal passages and through its flickering tongue, which picks up airborne particles. These

Venomous snakes like this rattlesnake have fangs they use to inject venom. Notice the drops of venom on the tips of its fangs.

particles are passed through special organs in the mouth alerting the snake to anything near.

Different species of venomous snakes live in different habitats. Some live in wet places along riverbanks and in woodlands. Some live in deserts and some live in the mountains. Like other reptiles, the snake is a cold-blooded animal and will hide away in a burrow or other places on very hot or very cold days.

Different words for "snake"—such as venomous snake, adder, asp, and viper—appear several times in the Bible. At least thirty-three different species have been found in Palestine. In the desert regions of Egypt, vipers, adders, and asps are very common. When the Bible refers to snakes or venomous snakes, we cannot be certain which type is mentioned unless the kind of snake is specifically named.

There are several passages in the Bible in which snakes play a key role. Here are a few of them:

A VIPER BITES PAUL

A viper is the master predator of the snake world. It has facial pits between the eye and nostril. These pits help the viper locate warm-blooded prey, especially at night. The viper can "feel" the heat of an animal and will strike warm targets. That was the kind of snake the apostle Paul once encountered.

Paul was on board a ship that was taking him over the Mediterranean Sea to speak to the high ruler in Rome. Suddenly, a storm came up. Before the ship could reach land, it was dashed against the rocks and broke apart. All the crew and passengers made it safely to land.

They found themselves on an island called Malta. It was cold and rainy, so the islanders made a fire so the crew and passengers could warm themselves. When Paul picked up some sticks to throw on the fire, a viper came out of the bundle and fastened itself on Paul's hand. He brushed the snake into the fire. The islanders thought Paul would die, but God took care of him.

A horned bush viper—a snake very much like the one that bit the apostle Paul's hand at Malta.

You can read the whole story in Acts 28.

SNAKE

A STICK BECOMES A SNAKE

God told Moses to go to Egypt to lead the Hebrew people out of slavery. Moses was afraid the people wouldn't listen to him, so God gave Moses a sign. He told him to throw his shepherd's staff on the ground. When he did, it became a snake. Moses ran from the snake at first, but God told him to pick it up by its tail. When he did, it became a staff again.

You can read the whole story in Exodus 4:1–7.

THE SERPENT ON THE POLE

Moses had led the Israelites out of Egypt. They were in the desert on the way to the Promised Land when they started to complain to God and to Moses. They cried, "Why have you brought us to the desert to die? We have no bread or water. We don't like the food God gave us."

God sent venomous snakes to bite the ungrateful people, and some of them died. The people came to Moses and said, "We have sinned against you and God. Ask God to take away the snakes."

So Moses prayed for the people. God told him to make a bronze snake and put it on a pole. When the people who had been bitten looked at the bronze snake on the pole, they lived.

See Numbers 21:4–9. Other Bible verses that mention snakes are Job 20:16; Proverbs 23:32; Isaiah 59:5; Mark 16:18; and 1 Corinthians 10:9.

DID YOU KNOW. . .

- Most snakes don't hunt but wait for prey to come to them.
- The average speed of a snake is less than 2 miles per hour.
- Snakes sleep with their eyes open because they have no eyelids.
- Horned viper snakes have structures to keep sand out of their eyes and protect them from the sun.
- A side-winding adder buries itself in the sand to escape the hot sun.

299

SPARROW

SUCH A TROUBLESOME BIRD TO BE SO SMALL!

Type of animal:
Bird

Find it in the Bible:
Matthew 10:29

The sparrow is a small, plump, brown gray bird with a short tail and a stubby, powerful beak. The short, pointed beak is ideal for seed cracking. The sparrow is a seedeater but will also consume small insects. It is part of a large group of birds called "perching birds." Its legs and toes are designed for perching on branches and other places where the bird chirps and twitters.

There are about 140 different species of sparrows, and they come in many different color patterns. Sparrows are flocking birds that gather by the thousands and take over feeding and roosting areas. They are sometimes aggressive and will force out other birds and take over their territories.

The sparrow is an intelligent bird that roosts in noisy flocks on branches of trees and bushes, under eaves of houses, and in attic vents. It can be troublesome to people when it nests in such places as gutters, drainpipes, and chimneys, causing water damage and even fires.

Sparrows are found in great numbers in Palestine and are of very little value to people. The Eurasian tree sparrow is very common throughout Europe and Asia and may be seen on Mount Olivet (also called the Mount of Olives) in Jerusalem.

In Matthew 10:29–31, Jesus used the sparrow to teach His followers how much God loves all His creatures—especially humans. If God cares for and feeds even the smallest birds, such as the sparrow, Jesus taught, how much more will He care for people?

OTHER BIBLE VERSES THAT MENTION SPARROWS ARE PSALM 84:3; PROVERBS 26:2; AND LUKE 12:6–7.

DID YOU KNOW. . .

- Because they are so often found in urban areas, the sparrow is considered one of the most familiar wild birds to humans.

- The house sparrow originally lived Europe and much of Asia, but it has followed humans all over the world and is now the most widely distributed bird on planet Earth.

- The American tree sparrow has a large crop (neck pouch) in which it can store up to one thousand seeds.

SPIDER

Type of animal: Arachnid

Find it in the Bible: Job 8:14

YUCK! A SPIDER THAT SUCKS UP GUTS!

The spider is a member of the "arachnid" family. It differs from insects, which have six legs and three body parts. Spiders have eight legs and only two body parts.

There are more than forty thousand known species of spiders living today. They are found anywhere in the world warm enough to support life. They come in different sizes and colors. Some are fuzzy, some smooth. Some spiders are poisonous, but some are not. Only about a dozen species of spiders are considered dangerous to humans.

Even though spiders have four pairs of eyes, they cannot see very well. They use tiny slits in their legs to sense vibrations. They also use chemical sensors to pick up taste and smell.

Nearly all spiders are predators that eat insects and other small animals. Some even eat small reptiles and birds! Many spiders build webs to catch their prey, but some hunt for their food. Those that build webs are called "orb web spiders." The spider uses its sticky web to trap its food.

When an unsuspecting insect or other bug gets caught in the web, the spider rushes over and wraps its victim in silk, turning it around and around. Then the spider pokes its fangs into its meal and injects poison that turns the prey's insides into a liquid. Once the spider has sucked all the liquid out of the victim, all that is left is a shell of the animal.

There are many species of spiders living in Palestine. Some spin webs, but some dig bottomless cells and make doors in them, and some chase their prey on the ground.

OTHER BIBLE VERSES THAT MENTION SPIDERS ARE PROVERBS 30:28 (KJV) AND ISAIAH 59:5.

DID YOU KNOW. . .

- The world's largest spider, the Goliath bird-eating spider, can grow to as large as twelve inches long.
- If a spider loses a leg, it can grow a new one.
- Some species of jumping spiders can leap up to seventy times their own body length.
- The young of some spiders feed on plant nectar.

STORK

Type of animal:
Bird

Find it in the Bible:
Leviticus 11:19

> I GUESS THE STORK REALLY DOES BRING BABIES.

The stork is a large, long-legged, long-necked wading bird. It is one of the most eye-catching of the wading birds, sometimes standing nearly four feet high. The stork is heavily built with broad, rounded wings. It is a strong flier that extends its neck and trails its legs behind when it is in the air. The adult stork makes no vocal noise. The only sound it makes comes from the clattering of its bill.

Storks build huge nests of sticks on cliffs, in trees, or even atop occupied houses. Some stork nests are as big as six feet wide and three feet deep. The female stork lays two or three eggs in the nest. Both male and female storks take turns incubating the eggs. Baby storks are naked when they are first born but later become covered with feathers. They remain in the nest after hatching. Both parents care for them.

The stork usually wades in shallow pools and marshes in search of food. Most storks eat fish, clams, frogs, insects, earthworms, and small birds and mammals that live in and around the water.

The stork is listed in the Mosaic Law as an unclean bird. Jeremiah 8:7 says that every year the stork knows when to migrate. Storks always stop in Palestine during their migrations. Both the black stork and the white stork are common in Palestine.

> OTHER BIBLE VERSES THAT MENTION THE STORK ARE DEUTERONOMY 14:18 AND PSALM 104:17.

DID YOU KNOW. . .

- While resting, the stork holds its long beak pointed downward.

- The stork's plumage is slate gray and white.

- The stork is punctual in returning to the same nesting area at the same time every year.

- The marabou stork has a wingspan of up to ten and a half feet, tying it with the Andean condor for the widest wingspan of all land birds.

SWALLOW

Type of animal: **Find it in the Bible:**
Bird Psalm 84:3

DOESN'T THAT SWALLOW EVER LAND?

The swallow is one of many members of a group of birds called "perching birds." It has a slim blue black body, short red brown neck, and pointed wings. It has a deeply forked tail that is uses for steering as it soars and twists in flight. It needs plenty of air room to make all of its maneuvers. It makes use of strong wings to migrate long distances.

Because it has short legs, the swallow can only hop around clumsily on the ground. It spends most of its life either perching or flying in the air. The swallow is an excellent flier that scoops up insects such as flies and mosquitoes that hover in the air. It even drinks in flight by snatching up rain water in its lower beak.

Some species of swallows nest in colonies. A pair of swallows, male and female, returns to the same nest site each year. The birds work together to build a new nest or repair the old one. Some species mix dirt and saliva together to build their nests. They create a hollow ball of mud with a ledge, where the female lays her eggs.

The swallow migrates to Palestine from March until winter. In biblical times, it made its nest in the temple eaves and was often seen with the common sparrow. It was sometimes confused with the swift or thrush, which some Bible translations use instead of the word swallow.

DID YOU KNOW. . .

- The names swallow and martin are used interchangeably, and there seems to be no difference between them.
- The arrival of the first swallow is sometimes seen as a sign that summer is near.
- The swallow spends most of the day in the air, but at night the family gathers together in a warm nest.
- One colony of barn swallows in Nigeria included 1.5 million individual birds.

SWAN

WHAT A MAGNIFICENT, GRACEFUL BIRD!

Type of animal:
Bird

Find it in the Bible:
Leviticus 11:18 KJV

The swan is a large water bird from the same family as geese and ducks. It has a boat-shaped body and webbed feet, which makes it a good swimmer. The swan's wide wingspan makes it a strong flier. Because it has difficulty taking off, it must paddle across the water surface with its feet as it flaps its wings to build up speed for takeoff.

Most swans have white feathers with a black beak and feet. To keep the feathers waterproof, the swan smears oil from a gland near the tail onto the feathers with its beak.

The swan lives near shallow water. It feeds on land and in the water. It eats mostly roots and shoots of plants that grow in the water, but it will eat small numbers of water animals.

When the swan feeds in the water, it uses its long neck to reach to the bottom of ponds and rivers in search of food. This is called "upending" or "dabbling," a funny-looking scene in which the swan's tail and backside stick out of the water while its head is submerged. When the swan feeds on land, it waddles along the water's edge to graze on grass and plants. It sometimes swallows small pebbles or sand to help it digest its food.

A pair of swans mates for many years—sometimes for life. The pair builds a nest of sticks on raised ground or on the water. Sometimes the nest is nine to twelve feet across and three feet deep. This helps keeps the baby swans safe from the water and from predators. Male swans help in incubating the eggs.

Some swan species are migratory, meaning they travel to warmer areas during the winter. A group of swans can migrate as far as one thousand miles, flying in a V formation. They fly as fast as 50 miles per hour—up to 70 miles per hour with a strong tailwind.

The Mosaic Law calls the swan an unclean bird. In biblical times, the bird lived along the banks of the Mediterranean.

DID YOU KNOW...

- The female swan is called a "pen" and the male is called a "cob."

- Once a year the swan loses its feathers and grows a new set.

- Some species of swans carry their young (called "cygnets") on their back to keep them warm and safe.

304

Type of animal:
Bird

Find it in the Bible:
Jeremiah 8:7

THAT BIRD IS GOING DOWN THE CHIMNEY!

The swift is a soft brown-colored bird similar in shape and size to the swallow, but it is unrelated to the swallow. The swift has a slender body and long, pointed wings with a wide span. It needs plenty of room between its shoulders and the ground to flap its wings when taking off.

Some of the birds have notched or forked tails. Some have short tails that make steering awkward. The bird must beat one wing more strongly than the other to change directions. The swift performs many loops and dips in the sky.

The swift has short legs and has difficulty walking. Because of this, it spends most of its life in the air. Swifts are among the fastest fliers of all birds, reaching air speeds of up to 70 miles per hour. They use their speed to catch insects to eat in the air.

There are several species of swifts, and they range in size from the pygmy swiftlet (three to four inches long) to the purple needletail (up to ten inches long).

The edible-nest swift lives in colonies of caves. It builds its nest of saliva and sticks it to the roof and walls of caves. It uses a kind of natural radar called "echolocation" to find its way in the dark caves.

The white-collared swift nests in vertical cliffs behind waterfalls. It flies in and out through the waterfall to get to its nest.

The prophet Jeremiah mentioned the swift, along with other birds, when he wrote about a time of migration. Some Bible translations use the word swallow instead of swift in the verse.

DID YOU KNOW. . .

- The swift is an expert flier and one of the fastest flying birds.
- The swift flies long distances at great heights when it migrates.
- The chimney swift gets its name because it likes to build its nest in chimneys.

305

TURTLE
(OR TORTOISE)

DOES A TURTLE EVER GO FISHING?

Type of animal:
Reptile

Find it in the Bible:
Leviticus 11:29 KJV

The turtle is a slow-moving reptile with a hard shell that serves sort of like a personal roof. It is the only reptile with a shell, and it protects the animal from heat and from predators.

A turtle's shell can be gray, brown, green, or a mixture of colors, depending on the species. The turtle has sprawling legs with short feet or flippers, depending on the species. It has good eyesight and seems to be sensitive to red. The turtle's ears are flat against the head with skin stretched over the opening.

The turtle has no teeth but uses its hard beak for tearing food apart and grinding it. The tongue is used for moving the food around in its mouth.

There are many kinds and sizes of turtles. Some turtles live on land only, and some live in the ocean. Still others spend part of their time in water and part on dry land. A tortoise is a type of turtle that lives its whole life on land.

The leatherback sea turtle can measure eight feet in length and weigh more than fifteen hundred pounds. The tiny freshwater turtle grows to about four inches long.

What a turtle eats depends on the species. Some turtles eat mostly vegetation, while others are meat eaters. Some eat both plants and meat.

The alligator snapping turtle has an extra tonguelike attachment in its mouth that looks like a worm. It opens its mouth and wiggles its tongue like a fishing lure. The fish thinks it is a worm and moves in to try to eat it. Then—snap!—the turtle has caught a fish for dinner!

The musk turtle, also known as stinkpot, produces a smelly liquid called "musk" to protect itself against predators.

The turtle, which is called a "tortoise" in Leviticus 11:29, is among the unclean animals. The New International Version calls it a "lizard."

DID YOU KNOW. . .

● Most turtles can go days, even weeks, without eating.

● All turtles, even those that live in the ocean, lay their eggs on land.

● Some sea turtles can swim up to 20 miles per hour and travel thousands of miles to return to their nesting sites each year.

VULTURE

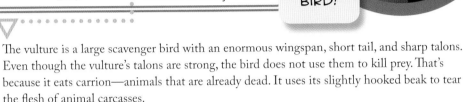

Type of animal:
Bird

Find it in the Bible:
Deuteronomy 14:13

SUCH AN UGLY BIRD!

The vulture is a large scavenger bird with an enormous wingspan, short tail, and sharp talons. Even though the vulture's talons are strong, the bird does not use them to kill prey. That's because it eats carrion—animals that are already dead. It uses its slightly hooked beak to tear the flesh of animal carcasses.

Many vulture species have long, naked necks. That allows the bird to reach deep inside carcasses without collecting flesh or blood on its feathers. After eating, the vulture sometimes stands with its wings spread to dry its wings and warm its body. This helps bake off bacteria that smeared on the body while it was feeding.

The vulture has keen eyesight that can detect food miles away by watching other birds in the sky. It also finds food by flying low to the ground to pick up the smell of dead animals.

The vulture's powerful wings allow it to fly long distances at high altitudes in search of food. When it finds a warm pocket of air, it holds its wings motionless. The warm air carries the vulture as it soars in circles in the sky, sometimes for hours at a time.

According to the Mosaic Law, the vulture is an unclean bird and not to be eaten. Some Bible translations replace the word vulture with "buzzard," "eagle," or "kite."

DID YOU KNOW. . .

- A group of vultures is called a "wake," "committee," or "venue."

- A vulture can fly up to 40 miles per hour.

- The vulture plays an important part in keeping the environment clean by eating dead animals.

307

WEASEL

MAKING A U-TURN IN A NARROW TUNNEL IS QUITE A TALENT!

Type of animal: Mammal

Find it in the Bible: Leviticus 11:29 NIV

The weasel is a meat-eating mammal with a long, slender body and a tail almost as long as its body. It has a small head with long whiskers. Most species have a dark brown upper coat and a white belly. Some weasels shed their summer coats and grow white ones during the winter. Depending on the species, the weasel grows from five to eighteen inches long.

The weasel makes its home in abandoned burrows and under rotting logs, tree roots, or rocks. The nest is made of grass and leaves and is lined with fur.

The weasel is very aggressive when its territory is invaded. Because it has such a slender build, it can chase prey such as mice or voles down their narrow tunnels. Its long, slender body can even make a U-turn in the tunnel if an exit is needed.

The weasel's speed, fierceness, and ability to crawl into tight spaces helps it cope with an array of predators. It also has a reputation for cleverness. The weasel uses its tail to help defend its food and territory against other weasels. Certain species of weasels perform the "weasel war dance" after fighting with other animals. During this "dance," the weasel arches its back and hops sideways and backward as it makes hissing noises.

The weasel was common in the Holy Land, although it is mentioned only once in the Bible. According to Mosaic Law, it is considered an unclean animal. The Hebrew word translated "weasel" probably translates as "mole." Several Bible translations use the word mole instead of "weasel."

DID YOU KNOW. . .

- A weasel can climb trees and is a good swimmer.
- The weasel releases a musk odor when it is frightened.
- A group of weasels is called a "boogle," "gang," "pack," or "confusion."

Type of animal:
Mammal
Find it in the Bible:
Genesis 1:21 KJV

WHALE

CAN A WHALE SING?

The whale is the largest animal in the world. Even though it lives in the ocean, it is not a fish. It is a mammal because it is warm-blooded, has lungs and breathes air, and has hair on its body.

When a whale breathes, it raises its head up out of the water high enough to take in air. It breathes in and out through its blowhole, which opens and lets out used air in a cough that looks like a waterspout. When the whale takes in new air, it shuts its blowhole and slides its head back under the water. The blue whale's "blow" can reach as high as thirty feet.

When a whale sleeps, it stays at the surface of the water with the blowhole above the surface. Because it must breathe air, it takes short naps instead of sleeping for long periods at a time.

The blue whale is the loudest animal in the world. It moans, groans, squeaks, and talks underwater where sounds travel great distances. The humpback whale has a song that lasts thirty-five minutes.

Some whales are quite acrobatic, making leaps out of the water called "breaching." The whale swims by moving its tail up and down and using its flippers to turn. It glides and takes long, deep dives. The sperm whale has been known to dive to depths of 655 to 980 feet.

There are two types of whales—

A giant blue whale expels moist air from its "blow hole."

those without teeth and those with teeth. The whale with teeth (called a "toothed whale") eats small fish and squid and hunts in groups called "pods." The sperm whale is a toothed whale.

The whale without teeth (called a "baleen whale") swims with its mouth open and takes in water filled with fish, plankton, and plants. It then pushes the water back out while straining out the food through the baleen in its mouth. The blue whale, the largest whale on earth at up to one hundred feet long, is a baleen whale.

A whale cannot see well underwater, especially when the water is dark and murky, so it depends on hearing. Toothed whales make clicking noises that sound like a very fast typewriter or high whistle. When they do that, they wait for an echo of the clicks to bounce off an object and come back to them. This tells the whale how far away an object is. This process is called "echolocation."

Whales are found in every ocean around the world. They migrate farther than any other animal. In warm summer months, they feast to build up blubber and other fat reserves. Then when weather and water cool, they migrate to warmer areas where they can find food. They do not stop to eat. They stop only for short periods to rest.

The first mention of the whale is in Genesis when God created the world and all things in it. The King James Version and The Message specifically refer to whales, but other translations call the animals God created "sea monsters" or "sea creatures."

When you see a whale's tail—also called a "fluke"—above water like this, you can bet the whale is probably beginning a dive deep into the water!

JESUS MENTIONS THE WHALE

The Pharisees and teachers of law came to Jesus one day and said, "Teacher, we want to see a miraculous sign from you."

Jesus answered and said, "Evil and unfaithful people ask for signs. I will not give you one except the sign of the prophet Jonah. Remember, Jonah was in the whale for three days and three nights. Something like this will happen to the Son of Man. He will spend three days and three nights in the grave"

See Matthew 12:38–41

WAS IT REALLY A WHALE THAT SWALLOWED JONAH?

Some Bible scholars do not believe that a whale could have swallowed Jonah. They speak of a big fish or a "sea monster." Perhaps God created a special fish that swallowed Jonah. The sperm whale has a gullet large enough to hold the body of a man. The only other animal capable of swallowing a man would be a large great white shark. The white shark was not uncommon in the Mediterranean Sea area.

DID YOU KNOW. . .

- The whale's flippers are very similar in design to a human hand.
- The grey whale migrates up to fifty-five hundred miles, the longest migration of any mammal on earth.
- When a whale rests, it lies still at the water's surface with its tail hanging down and part of its head near the surface. This is called "logging."
- Some whales can swim at speeds of up to 30 miles per hour.

WILD GOAT

Type of animal:
Mammal

Find it in the Bible:
Psalm 104:18

The wild goat resembles the common domestic goat, but it is much larger. The wild goat's horns are longer than the domestic goat's, sometimes a yard in length. Its horns are curved and surrounded by many rings and ridges. The wild goat uses its horns for spearing, thrusting, and warding off predators. It also uses its horns to fight off other wild goats during mating season.

In the wild, the female and young wild goats live in flocks of up to five hundred animals. Most grown males are solitary animals except when they are ready to mate.

Wild goats generally live in rugged mountain country. They climb up rough and narrow places and jump from one rock to another. Their small hooves are hollowed underneath and have a sort of ridge around them, which helps the goats cling to the rocks without slipping.

Wild goats migrate to higher ground in the spring and return to the lower ground in winter. They migrate in search of food—grass, twigs, berries, and bark. They are highly dependent on a source of water, because they need to drink every two or three days. If a source of water dries up, wild goats move to another area.

David wrote in the Psalms about the wild goats belonging to the high mountains. According to the Mosaic Law, the wild goat is a clean animal that the Israelites could eat. The wild goat is also called "mountain goat" in some Bible translations.

DID YOU KNOW...

- Both male and female wild goats have short beards.

- The life span of a wild goat is twelve to twenty-two years.

- The wild goat has heavy wool that helps it survive the harsh mountain winter climate.

WILD OX

Type of animal:
Mammal

Find it in the Bible:
Psalm 29:6

WHERE IS THE WILD OX TODAY?

The wild ox mentioned in the Bible is a mysterious animal. Different versions of the Bible call it different names—wild ox, unicorn, rhinoceros, or antelope. Job 39:9–12 describes this animal as being so large, powerful, and wild that no one could control it, tame it, or train it.

While it would be hard to know for certain what species of animal it really was, some Bible scholars believe it could be the gigantic aurochs, a huge bovine animal (in the same group of animals as modern-day cattle) that lived during biblical times but is now extinct. The aurochs was much larger than today's cattle, standing as tall as six and a half feet and weighing as much as twenty-two hundred pounds.

The aurochs had long, thick horns that pointed forward rather than sweeping out to the side. Cave paintings from various sites show the male aurochs as being mostly black, while the female and young were red in color.

This animal lived in the forest and open scrubland, but it could be found in grasslands as well. It grazed on grass, leaves, herbs, and fruit.

OTHER BIBLE VERSES THAT MENTION THE "WILD OX" OR "UNICORN" ARE NUMBERS 24:8; DEUTERONOMY 33:17; PSALM 22:21; 92:10; AND ISAIAH 34:7.

Since some Bible translations, including the King James Version, call the wild ox a "unicorn," some Bible scholars believe it was a rhinoceros. The fact that the rhinoceros is also large, strong, and has one large horn makes that a possibility.

The wild ox is mentioned in the Bible in connection with the strength of the nation of Israel (Numbers 24:8) and in connection with the goodness and power of God (Psalm 29:5–6).

DID YOU KNOW...

- The original Hebrew word for wild ox, *re'em*, refers to a wild, untamable animal of great strength with a mighty horn or horns.

- The Bible describes the wild ox as a very powerful, aggressive creature.

- The aurochs, which some believe is the wild ox of the Bible, became extinct in the early 1600s.

WOLF

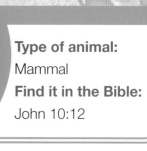

HOW CAN A WOLF
COMMUNICATE
WITHOUT MAKING
A SOUND?

Type of animal:
Mammal
Find it in the Bible:
John 10:12

The wolf is the largest member of the canine family of animals, which includes the domestic dog, the fox, the coyote, and other doglike animals. Its long, thick hair is mostly gray or a mixture of black, gray, tan, brown, and white.

The wolf is a fierce and dangerous hunter that usually feeds on small animals but will also attack and kill deer, sheep, and even cattle when it is hungry enough. If it is really hungry, a large adult wolf can eat as much as twenty-two pounds of meat at one time. But when food is scarce, it can go several weeks without eating.

The wolf is an intelligent animal that is loyal to other wolves. Though a few wolves are loners, they usually travel and hunt in packs. The packs usually include seven or eight members, but wolves have been known to run with packs of up to twenty animals. The wolf pack hunts over and over in the same territorial hunting routes.

Sometimes the wolf howls, but it can also bark, whine, yelp, and snarl like a domestic dog. A wolf can also communicate with another wolf without making a sound. When the wolf's ears point straight up and its teeth are bared, it is giving a warning. When it narrows its eyes and flattens its ears against its head, it is saying, "What's going on here?" When the wolf holds its tail high, it communicates the message, "I'm in charge!" When a wolf tucks its tail between its legs, it is saying, "I won't argue." When the wolf is happy, it tilts its head and wiggles its body from side to side.

The wolf has a keen sense of hearing and can detect sounds from up to six miles away. Touch and smell are important as it sniffs out prey. It has good eyesight to catch nearby movements.

The female wolf gives birth to litters of five or six babies in a den that is underground or dug into the side of a sandy hill. The baby wolves, which weigh about one pound at birth, are called "pups."

A wolf pack takes some time to rest before heading out to hunt.

The wolf was common in Palestine in biblical times. It was a constant threat to flocks of sheep and earned a reputation of being vicious as it stalked prey at night.

Wolves are mentioned in the Bible several times. Sometimes the Bible uses the word wolf to refer to cruel and evil leaders. The prophet Isaiah foretold the peaceful reign when Jesus returns to earth as a time when "the wolf will live with the lamb" (11:6 NIV). Jesus also spoke of those who opposed His message as "wolves."

JESUS' WARNING: YOU WILL ENCOUNTER THE WOLVES!

Jesus called His twelve disciples and gave them instructions about going out to teach and to heal the sick. He told them to heal the sick, raise the dead, heal people with leprosy, and drive out demons (see Matthew 10:8).

He instructed His followers to take no clothes or money with them but to rely on others to provide for them. Then Jesus said, "I am sending you out like sheep among wolves" (Matthew 10:16 NIV). Jesus warned His disciples so that they would be on their guard against people who would try to mistreat them because they preached the gospel message.

OTHER BIBLE VERSES THAT MENTION WOLVES ARE GENESIS 49:27; ISAIAH 65:25; JEREMIAH 5:6; EZEKIEL 22:27; HABAKKUK 1:8; ZEPHANIAH 3:3; MATTHEW 7:15; AND ACTS 20:29.

DID YOU KNOW. . .

- A wolf can run in short bursts at up to 38 miles per hour for hours without tiring.

- The wolf is known for howling, which it does mostly at night.

- A full-grown wolf can leap as high as a one-story building!

- Wolves are usually more frightened of humans than humans are of them.

315

WORM

WHY SO MANY WORMS ON THE GROUND AFTER A RAIN?

Type of animal:
Annelid (earthworm)
or insect (larva)

Find it in the Bible:
Deuteronomy 28:39

The worm is a soft-bodied animal without a backbone, arms, or legs. Some worms cannot move on their own but must wait on natural forces or animals to move them. Others have bristles or fins that help them move.

Worms are divided into three groups—flatworms, roundworms, and segmented worms. The flatworm has a flat, ribbon-shaped body with a pair of eyes at the front. The roundworm is found in damp soil and moss but can also live in water. The segmented worm has a body divided into segments or rings.

The best-known worms are the earthworms, which are from a group of animals called "annelids." They are valuable to gardens and farmer's crops. They tunnel deeply in soil, secreting slime that contains nitrogen, which helps plants grow.

Most worms need to live in moist places. If a worm's skin dries out, it will die.

Many worms do not die if they lose a body part. They can replace or repair any body segment but the head.

There are many Bible passages where insect larvae are called "worms." Larvae of insects, such as the moth, eat clothing made from wool. Some kinds of worms are destructive to grapevines and other crops.

The Bible also uses the worm as a symbol of lowliness or weakness (Psalm 22:6). In other verses, the worm is alive and working in a place for the unbeliever and wicked (see Mark 9:48).

DID YOU KNOW. . .

- Many earthworms are found above ground after a heavy rainfall because they can drown underground.

- In one acre of land, there can be more than a billion earthworms.

- Worms come in every size, from microscopic worms to the African giant earthworm, which can grow up to twenty-two feet long.

SCRIPTURE INDEX

Genesis
1:21. 309
8:1-7 286
8:6-12 206
15:9. . . . . .227, 294
18:7. 190
22:3. 203
24. 185
32-33 189
49:27 315

Exodus
4:1-7 299
7:19. 221
8 221
8:6 220
8:16-19 224
8:17. 258
9:3 188
10:18-20 257
14:9. 238
16:11-20 259
16:20 259
23:12 271
23:28 237
25:5. . . . . .172, 293
29. 188
29:36 190

Leviticus
1:5 188
1:14. 205
4:4 188
4:24. 228
5:7 278
5:7-11 205
11:9-12 212
11:13 267
11:14 244
11:16 232
11:17 194
11:18 . . . . .274, 304
11:19 . . . . .173, 236
11:21-22 230
11:22 . . . . 180, 196, 243
11:29 . . . . 265, 306, 308
11:30 210, 203, 255, 260, 295, 296
14:13 307
16:15 228

Numbers
6:10. 206

7:3 271
11:5. 212
11:31 281
13:26-33 230
13:33 229
14:15 197
15:8. 190
21:4-9 299
22:21 203
22:28 203
24:8. 313

Deuteronomy
8:15. . . . . .290, 297
14:5. . . . . 222, 241, 263
14:5-6 169
14:7. 283
14:12 268
14:13 . . . . .209, 244
14:15 231
14:15-17 270
14:17 274
14:18 . . . . .235, 245
22:10 . . . . .203, 271
25:4. 273
28:38 256
28:39 316
32:33 . . . . .192, 207
33:17 313

Joshua
6:4 . . . . .264, 293

Judges
13:19 228
14. 253
14:8. 177
14:14-18 178
15:1-8 219
15:4. 217

1 Samuel
6:4-5 265
8:37. 187
9:3 203
13:18 240
14. 179
16:1. . . . . .264, 293
16:20 203
17:32-37 175
17:34-35 253
17:34-37 294

17:37 253
24:2. 241
24:14 214
26:20 . . . . .214, 272
30:17 186

2 Samuel
1:23. 208
2:18. 189
8:1-4 239
17:8. 176
17:10 253

1 Kings
1:33. 266
4:23. 189
10:22 . . . . 170, 171, 273
10:29 239
17:1-5 286
18:16-39 189
19:19 271

2 Kings
2:23-25 176
2:24. 174

2 Chronicles
6:28. 187
7:5 294
9:21. . . . . .171, 273
29:23 . . . . .226, 228
33:14 213

Nehemiah
3:3 213
4 218

Job
1:3 184
8:14. 301
13:28 262
20:16 299
25:6. 259
30:29 207
39:9-12 313
39:13 273
39:13-18 269
39:26 232
39:27 208
40:15 181
40:16 181
40:17 181

SCRIPTURE INDEX

40:18 181
40:19 181
40:21 181
40:23 181
41:1-2, 14-15, 18-20, 22,
  24-26, 30, 33 249
41:1, 7 213

Psalms
8:8 213
17:12 253
22:6 316
22:21 313
29:5-6 313
29:6 313
39:11 262
42:1 198
44:19 207
55:6 206
58:8 296
78:42-52 216
78:45 221
78:46 187
84:3 . . . . .300, 303
91:13 . . . . .192, 207
92:10 313
102:6 . . . . .270, 274
104:18 . . . . .241, 312
105:30 221
105:31 . . . . . . 215, 224, 258

Proverbs
6:6 167
17:12 176
23:32 299
26:2 300
30:15 246
30:24-25 168
30:26 193
30:28 . . . . .254, 301
30:31 289

Isaiah
11:6 . . . . .248, 315
11:7 176
13:22 240
14:11 259
14:23 233
33:4 187
34:7 313
34:11 . . . . .183, 280
34:14 240

37:36-37 214
38:14 . . . . .195, 206
40:31 208
43:20 207
59:5 . . . . .299, 301
65:25 315

Jeremiah
2:23 186
5:6 315
8:7 . . . . .195, 305
13:23 247
15:3 240
48:40 208

Ezekiel
2:6 291
16:10 172
17:3 208
22:27 315
29:3 207

Daniel
6:22 251

Hosea
13:7 248

Habakkuk
1:8 315

Zephaniah
2:14 . . . . .183, 233
3:3 315

Matthew
3:1-4 179
4:18 213
6:19 261
6:19-20 262
7:15 315
8:28-34 277
10:8 315
10:16 . . . . .206, 315
10:29-31 300
12:38-41 311
21:1-11 204
21:2 203
23:24 . . . . .186, 224
23:37 234
26:31-35, 69-75 288

Mark
1:6 . . . . .186, 256
1:9-11 206
5:11 275
9:48 316
16:18 299

Luke
2:24 205
5:6 211
9:58 218
10:25-37 204
10:34 202
11:12 291
12:6-7 300
12:24 285
13:34 234
15:1-7 294
15:11-32 . . . . .190, 276
16:19-31 201
16:21 200
18:25 186
24:42 213

John
10:1-18 294
10:3 292
10:12 314
13:38 287
21:3-13 213
21:8 213

Acts
20:29 315
28 298

1 Corinthians
10:9 299

James
5:2 262

1 Peter
5:8 253

ART CREDITS

Art Resource: page 277

Big Stock photo: page 207 (top)

Creationism.org: page 219

Gary Nafis: page 254

istockphoto: page 167(both), 169-173(all), 175-178 (all), 180, 182-184 (all), 186-188, 190-198 (all), 200-203 (all), 205-206 (all), 207 (bottom), 208-211 (all), 214-215 (all), 217 (both), 218, 220 (both), 222, 223 (both), 226 (both), 227-229, 231-243 (all), 245-247 (all), 251-252 (all), 254 (top) 255-256 (all), 258-260 (all), 261 (top), 263 (both), 265-266 (all), 268-275 (all), 278, 280, 281 (top), 283 (both), 285 (bottom), 287 (both), 288, 290-293 (all), 295-298 (all), 301-304 (all), 306, 307, 309 (top), 310, 312, 314 (both), 316

Wikimedia: page 168, 174 (both), 181, 212, 219, 224 (both), 225, 230, 244, 248, 249, 250, 254 (bottom), 257, 261 (bottom), 267, 278, 279, 281 (bottom), 282 (both), 285 (top), 286, 289, 290, 300, 305, 308, 309 (bottom), 313

AUTHOR BIO

About Jane Landreth

Jane Landreth enjoys touching young lives with God's love. She taught school until her son, Eric, was born, then officially launched her writing career, using her son's adventures for her first story and article ideas. Later other ideas came from teaching children in church. She and her husband, Jack, reside in the Ozarks, where she continues writing for children and teaches writing in conferences and school classrooms. This is her third book for Barbour, having previously written *Bible Prayers for Bedtime* and *Bible Miracles for Bedtime*.